TREATMENT FOR POSTDISASTER DISTRESS

TREATMENT FOR POSTDISASTER DISTRESS

A Transdiagnostic Approach

Jessica L. Hamblen and Kim T. Mueser

 AMERICAN PSYCHOLOGICAL ASSOCIATION

Published by
American Psychological Association
750 First Street, NE
Washington, DC 20002
https://www.apa.org

Order Department
https://www.apa.org/pubs/books
order@apa.org

In the U.K., Europe, Africa, and the Middle East, copies may be ordered from Eurospan
https://www.eurospanbookstore.com/apa
info@eurospangroup.com

Typeset in Charter and Interstate by Circle Graphics, Inc., Reisterstown, MD

Printer: Sheridan Books, Chelsea, MI
Cover Designer: Gwen J. Grafft, Minneapolis, MN

Library of Congress Cataloging-in-Publication Data

Names: Hamblen, Jessica Liebergott, author. | Mueser, Kim Tornvall, author.
Title: Treatment for postdisaster distress : a transdiagnostic approach /
  by Jessica L. Hamblen and Kim T. Mueser.
Description: Washington, DC : American Psychological Association, [2021] |
  Includes bibliographical references and index.
Identifiers: LCCN 2020051936 (print) | LCCN 2020051937 (ebook) |
  ISBN 9781433836138 (paperback) | ISBN 9781433837296 (ebook)
Subjects: LCSH: Post-traumatic stress disorder. | Cognitive therapy. |
  Disaster victims. | Disasters—Psychological aspects.
Classification: LCC RC552.P67 H336 2021 (print) | LCC RC552.P67 (ebook) |
  DDC 616.85/21—dc23
LC record available at https://lccn.loc.gov/2020051936
LC ebook record available at https://lccn.loc.gov/2020051937

https://doi.org/10.1037/0000237-000

Printed in the United States of America

10 9 8 7 6 5 4 3 2 1

Contents

ADDITIONAL RESOURCES

Supporting materials for clinical use are provided in two online appendixes, available on the American Psychological Association website at http://pubs.apa.org/books/supp/hamblen, where they can be downloaded and printed out.

Foreword

Disasters are a regular part of our lives. Nearly every day we seem to be hearing about another disaster—either a flood, hurricane, forest fire, mass shooting, or more recently, a pandemic. These events can have a marked psychological impact on people affected by them. Not surprisingly, many mental health programs have been implemented over the years to address the widespread mental health effects of these disasters. Despite this proliferation of programs, most people with a persistent psychological reaction after a disaster never receive the evidence-based mental health assistance they need. A major reason for the lack of optimal mental health care is that there has not been a detailed manual to guide clinicians and practitioners working with disaster survivors that uses state-of-the-art evidence-based treatment strategies. This book fills this gap.

Evidence-based treatments are sorely needed in the management of persistent postdisaster mental health problems. For decades most of the attention has focused on early intervention after disasters, with a plethora of interventions offered to assist people in the initial days and weeks after the disaster. If there is one lesson we have learnt over the years, it is that putting all our efforts into early intervention efforts after disasters is not effective. We know from longitudinal studies that many of the persistent mental health problems following disasters only emerge in the months after the initial disaster. This pattern means that attempts to offer early intervention programs in the initial days or weeks may be premature. Further, many disaster survivors do not believe they need help in the initial weeks after a disaster because they are too shocked by events or are too distracted with competing demands that require their attention. Rebuilding homes, assisting family members, or trying to achieve financial security can be a disaster survivor's first priorities in the weeks after a disaster, and so it is only months later that a person is motivated to seek treatment. We should also not forget that there is a disheartening lack of evidence that any early intervention programs actually lead to better long-term mental health in disaster survivors. These factors lead to the conclusion that offering mental health programs that are relevant to disaster survivors when they need them and can be flexible enough to address changing needs is a highly sensible way to help disaster survivors to adjust to their experiences.

There are several features of this book that make it particularly useful for anyone working clinically with disaster survivors. First, it adopts a transdiagnostic approach. We know from much research following disasters that people can develop a range of mental health problems, and these problems do not remain the same over time; a person may have posttraumatic stress disorder (PTSD) several months after a hurricane, but their major problem may be depression 6 months later. Moreover, people will often present with an array of mental health issues at once, with some features of PTSD, depression, anxiety, or other conditions. It is not sufficient to apply a single treatment protocol to many disaster survivors because it may not address the entirety of their needs. As outlined in Chapter 3, the transdiagnostic approach adopted in this book uses evidence-based techniques to target the most common problems that people have after disaster, which makes this approach more applicable to most disaster survivors. One of the major limitations in how agencies and clinicians have traditionally attempted to address postdisaster mental health has been a near-myopic focus on PTSD. While this condition is an important potential sequela of a disaster, it is by no means the only problem people can have. A transdiagnostic approach provides clinicians and agencies with much more scope to deal with the common psychological problems that arise after disaster. The transdiagnostic paradigm also more accurately reflects our current understanding of the optimal ways to manage posttraumatic mental health. Rather than focusing on diagnostic categories and treating a person according to which *DSM-5* (*Diagnostic and Statistical Manual of Mental Disorders, Fifth Edition*) diagnostic label we place on them, recent research suggests that we should be targeting the clinical problems that they have by addressing the mechanisms underpinning each psychological problem. A transdiagnostic approach provides a useful framework to achieve this because it guides the clinician to use strategies that are common to many of the mental health problems that occur after a disaster and that have proven efficacy in improving mental health. The transdiagnostic approach adopted in this book serves the multiple purposes of reducing anxiety, persistent avoidance, passivity, social withdrawal, and depressive mood. A treatment protocol that does this is much more likely to achieve clinical benefits for many more disaster survivors than any disorder-specific program.

The other major advantage of this book is that it applies the treatment protocol in the context of the major problems faced by many disaster survivors. Many clinicians may be unfamiliar with the multitude of the issues that can arise for people in the aftermath of disaster. These may include ongoing stressors resulting from the event, social upheaval, stressors related to rebuilding, and financial or legal challenges. This book is written through the lens of assisting people to cope with mental health problems in the context of these potential confounding factors. The advice given regarding timing of treatment, helping people who have survived different types of disasters, and delivering treatment when the clinician may also have been directly or indirectly affected by the disaster is important for anyone providing therapy for disaster survivors.

Dozens of books are available on postdisaster mental health, and they can be generally categorized into two groups: one that provides scholarly reviews of the prevalence and nature of mental health conditions following disasters, and another that provides outlines of early intervention programs designed to achieve preventive benefits for disaster survivors. This book does not fall into either category. Following a concise summary of what is known from research about mental health responses following disasters and a very important primer on major mechanisms driving mental health after trauma, the book focuses exclusively on how to assess and treat distressed disaster survivors. This treatment manual is presented in a very detailed and practical manner, which will assist clinicians needing to deliver therapy to those affected by a disaster. To date, postdisaster mental health programs have given far too little weight to using evidence-based interventions. In this book, we have a much-needed balance between reliance on evidence, recognition of the range of problems arising after disasters, and practical application that is needed in the postdisaster context.

—*Richard A. Bryant, PhD, FAPS*

Acknowledgments

There are a number of people we would like to thank for their help in the development, evaluation, and dissemination of Cognitive Behavior Therapy for Postdisaster Distress (CBT-PD). First and foremost, our friend and colleague Stanley D. Rosenberg, who, along with Kim T. Mueser, encouraged the expansion of their treatment to be used in special populations. Their cognitive behavioral program for posttraumatic stress disorder served as the basis for the CBT-PD program. Many others provided insight and support in the development and implementation of the program, including Elisa Bolton, Matthew J. Friedman, Laura E. Gibson, Kari Gleiser, Jennifer Gottlieb, M. Kay Jankowski, Jennifer Price, Paula P. Schnurr, Susan Stevens, and Patricia J. Watson. We also thank Richard Bryant and Patricia Resick for comments on an early draft of the treatment program. Fran H. Norris has provided support and insight all along the way and has been integral to helping us evaluate the program. Similarly, April Naturale, who directed Project Liberty, the New York State Office of Mental Health's response to the September 11, 2001, attacks on the World Trade Center, has been a close friend and collaborator. After seeing the results of the CBT-PD program, she advocated for its use in other major national disasters.

We wish to thank the organizations that invited us in to train their providers, including the New York State Office of Mental Health, after the September 11th attacks; the Florida Department of Children and Families, after the 2004 Florida hurricanes; the Baton Rogue (Louisiana) Area Foundation, after Hurricane Katrina in 2005; and the Massachusetts Office for Victim

Assistance, after the Boston Marathon bombings in 2013. A special thank you goes to Rita Roncone, who thought the CBT-PD program was so effective that she had the treatment manual and workbook translated into Italian for use after the L'Aquila, Italy, earthquake in 2009.

We extend a special thank-you to the many therapists who have delivered CBT-PD and the hundreds of disaster survivors with whom they worked. We have been motivated by their strength and determination to overcome post-disaster challenges and get back to living their lives. Their willingness to share their experiences with the CBT-PD program and their feedback have helped us make improvements to the treatment program over the past 18 years.

INTRODUCTION

Development of a Transdiagnostic Treatment
for Postdisaster Distress

Why are there so many disasters on the news? Whether it's fires raging somewhere in the American West, a major earthquake or flood somewhere in the world, or the all-too-common shooting at a local mall, disasters seem to be happening, anywhere and everywhere. The reason why is twofold. First, disasters are headline news because they are sudden, dramatic, and unpredictable events that can seemingly affect anyone, thus drawing in viewers who can relate to the experiences of the survivors of disasters more easily than to the victims of other, more enduring destructive forces, such as war, disease, or poverty. Second, disasters are so frequently featured in the mainstream media in part because they are in fact relatively common. Depending on how you define the terms, a disaster or act of mass violence occurs practically every day, or even more often, across the world. For example, data collected over the 10-year period from 2008 to 2017 show that during that time frame natural disasters alone left nearly 2 billion people injured, homeless, or in need of emergency assistance (Ritchie et al., 2019). So, with the immediate aftermath of a disaster lasting anywhere from several days to weeks, months, and longer, there is much for the news media to choose from when it comes to reporting on disasters.

We have all seen pictures of the widespread destruction of a natural disaster: the rubble and remains left over after an explosion or a daring rescue in which a first responder saves a survivor. But the media and cameras often move quickly on to the next story, and mental health providers find themselves facing a serious public and mental health challenge as thousands of individuals are simultaneously in need of treatment. Most people who live through a disaster experience some posttraumatic symptoms. Between the fear and anxiety of the specific event; the grief and sadness associated with losing a loved one or one's possessions; and the subsequent difficulties associated with being displaced from one's home, physically injured, or lacking essential services, disaster survivors face myriad challenges and thus can benefit from the assistance of mental health providers. Some people's postdisaster symptoms improve on their own; however, others experience symptoms for months or years, especially if they do not seek professional treatment. These symptoms can lead to emotional distress as well as problems at work, at home, and with relationships. Despite the amply documented needs of these individuals, there are few treatments for people who have recently experienced a disaster, and the interventions that do exist focus primarily on posttraumatic stress disorder (PTSD).

PTSD is a psychiatric condition that can result from a life-threatening event. It is characterized by a combination of symptoms, including intrusive thoughts or memories of the traumatic event, avoidance of situations that remind the person of the event, negative thoughts and feelings about oneself and the world, and physiological overarousal (American Psychiatric Association, 2013). Depending on their level of direct exposure to the event and its effects on their lives, between 5% and 50% of people who experience a disaster develop PTSD (Neria et al., 2008). PTSD is the most extensively studied mental health consequence of disasters (Norris et al., 2002), and research indicates that trauma-focused cognitive behavior therapy is effective for people who meet the diagnostic criteria for PTSD after a disaster (e.g., Bryant et al., 2011; Difede et al., 2007; Duffy et al., 2007).

It is also clear, however, that a diagnosis of PTSD fails to capture the full breadth and depth of the impact of a disaster on most people's mental health functioning. In addition to subsyndromal PTSD symptoms, numerous other distressing symptoms occur in the wake of a disaster. Depression, anxiety, grief, anger, guilt, substance use problems, and suicidal thinking are just some of the additional problems disaster survivors report. Although these problems can occur with PTSD, they also occur on their own, in the absence of a PTSD diagnosis. Thus, there is a need for a psychological intervention for disaster survivors that does not narrowly focus on PTSD but instead addresses the broad range of negative reactions that can occur after a disaster and teaches skills for helping people rebuild and move on with their lives.

Our work in the mental health treatment of disaster survivors began after the September 11, 2001, terrorist attacks in New York City and Washington, D.C.

The New York State Office of Mental Health was in need of a treatment approach that would fill the gap between crisis counseling, which primarily comprises outreach and education provided by paraprofessionals and long-term treatment provided by specialists at traditional community mental health centers. Although a time-limited treatment focused on PTSD would technically satisfy this requirement, it would not meet the needs of the majority of disaster survivors experiencing other reactions, such as anxiety and depression. To address the need for a transdiagnostic treatment for disaster survivors that would be effective for people with both PTSD and other mental health reactions, we developed the Cognitive Behavior Therapy for Postdisaster Distress (CBT-PD) program, an eight- to 12-session intervention designed to be delivered by mental health professionals in typical community settings.

There are several advantages to the CBT-PD program's transdiagnostic approach to addressing the mental health problems that occur after a disaster. First, treating a broad range of postdisaster symptoms ensures that the maximum number of people affected by a disaster receive some psychological relief of their distress, including the significant number of people who do not meet diagnostic criteria for PTSD but are nevertheless suffering from mental health problems. Second, by virtue of being a transdiagnostic treatment, the CBT-PD program does not require the establishment of a formal psychiatric diagnosis, which may make it easier to implement and increase its acceptability to disaster survivors. Third, a single transdiagnostic intervention, which the CBT-PD program for disaster survivors is, has a higher potential for widespread dissemination to mental health providers than does a combination of interventions that target specific psychiatric disorders. It thus has increased efficiency because the time required to learn the intervention is shorter, and so people affected by a disaster can be helped more quickly.

THE COGNITIVE BEHAVIOR THERAPY FOR POSTDISASTER DISTRESS PROGRAM

The CBT-PD program is a flexible but structured individual-based treatment that involves teaching a broad range of strategies for facilitating recovery from a disaster. The program begins with psychoeducation about the nature of postdisaster reactions (including, but not limited to, PTSD); teaching relaxation techniques for reducing anxiety and physiological overarousal; and activity scheduling to reengage the client in enjoyable, meaningful activities to combat depression and help them avoid situations that remind them of the disaster. The majority of the program focuses on teaching cognitive restructuring as a strategy for dealing with negative feelings that follow a disaster. Clients are taught how to recognize and critically evaluate thoughts and beliefs that accompany their negative feelings and how to change them when those thoughts are determined to be inaccurate and maladaptive. In particular, clients are taught to recognize inaccurate thoughts related to the disaster, themselves, and the world in general that result in fear and anxiety, sadness and depression, anger, and guilt and to replace them with more accurate and less distressing ones. When the examination of an upsetting thought leads one to conclude that it is accurate—as is often the case after a disaster that results in real-life problems in areas such as housing, work, school, or basic needs—clients are taught how to create Action Plans in order to implement practical solutions to address their concerns.

As previously described, the CBT-PD program was first developed and implemented after the September 11th attacks in the United States. Our first trial of the CBT-PD program was successful, and we have continued to improve the program as we gained further experience with it after multiple other disasters, both in the United States, such as Hurricane Katrina in 2005 and the Boston Marathon bombing in 2013, and abroad, such as the earthquake in L'Aquila, Italy, in 2009. Most recently, the program has been offered through New York City's employee assistance program to assist front-line workers who are struggling to respond to the medical crisis associated with COVID-19. After each disaster in which CBT-PD has been used, we have gathered program evaluation data from survivors and treatment providers and honed the program so that today it is a robust and effective treatment for reducing postdisaster distress and symptoms and improving functioning in survivors.

ORGANIZATION OF THIS BOOK

The book is divided into three parts. Part I provides important background information on disaster-related mental health. We begin in Chapter 1 by reviewing the wide range of mental health consequences of surviving a disaster so as to lay the groundwork for the importance of a treatment that is transdiagnostic. Then, in Chapter 2, we review the theory underpinning the development of posttraumatic reactions, explaining how each component of the CBT-PD program targets specific mechanisms believed to underlie these reactions, before providing a comprehensive review of the research on treatment for disaster in Chapter 3. In Chapter 3, we also describe the development of the CBT-PD program and review the research on its effectiveness. Then, in Chapter 4, we provide an overview of the entire CBT-PD program, including logistical considerations. We end the chapter with a case vignette, based on composite cases that are a blend of information from multiple clients.

In Part II, we provide step-by-step instructions about how to deliver each of the major components of the CBT-PD program. Numerous case vignettes are used to illustrate the implementation of the different components of the program, using the composite approach described above. These vignettes give readers both a better feel for the specific issues facing these clients as well as demonstrations of how expert clinicians deliver the model. Issues related to screening and assessment, and the importance of using outcome monitoring to determine treatment effectiveness, are reviewed in Chapter 5. We begin Chapter 6 with a discussion of how to describe the treatment to clients and help them readily engage in the program. Provision of a clear treatment rationale and psychoeducation about the common postdisaster symptoms increases the treatment's credibility and creates client expectations for recovery. Once clients are engaged, the next step is to teach them resiliency skills to provide them with some immediate relief. Thus, in Chapter 7, we describe breathing retraining, which helps clients manage their anxiety as they begin to address their disaster-related symptoms, and activity scheduling, which helps improve clients' mood by increasing the number and quality of positive and meaningful experiences in which they engage.

In the next two chapters, we introduce cognitive restructuring, which is the core of the CBT-PD program. In Chapter 8, we describe how to introduce the basic rationale for cognitive restructuring, including how to explain to clients how inaccurate thoughts lead to negative feelings and how recognizing, examining, and changing inaccurate thoughts can reduce distress. Clients are then taught a basic cognitive restructuring skill that involves identifying specific patterns of inaccurate or distorted thinking when they feel upset—called "Problematic Thinking Styles"—and how to change those thoughts to more accurate ones. Then, in Chapter 9, we teach a new, richer, and more powerful skill that builds on the Problematic Thinking Styles, the 5 Steps of Cognitive Restructuring. The 5 Steps of Cognitive Restructuring can be used to deal with any negative feeling, including anxiety, depression, anger, and guilt, regardless of whether the thought or belief underlying the feeling is distorted or inaccurate or is quite reasonable and completely supported by the evidence. As with traditional cognitive restructuring, if a careful examination of the upsetting thought reveals that it is inaccurate, the client is taught to change it to a more accurate and less distressing one. If, however, the thought is found to be supported by the evidence and thus accurate, the client is taught how to create an Action Plan for dealing with the problematic situation. After describing in Chapter 9 the basics of teaching the 5 Steps of Cognitive Restructuring, in Chapter 10 we address solutions to common challenges that arise when teaching cognitive restructuring to disaster survivors. In the final chapter of Part II, Chapter 11, we provide guidance to therapists about terminating CBT-PD therapy with clients.

Part III of the book focuses on special considerations for therapists responding to a disaster and on applying the CBT-PD program to survivors of different types of disasters. We describe in Chapter 12 some of the unique challenges therapists face when responding to disaster, including the dual role played by mental health providers who are both disaster survivors and therapists. We consider how providers can ensure that they are managing their own reactions to a disaster before treating others as well as how they can use their own experiences to better connect with and assist their clients. Finally, in Chapter 13, we examine how the CBT-PD program can be tailored to address some of the unique challenges that arise with different types of disasters, such as the intentionality that is a component of terrorism and mass violence, the widespread destruction that is common after natural disasters, and the uncertainty associated with disease outbreaks.

Supporting materials are provided in two online appendixes. These materials are available on the American Psychological Association website at http://pubs.apa.org/books/supp/hamblen, where they can be downloaded and printed out for clinical use. Appendix A includes a measure of postdisaster distress that clinicians can use as a screening tool to help identify clients who may benefit from CBT-PD, measure treatment outcomes, and monitor progress over the course of therapy, and Appendix B includes all of the handouts that are included as part of the CBT-PD program. Handouts are referred to by name and number and are numbered sequentially so that providers can easily locate them online. There are two types of handouts: informational handouts and worksheets. The former describe key concepts taught in the CBT-PD program. They are given to clients at the end of the sessions and serve as a reminder of what has been taught. Worksheets are also given to clients at the end of a session, but they differ from handouts in that they require the client to complete them. Clients use the worksheets in between sessions to practice the skills they have been taught, and they are expected to bring the completed worksheets to the next session for review. At the end of the CBT-PD program clients can use their handouts and worksheets as a personalized self-help guide to support them as they continue to use the skills on their own.

In this book, we have tried to capture our many years of experience in helping people manage postdisaster reactions. We believe that the CBT-PD program is unique in both its flexibility and specificity. We hope that you, the reader, will find the program to be effective in your own work with disaster survivors and that it will provide your clients with the information and skills they need to recover from their experience and move on with their lives.

PART I BACKGROUND: WHAT WE KNOW ABOUT DISASTER MENTAL HEALTH

1 THE MENTAL HEALTH EFFECTS OF DISASTER

For Roseann Sdoia Materia, April 15, 2013 began much the same way every Patriots' Day had for the past 15 years. Her plans were always the same— to see the Red Sox play their only morning game of the season at Fenway and then, head over to one of her favorite Boylston Street bars to watch the [Boston] Marathon with friends. Everything seemed perfect, even the weather was cooperating on that beautiful sunny day. Then, the unthinkable happened. Two bombs exploded; Materia was just steps from the second blast. She remembers the flash by her feet and thinking it was too late to run. She remembers feeling that, if she closed her eyes, she might never wake up. And she remembers the selfless kindness of strangers, without whom, she may have lost her life instead of just part of her right leg. ("Boston Marathon Bombing Survivor," 2019)

A disaster occurs somewhere in the world nearly every day. Some are major, such as the September 11, 2001, terrorist attacks in New York City and Washington, D.C.; the Indian Ocean earthquake and subsequent tsunami in 2004; and Hurricane Katrina, which slammed into the Gulf Coast and New Orleans in 2005. Others are more local and attract little attention, such as some floods, storms, and fires. There are many different types of disasters.

https://doi.org/10.1037/0000237-001
Treatment for Postdisaster Distress: A Transdiagnostic Approach, by J. L. Hamblen and K. T. Mueser

Natural disasters include hurricanes, tornados, floods, storms, and wildfires. Accidents are another type of disaster that include transportation events, explosions, and industrial calamities. Terrorism and mass violence are also considered disasters because they are a specific type of event that affects a large group of people simultaneously. Disease outbreaks are considered disasters, too, even though they are ongoing events, as opposed to war and civil unrest, which can be ongoing events but usually are not.

What is unique about disasters compared with other life-threatening traumatic events is their acute and collective nature (Barton, 1969). Disasters occur with little or no warning; affect large numbers of people simultaneously; and often require assistance and resources that go beyond what a region, state, or even country can support. For example, disasters may disrupt community services such as power, communication, and transportation. In the immediate aftermath people may be stranded or cut off from assistance; after more significant disasters, services may be disrupted for weeks or even months. People may be unable to contact loved ones, get medical attention, or even obtain general information about what is happening. Cleanup after a disaster can be a years-long process. People's homes and businesses may need to be restored and, in some cases, rebuilt from the ground up.

In today's world, disasters are often breaking news. We can watch them unfold in real time as reporters comment on the impending destruction or the aftermath. Local human interest stories often provide details about the worst outcomes, but they also depict the experiences of survivors and rescue or reconstruction efforts. In this way disasters are different from individually experienced traumatic events, which tend to be private (as compared to public) and typically do not have a widespread impact on infrastructure or services.

In the past 10 years, there have been an average of 125 federally declared disasters per year (U.S. Department of Homeland Security, n.d.). Estimates suggest that half of all men and women in the United States will experience a disaster in their lifetime (Kilpatrick et al., 2013). Worldwide, each year more than 60,000 people die as a result of natural disasters, accounting for 0.10% of global deaths. Rates are highly variable, however, and the average is increased by a few highly impactful events, such as the 1983–1985 drought in Ethiopia that led to widespread famine; the 2004 Indian Ocean earthquake and resulting tsunami; and Cyclone Nargis, which hit Myanmar in 2008 (see Figure 1.1).

In the 10 years between 2008 and 2017, natural disasters caused more than 670,000 deaths, left almost 250 million people displaced, injured 1.2 million,

FIGURE 1.1. Global Deaths From Natural Disasters, 1978-2018

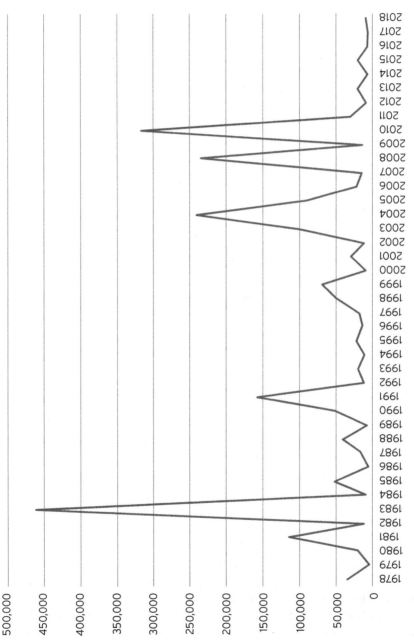

Note. This graph shows the absolute number of global deaths per year as a result of natural disasters (i.e., drought, floods, extreme weather, extreme temperature, landslides, dry mass movements, wildfires, volcanic activity, and earthquakes). From *Natural Disasters*, by H. Ritchie and M. Roser, 2019, Our World in Data (https://ourworldindata.org/natural-disasters#all-charts-preview). CC BY 4.0. Adapted with permission.

and affected nearly 2 billion people. The estimated economic costs are enormous, close to $1.5 trillion (in U.S. dollars). When terrorism and other disasters are added, the impact is even greater (Ritchie et al., 2019). But what impact do disasters have on people themselves?

POSTDISASTER PSYCHOPATHOLOGY

The majority of people are, fortunately, resilient after a disaster. Many experience difficulties immediately afterward, such as trouble sleeping or increased anxiety, but in most cases these symptoms improve rapidly and do not have a lasting impact on their ability to function at work or with their families. Others, however, experience more pronounced, adverse, and enduring mental health effects, including fear, anger, and sadness, and often meet criteria for psychiatric diagnoses such as posttraumatic stress disorder (PTSD) and major depression. Given that disasters affect many people, even if only a minority experience long-term mental health problems a disaster often means a large number of affected individuals will need help.

In 2002, Fran Norris and her colleagues published the most comprehensive study of the effects of disaster to date, an article titled "60,000 Disaster Victims Speak." It was an empirical review of the literature on mental health consequences of disasters covering the years 1981 to 2001, and it was later updated to include new studies published through 2004 (Norris & Elrod, 2006). They examined 225 distinct samples of disaster victims covering 132 different events. One of the aims of the review was to learn about which outcomes had been evaluated. More than three quarters (77%) of the studies reported on specific psychological problems that followed the disaster. PTSD symptoms were the most common problem reported, in 68% of the studies, followed by depression and anxiety, which were reported on somewhat less frequently (36% and 20% of studies, respectively). "Nonspecific distress," defined as stress not related to a specific psychiatric disorder, was reported in 39% of studies. Physical health problems, which included general health complaints as well as problems sleeping and with alcohol and drug use, were reported in 23% of studies. Chronic problems in living, including secondary stressors, such as work and financial difficulties, family and interpersonal conflicts, and housing or other rebuilding efforts, were examined in 10% of the studies. Finally, 9% of the studies reported on the loss of psychosocial resources, such as social support, optimism, and perceived control (Norris et al., 2002). In the next paragraphs, we examine some of these areas in greater depth.

Posttraumatic Stress Disorder

PTSD is a psychiatric condition that can develop after one has experienced a life-threatening event, such as combat, assault, and disasters. According to studies of the general U.S. population, an estimated two thirds to three quarters of adults will experience a traumatic event at some time in their life (Goldstein et al., 2016; Silove et al., 2017). Epidemiologic surveys indicate that the prevalence of PTSD in the U.S. population is approximately 5% (Goldstein et al., 2016). Although men and women are equally likely to experience a traumatic event (Kessler et al., 1995; Silove et al., 2017), women have a greater chance of developing PTSD (Goldstein et al., 2016; Silove et al., 2017). The higher rates in women appear to be due both to women's greater susceptibility to PTSD (Tolin & Foa, 2006) and to the types of traumas they experience. A large meta-analysis found that when type of trauma is controlled for, women are still more susceptible to developing PTSD (Tolin & Foa, 2006). In addition, women are more likely to experience the types of traumas that increase the chances of developing PTSD, including interpersonal trauma, such as sexual abuse and assault, intimate partner violence, and stalking, whereas men are more likely than women to experience serious injury and other types of physical violence (Goldstein et al., 2016; Silove et al., 2017). One reason for the higher prevalence of PTSD in women is that the aforementioned interpersonal traumas are associated with stigma, shame, and self-blame (Silove et al., 2017), as well as intentionality. Whereas some disasters also have intentionality associated with them, such as terrorism, others, such as hurricanes, are not typically perceived to be intentional. Culpability may also be a factor in man-made traumatic events, such as a toxic waste spill, or the 2018 Camp Fire in northern California, which may have been the result of negligence on the part of an electric utility company.

PTSD can be thought of as an inability to recover after a life-threatening event. During and shortly after a traumatic event it is appropriate to be on the lookout for threat and to be prepared to escape or defend oneself. Once the threat has passed, however, those feelings frequently go away. In contrast, for people with PTSD the world continues to feel threatening, and feelings of fear and anxiety actually intensify. This "normalizes" PTSD reactions a little more.

PTSD was not formally recognized in psychiatric diagnostic systems until 1980, in the third edition of the *Diagnostic and Statistical Manual of Mental Disorders* (*DSM*) published by the American Psychiatric Association. Over the years, there have been relatively minor changes to the diagnostic criteria. According to the fifth edition of the *DSM* (*DSM-5;* American Psychiatric

Association, 2013), PTSD is one of several trauma- and stressor-related disorders, whose criteria are specified as follows:

> Exposure to actual or threatened death, serious injury, or sexual violence in one (or more) of the following ways: 1) directly experiencing the traumatic event(s), 2) witnessing, in person, the event(s) as it occurred to others, 3) learning that the traumatic event(s) occurred to a close family member or close friend. In the case of actual or threatened death of a family member or friend the event(s) must have been violent or accidental, or 4) experiencing repeated or extreme exposure to aversive details of the traumatic event(s) (e.g., first responders collecting human remains; police officers repeated exposed to details of child abuse). (p. 271)

To be diagnosed with PTSD, a person must also experience symptoms at least 1 month after the traumatic event from each of four different symptom categories: (a) intrusive thoughts or feelings, (b) avoidance, (c) negative alterations in cognition and mood, and (d) overarousal. The diagnosis requires at least one *intrusive* symptom, including involuntary and distressing memories of the event, trauma-related nightmares or flashbacks, or psychological or physiological distress at reminders of the event. The person must also have one *avoidance* symptom, including avoiding thoughts, feelings, activities, people, or places that remind them of the trauma. Two symptoms indicative of *negative alterations in cognition or mood* are required, including forgetting parts of the traumatic event; negative beliefs about oneself, others, and the world; distorted cognitions about the causes and consequences of the event; persistent negative feelings; diminished interest; feeling detached or cut off from others; and an inability to experience positive feelings. Finally, a PTSD diagnosis requires at least one symptom of *overarousal*, including irritability, reckless or self-destructive behavior, hypervigilance, an exaggerated startle response, difficulties concentrating, or problems sleeping. The symptoms must last for at least 1 month and cause significant distress or impairment (American Psychiatric Association, 2013).

A 2008 review of the disaster literature examined 284 reports of disaster-related PTSD (Neria et al., 2008). The results indicated that 30% to 40% of direct victims, 10% to 20% of rescue workers, and 5% to 10% of the general population develop PTSD after a disaster. Children were at higher risk of PTSD than adults. The review also indicated that severity of exposure, which included injury, life threat, property destruction, and fatalities, was most predictive of PTSD. In addition, there was a general trend for symptoms to improve over time, but not for everyone.

Immediately after the September 11th attacks a question arose about whether the entire country might develop PTSD just from watching news coverage of the event. Although *DSM-5* later specified that exposure to an event via the media does not count as a traumatic event for the formal diagnosis of PTSD, there is evidence that such exposure can lead to symptoms of PTSD. One national study found high levels of posttraumatic stress symptoms: Of adults living in the United States, who by and large learned about the event from the media, 44% reported experiencing at least one symptom of PTSD "quite a bit" or "extremely" (Schuster et al., 2001). The most common symptom was feeling very upset when something reminded them of what had happened. PTSD itself could not be diagnosed because of the 1-month-duration requirement; however, about a month later another national study found that only about 4% of U.S. adults reported probable PTSD, suggesting that although there was widespread distress immediately after the attacks, most people who were not directly affected recovered quickly (Schlenger et al., 2002). In contrast, residents of Manhattan, who had the greatest exposure to the disaster, had higher rates of PTSD. Five to 8 weeks after the attacks, 7.5% reported symptoms consistent with a probable diagnosis of PTSD (Galea et al., 2002). By 4 months, the PTSD rates in these same residents had dropped to 1.7%, and by 6 months only 0.6% reported significant PTSD symptoms (Galea et al., 2003). Among those who were most directly affected, however, rates were about double. These included people who were either inside the World Trade Center or injured during the attack, those who lost possessions or property as a result of the attack, had a friend or relative killed, lost a job as a result, or were involved in rescue efforts.

A longitudinal study conducted in Sweden after the 2004 Indian Ocean tsunami supports the high prevalence of PTSD after a disaster (Arnberg et al., 2015). Sweden was uniquely poised to examine the impact of the tsunami on repatriated Swedish survivors because the government has complete population registries of medical and mental health diagnoses for all of their residents, and therefore it was possible to look longitudinally at the impact of the disaster and to statistically control for preexisting psychiatric disorders. Five years after the tsunami, the risk of having PTSD was seven times higher in the exposed population than in the matched controls. In addition, as in the studies of the September 11th attacks, there was a dose–response relationship between exposure and symptoms: Swedes who had been directly exposed to the tsunami (i.e., were caught or chased by the tsunami, felt their life was in danger, or required care for an injury) were 14 times more likely to develop PTSD than matched controls, whereas those with indirect exposure (i.e., experienced bereavement of a relative; sustained a minor injury; or witnessed distressing disaster scenes, like dead bodies) were 3.5 times more likely to develop PTSD. Bereavement was also found to be related to PTSD (Arnberg et al., 2015).

Depression and Suicidality

Disaster survivors often experience significant stressors and losses. For example, when there is widespread destruction, disaster victims often must find a new place to live, locate and hire contractors to complete home repairs, negotiate with insurance companies, commute farther distances to work or school, or look for a new job. At the same time, they may be dealing with ongoing health problems, physical injuries, and, in the worst cases, the loss of a loved one. They may be separated from neighbors, friends, or family because people have been displaced. They may also experience loss of their homes, property, and/or possessions. Finally, there can also be a loss of faith in others and in the world. Beliefs about the world being a safe place can be threatened. All of this can make people feel hopeless and overwhelmed, which can result in depression.

People who are depressed experience both sadness and a loss of interest or pleasure in activities they used to enjoy. In addition, they may experience other symptoms, such as changes in weight or sleep, feelings of agitation or lethargy, trouble concentrating, feelings of worthlessness, and thoughts of death with or without any suicide attempts. As with PTSD, rates of depression vary according to the specific disaster and the degree of the person's exposure to it. About 1 month after Hurricane Ike in 2008 hit Galveston, Texas, as a Category 4 storm, approximately 5% of individuals living in that area reported feelings of depression (Pietrzak et al., 2012), which is close to the expected 6% rate of current depression in the general population (Kessler et al., 1995). In contrast, 10% of Manhattan residents met criteria for depression during that same postdisaster period after the September 11th attacks (Galea et al., 2002). These differences may be due to the type of event (natural disaster vs. terrorism), the degree of exposure, or the aftermath.

The extent of disruption in people's lives has important implications for postdisaster symptoms and their long-term course. Rates of depression were higher after Hurricane Katrina than some other disasters, probably because of the greater personal destruction and widespread displacement the storm caused. Approximately 6 months after Katrina, 31% of the residents who lived in affected areas reported symptoms suggesting a diagnosis of depression or anxiety according to a brief psychiatric screen, 2.8% reported thinking about suicide in the last year, 1.0% reported a plan to kill themselves, and 0.8% reported having made an attempt to kill themselves (Kessler et al., 2008). One year later, these symptoms mostly persisted and or had worsened: Thirty-four percent reported symptoms of anxiety and depression, 6.4% reported having thought about suicide in the past year, and 2.5% reported having made a suicide plan. In contrast, however, there was a decrease in suicide attempts, to 0.2% (Kessler et al., 2008). It may be that, for residents struggling the most after Hurricane Katrina, the ongoing stressors began to wear them down, and the resulting helplessness and hopelessness became overwhelming.

It is interesting to note that in the population study of the 2004 Indian Ocean tsunami, repatriated survivors from Sweden did not exhibit increased rates of depression or anxiety (Arnberg et al., 2015). Although depression and anxiety were present in survivors who had been exposed to the tsunami, the rates were not higher than those in matched controls. The authors suggested that this may be because, unlike many disasters that happen where people live or work, in this case survivors returned to intact homes and support networks. There was, however, an increase in suicide attempts in Swedish women: Those exposed to the tsunami were 1.65 times more likely than matched controls to have made a suicide attempt.

A systematic review of risk factors for suicide after natural disasters (most commonly earthquakes) supported the fact that suicide rates generally increase after a disaster (Jafari et al., 2020). Being female and having a serious preexisting mental health problem were the most frequently identified risk factors. A number of other factors were also shown to increase the risk of suicide, including age (in particular, being an adolescent or being older), developing PTSD or depression after the disaster, low socioeconomic status, injury to oneself or a loved one, and low social support (Jafari et al., 2020).

Grief

Grief is a natural response when someone loses a loved one; however, when grief persists over an extended period of time and interferes with the person's ability to get on with their life, they may meet criteria for a psychiatric disorder. When a disaster survivor loses a loved one, therefore, there is a risk of a prolonged grief reaction. There are two overlapping conceptualizations of disorders resulting from grief reactions. The first, *prolonged grief*, is defined as a period of normal grief that lasts longer than 6 months and results in functional impairment (Prigerson et al., 2009). The second, *complicated grief*, is defined as when the bereaved person has trouble accepting the death of a loved one and experiences intense yearning for the deceased, emotional pain, and preoccupation with thoughts about the death or the deceased (Shear et al., 2013). The *DSM-5* proposed *persistent complex bereavement disorder* as a diagnosis for further study (American Psychiatric Association,

2013) and currently has a new proposal for *prolonged grief disorder* under review (American Psychiatric Association, 2020).

Because of variability in definitions of prolonged grief disorder, as well as differences between disasters, populations, and time since event, the prevalence estimates of it vary substantially. For example, among survivors of Hurricane Katrina, 19% of those who were bereaved reported moderate to severe symptoms of complicated grief approximately 6 months after the disaster (Shear et al., 2006). In contrast, in a sample of survivors from the 2008 Sichuan earthquake in China, approximately 1 year later 71% of bereaved survivors scored above a cutoff for a diagnosis of complicated grief (Li et al., 2015). Other studies fall in between. For example, 43% of those who lost a loved one during or after the September 11th attacks screened positive for a diagnosis of complicated grief 2.5 to 3.5 years later (Neria et al., 2007).

One study allowed for a comparison of complicated grief in survivors who were directly or indirectly exposed to the disaster. In this study, 130 Norwegians who lost a loved one in the Indian Ocean tsunami were screened for complicated grief 2 years later. Overall, 47% screened positive for complicated grief (66% of those directly exposed and 41% of those indirectly exposed), but there was no significant difference between the groups when other variables, such as loss of a child, were controlled for (Kristensen et al., 2010). In several studies, loss of a child was particularly likely to result in complicated grief reactions (e.g., Kristensen et al., 2010; Li et al., 2015; Neria et al., 2007).

Substance Use

Another problem that can occur after disaster is substance use. *Substance use disorder* is defined as a problematic pattern of alcohol or drug use that results in difficulty fulfilling work or family obligations, social or interpersonal problems, hazardous behavior, tolerance, withdrawal, and failure to quit. Research on the effects of disaster on substance use problems is mixed. In the next paragraphs we describe research on the effects of three large-scale disasters on substance: the September 11th attacks, the Indian Ocean tsunami, and the COVID-19 pandemic.

Some survivors reported an increase in substance use after the disaster. For example, after the September 11th attacks a survey of more than 1,500 residents living in New York City found that 10% of residents reported an increase in smoking, 17% reported increased drinking, and 3% reported increased marijuana use in the month immediately following the attacks (Vlahov et al., 2004). When the researchers examined drinking in these same individuals in the 6 months before and after the attacks, they still found a small, nonsignificant increase in drinking, from 3.7% in the 6 months before to 4.2% in the 6 months after (Vlahov et al., 2006). This study also allowed the authors to examine whether having a preexisting drinking problem increased severity of use after the disaster. The results indicated that 2.0% of people with drinking problems before the attacks continued to have problems, whereas 2.2% developed a new drinking problem. Thus, the modest increase in drinking appears to be in people with new cases of problematic drinking. Younger age, being single, and having a panic attack in the hours after the attack were significantly associated with new-onset drinking problems. People with drinking problems were also more likely to have symptoms of PTSD and depression (Vlahov et al., 2006).

A study of Norwegian survivors of the Indian Ocean tsunami found that 6 months after the disaster some directly exposed people retrospectively reported an increase in drinking relative to nonexposed people, whereas others reported a perceived decrease. There were no differences in current drinking between the groups, however, which calls into question whether temporary changes occurred or whether there was a recall bias in the retrospective ratings (Nordløkken et al., 2013). Furthermore, in a related study the authors found that current alcohol consumption 6 months to 24 months after the tsunami was not related to severity of disaster exposure or PTSD symptoms (Nordløkken et al., 2016). On the other hand, in a study of repatriated Swedish survivors of the tsunami, 5 years after the event drinking was significantly, but only modestly, elevated in exposed people compared with nonexposed controls. Those directly exposed to the tsunami were 1.27 times more likely to meet criteria for alcohol abuse or dependence, controlling for preexisting psychiatric conditions, than nonexposed controls (Arnberg et al., 2015).

A study that examined alcohol use during the COVID-19 pandemic, a prolonged rather than sudden disaster, also found an increase. In this study, alcohol use in a large, nationally representative sample from the United States was compared from 1 year before the pandemic to a period during the pandemic when there were substantial statewide social distancing measures in place (Pollard et al., 2020). Overall, there was a slight increase in both the number of drinking days and the amount that was consumed. On average, people drank on 0.74 more days a month then the year before (a 14% increase); increases were higher for women, for adults between ages 30 and 59, and for non-Hispanic Whites. In addition, women had a 41% increase in heavy drinking days, which were defined as days when they consumed four or more drinks at one time (Pollard et al., 2020). Taken together, these results suggest that after both sudden and prolonged disasters there may be at least a temporary increase in substance use and a small but more persistent increase in new problematic substance use.

Other Psychiatric Problems

The disaster literature includes individual studies documenting the development or exacerbation in disaster survivors of many other psychiatric problems or disorders, such as panic attacks (Wood et al., 2013), generalized anxiety disorder (Ghafoori et al., 2009), specific phobias (Arnberg et al., 2013; Meewisse et al., 2011), impaired eating (Carmassi et al., 2015); somatic symptoms (Carmassi et al., 2020), mania (L. Dell'Osso et al., 2014), and sleep problems (Thordardottir et al., 2015). However, larger epidemiologic surveys of these conditions have not been conducted.

Comorbidity

In general, it is not unusual for people who have one mental health problem to have more than a single disorder, or *comorbid disorders*. The National Comorbidity Survey, a large, nationally representative sample of U.S. adults, found that among respondents with any mental health problem, 50% had only one disorder, 23% had two, and 27% had three or more (Kessler et al., 2005). Compared with other psychiatric conditions, PTSD tends to be associated with even higher rates of other comorbid disorders. For example, in the National Comorbidity Survey 88% of men and 79% of women with PTSD also had another disorder (Kessler et al., 1995). Men with PTSD were most likely to have comorbid alcohol use disorders (52%) and major depression (48%), whereas women with PTSD were more likely to have comorbid alcohol (34%) or drug (15%) use disorders, conduct disorder (16%), or major depression (12%). These results replicate those of other nationally representative surveys both within and outside the United States (Creamer et al., 2001; Jeon et al., 2007; Pietrzak et al., 2011).

As expected, studies of disaster survivors also have found high rates of comorbidity, most notably between PTSD and depression. A study conducted after the 1995 Oklahoma City bombing of the Alfred P. Murrah Federal Building assessed survivors for a range of disorders and found that nearly half the sample met criteria for more than one psychiatric diagnosis, and 63% of those with PTSD met criteria for another disorder, most often depression (North et al., 1999). In a longitudinal study of survivors of the 2000 Enschede fireworks disaster in the Netherlands, 66% of survivors with PTSD had one or more comorbid disorders (most often a specific phobia or depression) 2 years after the event (Meewisse et al., 2011). Similarly, a study of firefighters who responded to the 1983 Ash Wednesday bushfires in South Australia indicated that 77% of those with PTSD had a comorbid disorder, the most common of which was depression (McFarlane & Papay, 1992), and a study of survivors of the Indian Ocean tsunami found that 88% of exposed disaster survivors with PTSD met criteria for depression (Arnberg et al., 2013). A 2005 study of Hurricane Katrina survivors, however, suggested that comorbidity might be higher among those with depression than those with PTSD: Results from a sample of 810 people living in southern Mississippi indicated that among those with PTSD, 44% had depression, whereas among those with depression 72% had PTSD (Nillni et al., 2013).

Course of Symptoms

The general course of symptomatology for people experiencing postdisaster distress is for the severity of symptoms to be greatest immediately after the event and to gradually improve, to the point of full recovery, in the weeks and months that follow; however, a closer look at the patterns of psychological response after a disaster suggests that there are at least five different trajectories: (a) resistant, (b) resilient, (c) recovered, (d) chronic dysfunction, and (e) delayed dysfunction.

Norris et al. (2009) examined two large population-based surveys: One followed 561 people who had experienced the 1999 severe floods in Mexico, and another followed 1,267 residents of the New York City metropolitan area after the September 11th attacks. Both surveys were initiated 6 months after the disaster. One third of those in the Mexico floods, and one half of the New York City residents, experienced few or no PTSD symptoms during the 1.5- to 2.5-year follow-up period after the disaster, which they described as a *resistant* group. A second, *resilient*, group experienced symptoms of PTSD immediately after the disaster followed by rapid improvement; this was observed in 32% of the Mexico sample and 10% of the New York City sample. A third group of people, who comprised about 10% of these study samples, were described as *recovered*; they exhibited symptoms immediately after the disaster but gradually improved over the course of several years.

The people who followed the final two trajectories did not improve. The fourth group was characterized as having *chronic dysfunction*, which involved moderate to severe PTSD symptoms that were stable over time. Between 13% (New York City) and 22% (Mexico) of respondents showed this trajectory. The fifth group had *delayed dysfunction*; they were characterized by few PTSD symptoms immediately after the disaster but then experienced an increase in symptoms that did not remit. Of the New York City sample, 14% were on this trajectory.

Overall, the data from the studies Norris et al. (2009) examined indicate that only 30% to 50% of disaster survivors experienced few to no symptoms, and the remaining survivors experienced symptoms for prolonged periods of time. These findings suggest that many survivors could benefit from treatment that focuses on their postdisaster reactions. They also are consistent with the results from a study of Swedish survivors of the Indian Ocean tsunami that found that 39% of people directly exposed to the tsunami had chronic symptoms over the following 6 years that either resolved slowly or did not resolve at all (Johannesson et al., 2015).

RISK FACTORS

An important question to answer is, who is most at risk for negative reactions after a disaster? Knowing who is at risk can help health care professionals identify the people who are most likely to need help. Understanding different risk factors for negative reactions can also help in estimating the overall mental health need of a population after a disaster. Finally, the knowledge of what contributes to risk as well as what protects against risk and promotes resilience can help in the development of programs that target the protective and resiliency factors.

Vulnerability to the psychological and behavioral effects of disaster is related to several different types of characteristics: personal characteristics, event characteristics, and recovery environment characteristics (see Exhibit 1.1). We discuss each of these characteristics next.

EXHIBIT 1.1. Factors That Increase Vulnerability to the Mental Health Effects of Disasters

Personal characteristics	Event characteristics	Recovery environment characteristics
Gender	Severity of exposure	Secondary stressors:
Age	Bereavement	• Displacement
Ethnicity	Injury	• Unemployment
Socioeconomic status	Home loss	• Health problems
Marital status	Intentionality of event	• Interpersonal problems
Children in the home		Loss of social support
Psychiatric history		

Personal Characteristics

The term *personal risk factors* refers to characteristics of the people who experienced the disaster. A number of demographic risk factors have been identified, including female gender; racial/ethnic minority group membership; poverty or low socioeconomic status; little previous experience in coping with disasters; psychiatric history; presence of children in the home; being middle aged or older than 65; and being sick, economically disadvantaged, affected by evacuation procedures, or frail (Goldmann & Galea, 2014; Lowe & Galea, 2017; Norris & Elrod, 2006; Tang et al., 2017). Children are particularly vulnerable (Goldmann & Galea, 2014). Being married appears to be a risk factor for women but a protective factor for men (Norris & Elrod, 2006). One explanation is that middle-aged married women with children may feel more caretaking responsibility after the disaster and thus experience more overall stress and burden.

Event Characteristics

The term *event characteristics* refers to what happens at the time of the disaster, and they are among the most predictive of postdisaster mental health problems. Severity of exposure has consistently been found to be the strongest predictor (Goldmann & Galea, 2014; Lowe & Galea, 2017; Norris & Elrod, 2006). For example, in a review conducted by Neria et al. (2011) of highly exposed people after the September 11th attacks, those with the greatest level of exposure consistently reported higher symptoms. Of World Trade Center evacuees, 15% met criteria for PTSD 2 to 3 years later, and 17% of primary care patients who knew someone who was killed in the attacks had PTSD around 1 year later. This stands in contrast to studies of adults living in New York City at the time of the attack, of whom only about 4% to 5% met criteria for PTSD (Neria et al., 2011).

Another study, which examined New York schoolchildren after the September 11th attacks, also showed that greater exposure was related to a higher prevalence of PTSD (Rosen & Cohen, 2010). For example, 16% of children in Grades 5 through 12 who knew someone who died during the attacks had PTSD, compared with 7% who did not know someone. Data from a Swedish study of tsunami survivors also indicate that exposure predicts symptoms. In that study, both life threat and loss of a friend or relative were predictive of having a worse outcome (Bondjers et al., 2018).

In a meta-analysis of 37 earthquake studies that focused on adults, those who were trapped or experienced fear, injury, or bereavement were significantly more likely to have PTSD (Tang et al., 2017). Fear was most predictive (those who reported fear were 2.97 times more likely to have PTSD than those who did not), followed closely by bereavement (2.49 times more likely). Adults who had been injured or trapped were 2.06 and 1.81 times more likely to develop PTSD, respectively (Tang et al., 2017).

The type of disaster has also been shown to be predictive of the development of mental health problems. Norris and Elrod (2006) found in their updated review of the disaster literature that, with all other characteristics held constant, severe levels of impairment were reported in 67% of the samples who experienced mass violence, compared with 39% of the samples assessed after technological disasters and 34% of samples assessed after natural disasters (Norris & Elrod, 2006). This may be due to presumed levels of intent. Disasters that are seen as intentional are experienced as being worse than those that appraised as being accidental or due to an act of nature.

Recovery Environment Characteristics

The recovery environment is the third category of risk factors. What happens after the disaster comprises in some ways the most important group of risk factors because they are the only ones that we can potentially change. The two risk factors that have the strongest effect are secondary stressors and lack of social support. *Secondary stressors* include all the problems that can happen after a disaster, such as unemployment, health troubles, being displaced from one's home or dealing with house repairs, transportation issues, taking care of other family members or friends who may have been affected, marital stress, and school adjustment problems (Goldmann & Galea, 2014; Lowe & Galea, 2017; Norris & Elrod, 2006; Tang et al., 2017). All of these can be consequences after major disasters and can increase the level of stress individuals feel.

Lack of social support is also a risk factor. Immediately after a disaster there is often a surge in support, both locally and nationally. This support may be tangible, such as money, a place to live, or property; informational, such as directions regarding how and where to get help; or emotional, such as expressions of concern or provision of comfort (Kaniasty & Norris, 2012). A study of low-income mothers after Hurricane Katrina found that those who perceived more support after the hurricane had fewer postdisaster psychological problems (Lowe et al., 2010).

There is, however, an important difference between received social support and perceived social support. *Received social support* is the actual support provided, whereas *perceived social support* refers to the belief that the support will be provided when needed (Norris & Kaniasty, 1996). Because disasters often happen to communities, local support networks that provide much of the perceived support may be disrupted when their members are either displaced or dealing with their own immediate needs (Kaniasty & Norris, 2012). In addition, even if the social networks remain intact, those not directly affected may not be able to sustain the support, and disaster survivors may feel forgotten or disappointed (Kaniasty & Norris, 2012). Norris and Kaniasty (1996) tested a model in survivors of Hurricanes Hugo and Andrew showing that both received and perceived support affect post-disaster mental health.

CONCLUSION

Disasters are an unfortunate but relatively common part of life. Both natural and man-made disasters affect entire communities, who are left to rebuild both literally and figuratively. The majority of people who survive a disaster experience some psychological symptoms. Although for most people these problems resolve on their own, others may continue to experience distress for years. This is particularly true of those with greater levels of exposure, such as people who have almost died, have been injured, or have lost a loved one. For these individuals, especially those with preexisting mental health problems and less social support, the symptoms are more likely to continue.

The ways people respond to disasters vary greatly. PTSD is the most-studied psychological consequence of surviving a disaster, and research suggests that it is the most common psychiatric diagnosis. But there are numerous other negative responses to a disaster, including other psychiatric disorders, which often occur together with PTSD but may also occur on their own. After PTSD, depression, which can immobilize a person and impede their recovery from the event, is the most common response to a disaster. As depression grows and people begin to lose hope in the world and themselves, or believe that things will never be the same, suicidal thinking may develop, and it may culminate in suicide attempts. People who have lost loved ones may experience significant bereavement in addition to PTSD and depression symptoms, and this bereavement, if not resolved, can evolve into prolonged grief disorder. Others may find that they are worrying more about their safety or the safety of loved ones. Some may discover they are using substances more.

Disasters also can result in secondary stressors that can worsen reactions. For example, disaster survivors may find themselves out of work, unable to access transportation, or dealing with issues related to being sick or injured. They may be temporarily displaced or even homeless. They may have financial problems, trouble with relationships, or difficulty at work. Some may suffer from ongoing health concerns. Also, although disasters may initially result in increased attention and social support, over time this attention may dissipate, leaving people feeling isolated and alone.

Over the course of the next several chapters, we describe the theory underlying the development of postdisaster reactions and what is known about treatment for these reactions. We then describe in detail the Cognitive Behavior Therapy for Postdisaster Distress (CBT-PD) program, which was specifically designed to target the wide range of symptoms and problems that can follow a disaster. We start by providing an overview of the program, which takes a transdiagnostic approach to helping people overcome the broad range of psychological consequences of exposure to a disaster. The CBT-PD program is a flexible but structured one that incorporates multiple strategies for facilitating recovery from a disaster, including psychoeducation, teaching relaxation techniques (breathing retraining), and activity scheduling to facilitate and reengage people in enjoyable and meaningful activities. The majority of the program is devoted to teaching cognitive restructuring as a self-management skill for dealing with negative feelings that follow a disaster; this involves learning not only how to challenge and change inaccurate, distressing thoughts and beliefs related to the disaster but also how to identify and implement practical solutions for addressing real-life problems and concerns. The CBT-PD program is appropriate for people with moderate or severe postdisaster distress and symptoms, and it can be delivered as soon as the immediate threat and disruption of the disaster has ended (e.g., 1–3 months later), or after a more extended period following the disaster (e.g., 6–12 months or longer). Subsequent chapters address each component of the treatment with case vignettes. An additional chapter delves deeper into the challenges of teaching cognitive restructuring to clients with suggestions for how to work through these challenges. We end with a discussion of some of the unique aspects of disasters therapists should be aware of and a discussion of how the program can be applied across different types of disasters.

2 TRANSDIAGNOSTIC TREATMENT OF POSTDISASTER REACTIONS

In Chapter 1, we examined the range of mental health effects that are common after a disaster, with a primary focus on posttraumatic stress disorder (PTSD). We begin this chapter by providing a rationale for using a transdiagnostic approach to the treatment of psychological consequences that follow a disaster. We then consider how behavioral, cognitive, and physiological theories of trauma, PTSD, and posttraumatic reactions can help explain the development of symptoms of distress and their clinical implications. On the basis of these theories, we identify four different guiding principles of transdiagnostic treatment for postdisaster distress and elucidate each principle in terms of how it is addressed in our treatment, Cognitive Behavior Therapy for Postdisaster Distress (CBT-PD).

A TRANSDIAGNOSTIC APPROACH TO TRAUMA AND POSTTRAUMATIC STRESS DISORDER

After a traumatic event, such as a disaster, PTSD is highly prevalent, but other mental health problems, such as depression, anxiety, and substance use, are also common, as are problems related to secondary stressors. Moreover,

https://doi.org/10.1037/0000237-002
Treatment for Postdisaster Distress: A Transdiagnostic Approach, by J. L. Hamblen and K. T. Mueser

significant symptoms often emerge after a natural disaster or an act of violence, either alone or in combination with each other, in people who do not meet full diagnostic criteria for PTSD. Despite this, most research on the treatment of psychological consequences of exposure to a disaster has focused only on PTSD symptoms and diagnosis, excluding the broader population of persons with subclinical PTSD who experience a range of other debilitating symptoms.

The transdiagnostic approach to the treatment of psychiatric disorders provides a useful alternative to traditional diagnosis-bound interventions by addressing the fuller range of symptoms and disorders often present in people who need treatment (Fusar-Poli et al., 2019). There is a need for a broader, transdiagnostic approach to the treatment of postdisaster reactions that is more responsive to the multitude of psychological consequences people experience (Hamblen, Norris, et al., 2009). The transdiagnostic program described in this book, CBT-PD, addresses the full range of cognitive, emotional, and behavioral reactions that follow exposure to a disaster and attends to both the symptoms of PTSD and to depression, sensitivity to stress, and functional difficulties.

There are several advantages to a transdiagnostic approach. First, by its very nature a transdiagnostic approach is designed to treat not only symptoms in people who meet diagnostic criteria for PTSD but also subclinical PTSD symptoms in those who do not meet the full diagnostic criteria, as well as those who experience other primary reactions to a disaster that may be even more debilitating, such as depression or anxiety. Thus, a transdiagnostic approach has the potential to alleviate the suffering of a larger number of people experiencing the psychological consequences of exposure to a disaster.

Second, a transdiagnostic approach can facilitate the adoption and dissemination of empirically supported interventions in community settings (McHugh et al., 2009). The need for treatment after a disaster often overwhelms local resources, and community providers usually lack the experience necessary to respond to the demand, including both assessment and treatment expertise. A transdiagnostic approach to treating the psychological sequelae of exposure to a disaster eliminates the need for expertise in psychiatric evaluation and diagnosis and streamlines the requirements for the training of clinicians to treat the associated problems. A transdiagnostic treatment that targets a variety of postdisaster stress reactions but does not require training in psychiatric diagnosis can be disseminated to clinicians in the community through a single training rather than through multiple trainings that focus on psychiatric assessment and treatment of specific disorders, making it a more cost-effective way of preparing a large number of clinicians to respond to a disaster. Furthermore, the transdiagnostic program we describe in this book can be used across a wide range of different disasters, regardless of whether it resulted in great loss of possessions, such as in a hurricane, or primarily resulted in significant fear and loss of life, such as in a mass shooting, facilitating its broadscale implementation.

Third, adopting a transdiagnostic approach can reduce the stigma associated with seeking treatment for postdisaster psychological symptoms. Stigma is a major barrier to seeking care for psychological disorders (Clement et al., 2015; Corrigan, 2004), including PTSD (Mittal et al., 2013). Fewer than half (45%) of people with a mental health problem seek treatment (Park-Lee et al., 2017), because of both public stigma (e.g., beliefs that people with mental illness are dangerous, weak, or unpredictable) and self-stigma (the endorsement of stereotyped beliefs about mental illness), leading to a worsening in symptoms and associated functional impairment (B. Dell'Osso et al., 2013). Conceptualizing posttraumatic stress reactions after a disaster as normal responses rather than pathological ones indicative of a disorder or disease can reduce stigma-related barriers to seeking help, especially when these reactions persist or worsen over time.

THEORIES OF POSTTRAUMATIC STRESS DISORDER AND POSTTRAUMATIC DISTRESS

Theories of the etiology of PTSD and related posttraumatic reactions have evolved over the past 80 years, with a growing consensus about the most central factors emerging in more recent decades (Lissek & van Meurs, 2015). A general framework for understanding the development of posttraumatic distress has been provided by the work of Horowitz (1975, 1986) and Janoff-Bulman (1989, 1992), who conceptualized the effects of psychological trauma in terms of the shattering of valued assumptions that people have about the world, other people, and themselves. *Valued assumptions* are thoughts and beliefs that influence a broad range of interconnected behaviors and feelings and are broadly defined as *schemas*. After a traumatic event that challenges these beliefs, the person's task is to incorporate the experience into their existing schemas or to modify or change these schemas.

PTSD and other symptoms of posttraumatic distress emerge when people have difficulty incorporating the traumatic experience into their worldview (Mueser et al., 2009). Instead of a memory of the event forming and being encoded into the person's schemas, where it can be accessed as needed, the person continues to relive the event, leading to a reexperiencing of symptoms (e.g., intrusive images, flashbacks). An inability to form a coherent, temporal, organized memory of the traumatic event results in fragmented and disjointed memories in survivors. Situations that trigger memories of the event lead to confrontations with unresolved challenges to the person's worldview and associated negative feelings (e.g., anxiety, depression, shame), resulting in avoidance symptoms. The alternations between trying to avoid or escape situations that remind the person of the traumatic event, and constantly being bombarded by reexperiencing the event as though it were happening all over again, lead to a state of chronic vigilance and hyperarousal, a prominent symptom of PTSD.

The challenge of incorporating a traumatic event into one's worldview is shared by all trauma survivors, and most experience posttraumatic distress in the days and weeks afterward; however, as they struggle with and succeed at integrating or accommodating the event into their schemas they usually experience a reduction in or resolution of their symptoms. Learning, cognitive factors, and physiological factors all play a role in determining how people respond to a traumatic event and cope with the experience and whether they experience persistent symptoms of posttraumatic distress. Understanding these factors can inform the treatment of posttraumatic reactions after a disaster, and in the following sections we review the theories that underlie such an understanding.

Learning Theory

Two different types of learning are involved in the development of PTSD and other posttraumatic reactions: (a) associative learning and (b) instrumental learning.

Associative Learning
Associative learning is broadly defined as a conception of learning as a process whereby the individual forms associations between different stimuli and responses, including in contemporary theories of cognitive representations. The most well-known example of associative learning is *classical conditioning* (or *Pavlovian conditioning*), in which a neutral stimulus is paired with another stimulus that has a positive or negative valence and that leads to a natural response (e.g., a shock, causing fear and escape attempts), resulting in a learned association among the neutral stimulus, the valenced stimulus, and the natural response. In Pavlov's classic experiment he paired the ringing of a bell with the subsequent feeding of dogs in his laboratory. After multiple pairings, the bell ringing (the *conditioned stimulus*) became associated with the food (the *unconditioned stimulus*), and the dogs began to secrete gastric juices as soon as the bell rang, a response that had formerly occurred only during feeding. Here, the *unconditioned response* of secreting gastric

juices during feeding became the *conditioned response* to the ringing of the bell. Although multiple pairings of the bell and the food were required to form this association in Pavlov's experiment, strong associations between two previously unrelated stimuli can occur in one trial. For example, aversions to a specific food can be acquired by animals after a single instance of poisoning (Garcia et al., 1985).

In the case of PTSD, the traumatic event is an unconditioned stimulus, which leads to the unconditioned response of fear and anxiety. Other neutral stimuli that were present during the event (e.g., the location, objects, sounds, smells) become associated with the trauma (or conditioned stimuli). Then, the next time the person is exposed to those previously neutral stimuli they experience similar feelings of fear and anxiety (or conditioned responses), even in the absence of further trauma. For example, a woman who was in a car when an earthquake struck feels afraid the next time she gets in a car; a man who was in a nightclub where a shooting took place is anxious the next time he returns to that bar. Experiencing negative feelings when exposed to cues that remind the person of the traumatic event is a common symptom of PTSD.

Instrumental Learning

Instrumental learning (also called *operant conditioning*) is any form of behavior change (either increases or decreases) that occurs as a function of the consequences of the behavior. The likelihood that a behavior will be repeated is influenced by two broad types of consequences that follow: *Adverse consequences* (or *punishment*) reduce the chances of the behavior in the future, whereas *positive consequences* (or *reinforcement*) increase the chances. Two types of positive consequence are also important to distinguish: positive versus negative reinforcement. *Positive reinforcement* occurs when a behavior is followed by a consequence with positive valence, such as providing food, praise, or money. *Negative reinforcement* is when a behavior is followed by the reduction or removal of something negative or unpleasant, such as pain, hunger, fear, or anxiety. Thus, behaviors that result in a tangible reward or positive feeling (positive reinforcement), or that lead to a reduction in something unpleasant (negative reinforcement), are more likely to occur again in the future. As we describe in the next section, associative learning and instrumental learning together play a major role in causing the avoidance behaviors of posttraumatic reactions.

Interactions Between Associative and Instrumental Learning

In the aftermath of a traumatic event, previously neutral stimuli become associated with the event, leading to distressing memories the next time the person is exposed to those stimuli. People respond to this distress by trying to escape or avoid situations and stimuli that evoke the upsetting memories, because escape or avoidance results in a momentary reduction in distress (or negative reinforcement). This relief is only temporary, however, because successful avoidance sets the stage for the generalization of newly learned feared stimuli to other neutral stimuli that are even less related to the traumatic event.

An information-processing model for how avoidance behavior in PTSD is learned and generalized can illustrate this process (Foa & Kozak, 1986). After a traumatic event, cues in different situations that remind the person of the event serve as "danger signals" that the person is unsafe and needs to escape. When escape is successful, however, additional neutral stimuli now become danger signals, triggering escape, which is again accompanied by immediate relief. This creates a vicious cycle in which increasingly higher numbers stimuli that are only distantly related to the traumatic event become danger signals, triggering negative feelings and precipitating further avoidance behavior.

Recall the example of the woman who was in a car during an earthquake. The next time she has to drive somewhere she feels anxious approaching the car because of the associated memory of the event. As soon as she decides *not* to drive, she feels relieved, which reinforces her avoidance of driving; however, the next time she even *thinks* about driving, that thought becomes a warning signal that triggers anxiety, without even seeing her car. She may respond by deciding not to drive, temporarily putting the thought out of her mind and experiencing relief. The process of increased avoidance in response to a growing variety of cues that evoke anxiety in different situations is called *generalization*, and it may result in fear and avoidance of situations only remotely related to the traumatic event, such as, in this example, avoiding all forms of transportation.

A similar process can be illustrated with the example of the man who was in a bar when a shooting occurred. He initially may avoid returning to that same bar and, over time, other, previously neutral stimuli may become danger signals that provoke anxiety and escape, such as being in the same part of town where the bar is located, going to any bar, or just going out at night. As each situation that evokes anxiety is successfully avoided, more and more stimuli become "danger signals" warning of the need to escape.

These theories of learning not only help explain the avoidance symptoms common in posttraumatic reactions but also account for how memories of the event become more distressing over time. Memories form immediately after a traumatic event occurs. Although the memories themselves pose no bodily harm to the person, they evoke negative feelings related to the event, which are responded to by avoidance, accompanied by the usual relief. As with the growth of trauma-related cues that lead to increasing avoidance, even momentary recollections of the event become danger signals that precipitate distress and avoidance.

Cognitive Factors

Theories of learning provide useful insights into the avoidance symptoms of PTSD, but they do not account for important cognitive aspects of posttraumatic reactions. The development of posttraumatic distress is also influenced by how the person construes the event and the attributions they make about those events. The importance of cognition to understanding differences in how people respond to events, including traumatic ones, has long been recognized, as exemplified by the Greek philosopher Epictetus, who observed, "People are not disturbed by things, but by the view that they take of them."

Cognitive theories of posttraumatic distress emphasize the importance of the person's appraisal of a traumatic event in shaping their response to it (Ehlers et al., 2012). *Appraisal* is a multidimensional process that involves the perception, evaluation, and integration of information into personal schemas that influences the motivations and goals people have (Mueser et al., 2009). The unexpected and threatening nature of a traumatic event frequently leads to exaggerated and generalized appraisals of imminent danger or increased risk of harm in a variety of situations, and accompanying fear. For example, it is not uncommon for people to believe "the world is an unsafe place" immediately after a natural disaster or terrorist attack, and this belief may persist or worsen for those who go on to develop PTSD and other posttraumatic reactions. A person who has been traumatized by one or more people often believes "nobody can be trusted." When this and related beliefs persist, the accompanying fear often prevents them from participating in formerly enjoyable and meaningful activities (e.g., recreational activities, relationships, work) and contributes to depression, the most common mental health problem associated with exposure to traumatic events (Flory & Yehuda, 2015; Shah et al., 2012).

Although concerns about increased danger are common in the aftermath of a traumatic event, they often give way to other interpretations as people struggle to make sense of what happened. These thoughts and beliefs can be focused on a broad range of factors related to the event, including those related to oneself, and they can be just as distressing, or more so, than the fear-based appraisals they replace. Some people blame themselves after a traumatic event in the mistaken belief that they were partly or wholly responsible for it. This is a natural temptation given the notion that "hindsight is always perfect." For example, a woman whose son was playing at a friend's house when a tornado struck and injured him may blame herself for not having kept him at home to do his homework that afternoon.

Self-blame can also focus on how the person responded to the event, either during it or afterward. For example, someone who survived a house fire might blame himself for going back into the house to rescue other family members and thereby suffering extensive injuries. People who develop posttraumatic reactions after a traumatic event often blame themselves for not having "gotten over it," believing that if they were stronger that they would have recovered by now. These individuals see their symptoms of posttraumatic distress as evidence of personal weakness.

Appraisals of self-blame or inferiority go to the heart of the individual's concept of who they are as a person, including their self-worth, their capabilities, and their flaws. Posttraumatic appraisals may also focus on the person's future, such as the belief that they have no future to look forward to or have little influence over what will happen (Ratcliffe et al., 2014). Examples of common thoughts are, "I'll never be able to have a normal life again," "My life has forever been changed by the event," and "I have no control over my life."

The specific appraisals that emerge after a traumatic event reflect the person's life experiences, beliefs, and vulnerabilities. Thus, people who have experienced much hardship and loss in their life are more prone to viewing a natural disaster as just one more piece of evidence that the world is a cruel, unsafe place. People who lack social support and have low self-esteem may focus on their own perceived inadequacies and limitations in responding to a traumatic event. For people who have previously struggled with depression, the event may tap into existing schemas of hopelessness and helplessness, leading to appraisals of the event as signifying irreparable loss and portending a bleak future.

The importance of cognitive appraisals to posttraumatic distress is reflected by the inclusion of altered thoughts and feelings as one of the core symptom clusters of PTSD in the *Diagnostic and Statistical Manual of Mental Disorders* (American Psychiatric Association, 2013). Furthermore, research shows that negative cognitions after a traumatic event are strong predictors of the development or persistence of PTSD, including cognitions not related to perceived danger and fear (Cyniak-Cieciura et al., 2015; Ehring et al., 2008; Kindt & Engelhard, 2005; Ready et al., 2015). There is also evidence from studies of PTSD that changes in trauma-related cognitions over the course of treatment predict reductions in posttraumatic distress (Holliday et al., 2018;

Kleim et al., 2013; Kumpula et al., 2017; McLean et al., 2015; Schumm et al., 2015; Zalta et al., 2014).

Physiological Factors

Heightened physiological reactivity has long been described as a characteristic of posttraumatic reactions, such as the typical overarousal symptoms of PTSD, including hypervigilance, an exaggerated startle response, difficulty sleeping, problems with concentration, irritability, and angry outbursts. The cycle of reexperiencing symptoms and avoidance of places, people, or things after a traumatic event, combined with negative emotions and cognitions, can contribute to a chronic state of anxious overarousal. Overarousal, however, is not just a by-product of posttraumatic distress; it also plays a critical role in its development and persistence.

A useful framework for understanding the role of these physiological factors is provided by *polyvagal theory*, which addresses interactions between different circuits that comprise the vagus nerve (Porges, 2011; Sullivan et al., 2018). This theory focuses on three distinct neural circuits in the autonomic nervous system, which evolved in mammals to regulate adaptive behaviors and responses in dangerous situations. The oldest circuit is the *unmyelinated vagus*, which is involved in fear-immobilization behaviors in extreme danger through rapid reductions in cardiac output. The next oldest circuit is the *sympathetic nervous system*, which controls fight–flight reactions to threat through increased metabolic and cardiac output. The newest circuit is the *myelinated vagus*, which inhibits sympathetic nervous system effects on the heart when danger is not perceived and serves as a social engagement system of sorts to permit human connection and more adaptive, flexible responses to situational challenges. Conversely, activation of the sympathetic nervous system inhibits this social engagement system until the perceived threat has passed.

Traumatic experiences can result in prolonged overactivation of sympathetic defensive responses (McEwen, 2017), reflected by inflated, inaccurate, and pervasive appraisals of threat. The consequences of persistently elevated arousal and perceived threat are reduced engagement with the environment and people, rigidity and impaired problem-solving, and poor control over emotions. The posttraumatic reactions contribute to common problems in social relationships (Westphal et al., 2011; Zlotnick et al., 2003), work functioning (Davis et al., 2018), and emotional stability (Jerud et al., 2014).

Polyvagal theory explains why the overarousal symptoms of posttraumatic reactions are not simply the consequence of reexperiencing, avoidance, and cognitive appraisal symptoms but instead play a primary role in contributing to and exacerbating those symptoms. Chronic overactivation of the sympathetic nervous system leads to exaggerated perceptions of threat and greater intensity of negative emotions, increasing avoidance behavior and distress related to the reexperiencing of symptoms. At the same time, the heightened physiological state and sense of being in constant danger prevents people from more flexible and adaptive engagement with their environment and others and experiences that could help them process the traumatic event, connect with others, get on with their lives, and resolve their PTSD and related symptoms. The implications of polyvagal theory, which we discuss further in the next section, are that decreasing sympathetic nervous system overactivation and stimulating the social engagement system can reduce negative cognitions and feelings, avoidance, and intrusive memories of the traumatic event.

Building on these theories, we developed CBT-PD, a manualized, time-limited, transdiagnostic treatment for postdisaster distress. The primary focus of the program is on identifying and challenging maladaptive disaster-related beliefs (i.e., cognitive restructuring) while also providing psycho-education about common reactions to disaster and strategies for reducing the common problems of anxiety and depression (i.e., breathing retraining and behavioral activation).

CLINICAL IMPLICATIONS OF THEORIES OF TRAUMA AND POSTTRAUMATIC STRESS DISORDER

The theories reviewed above have important clinical implications for the treatment of posttraumatic distress after a disaster. (Note that we are again using the term "disaster" because we are focusing more narrowly on the CBT-PD program.) Understanding these implications can help clinicians customize treatment to a specific client's circumstances and thus optimize outcomes. Four broad principles of treatment can be drawn from theories of development of posttraumatic reactions. Each of these principles is integrated into the CBT-PD program. We discuss them each in their own section.

1. Educate the Person About Posttraumatic Stress Disorder and Other Posttraumatic Reactions

Cognitive theory points to the important role of appraisals in how people react to a traumatic event such as a disaster and cope with the psychological aftermath. For example, people often struggle to understand symptoms they experience afterward, such as intrusive memories, difficulty sleeping, and emotional numbness. They do not recognize these experiences as common "symptoms" of an established syndrome, or a posttraumatic reaction. Even people who know about PTSD usually do not recognize all of the symptoms (e.g., altered thoughts and feelings), and they may be puzzled by other symptoms they experience, such as depression. They often think that something is wrong with them, or that they are going crazy, or they blame themselves for not having recovered from the effects of a traumatic event by now. These appraisals can contribute to significant distress and dysfunction, and yet they can often be modified simply by the provision of basic factual information.

In the CBT-PD program, clients are provided with information about the nature of PTSD and other posttraumatic reactions in an interactive and personally meaningful way that enables them to change pathologizing, self-blaming appraisals to more accurate and benign interpretations. Providing this information (or *psychoeducation*) lets clients know they are not alone in experiencing their symptoms, that posttraumatic distress is both common and normal after a traumatic event, and that the symptoms are not their fault or a sign of personal weakness. This normalization of posttraumatic reactions helps them integrate the disparate symptoms they have been experiencing into an understanding of posttraumatic distress as a syndrome related to a traumatic event. The information also conveys to the client that scientists and clinicians understand this syndrome and know how to treat it; this can instill hope for recovery and increase investment in treatment.

Psychoeducation about the nature and treatment of specific mental illnesses is a common feature of numerous interventions for a wide range of different disorders (Barlow & Craske, 2000; Gingerich & Mueser, 2011; González-Pinto et al., 2004). Education about trauma and PTSD is also a common feature of PTSD treatment programs. For example, widely used treatment programs for PTSD, such as cognitive processing therapy (Resick et al., 2017) and prolonged exposure therapy (Foa et al., 2019), provide clients with information about PTSD, such as how common it is, the characteristic symptoms, and other problems that often occur with the disorder.

Psychoeducation plays an important role in the CBT-PD program, especially early on, when it facilitates the client's engagement by instilling hope for change and investment in the program. After the assessment and orientation to the CBT-PD program, the majority of the first treatment session is devoted to providing the client with basic information about posttraumatic reactions. An interactive teaching style is used, guided by a series of educational handouts and worksheets, to help the client understand the information and relate it to their own experiences. Although the majority of psychoeducation takes place during the first session of CBT-PD, the clinician should be alert to opportunities later in the program to reinforce or review pertinent information about posttraumatic reactions that the client may have forgotten or did not fully assimilate. This helps the client learn more about PTSD and related reactions during the overall program than if they received only psychoeducation at the start (Mueser et al., 2015).

2. Teach the Person the Individual Strategies for Reducing Physiological Overarousal

As we described in the section titled Physiological Factors, overarousal symptoms are a primary characteristic of PTSD and posttraumatic reactions that can contribute to or worsen other posttraumatic symptoms. To be specific, according to polyvagal theory, overactivation of the sympathetic nervous system (i.e., as indicated by overarousal symptoms) results in frequent misperceptions of threat and a chronic fight–flight reaction, which inhibits the more flexible, accurate, and adaptive thinking required for social connection with others. The clinical implication is that teaching people how to reduce their overarousal symptoms can lead to more accurate perceptions of threat and safety, reducing their fear and avoidance and increasing their capacity to engage with others and their environment.

In the CBT-PD program, *breathing retraining* is taught to clients as a strategy for helping them reduce their sympathetic overarousal. Breathing retraining involves teaching clients how to slow down their rate of respiration, resulting in a reduced flow of oxygen to the brain and subsequent decreases in arousal level and associated anxiety (Krygier et al., 2013; Tan et al., 2011). Breathing retraining is frequently taught in treatment programs for anxiety disorders (Barlow et al., 2002) as well as in stress management programs (Woolfolk et al., 2008), self-management programs for serious mental illnesses (Gingerich & Mueser, 2011), and PTSD treatment programs (e.g., Foa et al., 2019). There are many other approaches to reducing overarousal symptoms as well. For example, breathing-based meditation and yoga have established effects on reducing sympathetic arousal, and a growing body of research suggests they may be beneficial in the treatment of PTSD (Hilton et al., 2017; Seppälä et al., 2014; van der Kolk et al., 2014).

In the CBT-PD program, breathing retraining is used as the primary approach for reducing overarousal symptoms because it requires relatively little time to teach and clients often develop proficiency after just a few weeks of practice. Breathing retraining is demonstrated and taught in the second CBT-PD session along with behavioral activation. Clients are asked to practice the skill between sessions, and their use of breathing retraining is followed up in subsequent sessions, with additional teaching and tailoring of the skill to the client as needed.

3. Facilitate the Person's Reengagement in Enjoyable, Meaningful, and Functional Activities, and Reduce Their Avoidance of Feared Situations

Avoidance is a cardinal feature of posttraumatic reactions. Although people initially avoid trauma-related situations after a traumatic event, learning theory explains why these avoidance behaviors rapidly generalize to a wide range of situations, including ones that have little or no relationship to the traumatic event. As a result of the generalization of avoidance behaviors, people often reduce their engagement in activities that were formerly rewarding (e.g., going to the movies or working out), meaningful (e.g., close relationships, family life, spirituality), and functional (e.g., working, going to school, or parenting). The consequences of this avoidance are depression, loss of sense of purpose, and functional impairment.

In the CBT-PD program, *behavioral activation* is used as the primary approach to increasing clients' engagement in rewarding, meaningful, and functional activities. Behavioral activation involves having clients routinely identify and schedule enjoyable and meaningful activities that are consistent with their values and goals. It was first developed as a treatment for depression, on the basis of the theory that depression results when life events interrupt a person's routine engagement in reinforcing activities (Lewinsohn, 1974). When depression emerges as a result of this loss of reinforcement, the associated low mood and negative expectations for future events hinder reengagement in these activities, which causes the depression to become further entrenched. When someone has PTSD, formerly reinforcing activities are avoided because they trigger trauma-related memories, which, as described above, contributes to further avoidance. Behavioral activation targets both depression and avoidance in PTSD by reengaging clients in rewarding and meaningful activities, which at the same time exposes them to situations that may evoke trauma-related memories. As clients resume participation in personally important activities they learn that their diminished expectations for how rewarding the activities will be are often inaccurate and that the situations are safe despite any memories of traumatic events they may trigger. Over time, and with regular participation in reinforcing activities, clients with PTSD learn that their trauma-related memories cannot hurt them, which reduces their avoidance of those memories and the distress associated with them.

Behavioral activation is a widely used strategy with a strong evidence base for the treatment of depression (Dimidjian et al., 2011; Kanter et al., 2010). The approach has also been incorporated into PTSD treatment programs (Wagner et al., 2007; Zatzick et al., 2011), and recent research suggests that it is effective on its own in the treatment of PTSD (Wagner et al., 2019).

Reengaging in activities that used to be part of one's usual life can arrest the cycle of increasing avoidance and provide valuable evidence that contradicts unfounded safety concerns or beliefs of helplessness and hopelessness.

In the CBT-PD program, behavioral activation is introduced in the second session. Clients are encouraged to consider a wide range of formerly enjoyable or personally important activities in which they previously engaged but now avoid. Then they are asked to schedule specific days and times for engaging in at least five activities over the next week and to track what happened and what it was like. For example, a client who is feeling isolated might select getting together with friends for lunch, or even just initiating a conversation with a coworker in the break room. A client who feels exhausted and concerned about weight gain might select joining a fitness class, and a client who feels hopeless might try volunteering. These experiences are reviewed with the client in the next session, with troubleshooting conducted as needed and additional events planned for the following week.

Most trauma-focused programs for PTSD include either cognitive restructuring or some type of exposure therapy to reduce avoidance of trauma-related situations. Cognitive restructuring, which is described in more detail in the section that follows, involves teaching people how to examine and change inaccurate thoughts and beliefs that underlie distressing feelings, including feelings of anxiety that lead to the avoidance of trauma-related situations. Cognitive restructuring is used in the CBT-PD program to address a broad range of inaccurate thoughts and beliefs that follow a traumatic experience, including the avoidance of trauma-related situations. *Exposure therapy* involves systematically exposing people to distressing memories of traumatic events and feared but safe situations that evoke trauma-related memories (e.g., Foa et al., 2019). Exposure to different memories and situations is done for long enough periods of time that the client's anxiety habituates (decreases) as they come to understand that the feared memories and situations cannot hurt them, and the client stops avoiding them. Exposure therapy is not included in the CBT-PD program because research has shown that exposure therapy and cognitive restructuring are equally effective in reducing avoidance and other symptoms of PTSD (Marks et al., 1998; Resick et al., 2002; Tarrier & Sommerfield, 2004) and that providing both interventions is not more effective than providing either one alone (Foa et al., 2005; Resick et al., 2008).

4. Help the Person Correct Inaccurate Thoughts and Beliefs Related to the Traumatic Event

As reviewed in the Cognitive Factors section of this chapter, the way a person appraises a traumatic event plays a critical role in determining whether they develop prolonged posttraumatic reactions afterward. Cognitive appraisals develop in the weeks and months that follow the event, as the person tries to make sense of their experience and reestablish a stable worldview that allows them to get on with their life. These appraisals frequently extend far beyond the traumatic event itself and can address concerns about the world (e.g., one's safety, the belief that the world is a cruel place), other people (e.g., ability to trust), oneself (e.g., personal strength, competency, self-worth, self-efficacy), and one's future (e.g., ability to control the future, bleakness). These appraisals are often distorted, or even dead wrong, but they contribute to strong negative feelings (e.g., anxiety, depression, guilt, shame) and avoidance of trauma-related situations. Helping people change inaccurate trauma-related thoughts and beliefs can facilitate their recovery from the traumatic event and posttraumatic distress.

As described in our explanation of Principle 1, psychoeducation about the nature of PTSD and its treatment can change inaccurate and harmful beliefs about the meaning of the traumatic event (e.g., "The world is unsafe"), its effects on the client (e.g., "I must be going crazy"), and how they coped in the aftermath (e.g., "I'm weak and should have gotten over this by now"). However, more than psychoeducation alone is often needed to change destructive cognitive appraisals that lead to or worsen posttraumatic reactions, including avoidance. To address this need, *cognitive restructuring* is taught in the CBT-PD program to clients to help them learn how to recognize and change inaccurate thoughts and beliefs, including trauma-related ones that are the basis for postdisaster reactions.

Cognitive restructuring, which is at the heart of cognitive behavior therapy (A. T. Beck, 1952; J. S. Beck, 1995), is a powerful method for giving people more control over their thoughts, feelings, and behaviors. It has been used successfully in the treatment of a broad range of psychiatric conditions, such as depression, anxiety disorders, borderline personality disorder, schizophrenia, and PTSD. Research has shown that cognitive restructuring for PTSD is not only equally effective as exposure therapy (as we discussed in the previous section), it also is more effective than other psychotherapeutic approaches to the treatment of PTSD (Bisson et al., 2013; Courtois et al., 2017).

Cognitive restructuring is the linchpin of the overall CBT-PD program, with more sessions devoted to teaching it than to any other component. It is taught in the third and fourth sessions of the program, with most of the remaining sessions primarily focusing on applying it to specific thoughts. Cognitive restructuring is taught to clients as a skill for dealing with negative feelings, with initial sessions focusing on helping them apply the skill to any distressing feelings they may be experiencing and later sessions gradually shifting the focus to more trauma-related thoughts and feelings. The skills are designed to help clients recognize when negative feelings are due to inaccurate thoughts and beliefs (whether trauma related or not), how to change those thoughts or beliefs, and when the feelings are in fact accurate and signal the presence of a problem, and then how to take steps to solve the problem. Clients practice using the skill on their own between sessions, with in-session work focusing on the review of home practice and the honing of skills.

CONCLUSION

As we discussed in Chapter 1, although PTSD is common after a disaster, it is not the only reaction. Disaster survivors may present with subsyndromal PTSD symptoms or a range of other reactions, such as depression, anxiety, or suicidal thinking, or just difficulty coping. Furthermore, interventions that focus specifically on a psychiatric disorder such as PTSD may be perceived as more stigmatizing and solidify the barrier to seeking help. For these reasons, the CBT-PD program was developed.

Over the past several decades, behavioral, cognitive, and physiological theories of PTSD and other posttraumatic reactions have been developed, refined, and tested. On the basis of these theories, four principles of treatment were identified that guide the transdiagnostic CBT-PD program: (1) educate the person about PTSD and other posttraumatic reactions; (2) teach the person the individual strategies for reducing physiological overarousal; (3) facilitate the person's reengagement in enjoyable, meaningful, and functional activities, and reduce their avoidance of feared situations; and (4) help the person correct inaccurate thoughts and beliefs related to the traumatic event.

In the CBT-PD program, Principle 1 is addressed by providing psycho-education about PTSD and other distressing responses to disaster, to normalize the client's reactions, to let them know they are not alone, and to foster hope for relief from their symptoms. Principle 2 is addressed by teaching breathing retraining, a widely taught skill that involves slowing down the rate of respiration in order to reduce arousal and anxiety, and to increase sense of calmness. Two approaches are used in CBT-PD to address Principle 3. First, behavioral activation, or the routine scheduling of participation in enjoyable, functional, or other personally meaningful activities, is incorporated in order to reduce the depression and functional impairment that are associated with reduced involvement in, or avoidance of, formerly enjoyed activities or important roles. Second, cognitive restructuring, or teaching people how to identify and correct inaccurate thoughts or beliefs, is used to reduce avoidance of feared but safe trauma-related situations and stimuli. Principle 4 is also addressed in CBT-PD by teaching cognitive restructuring, a skill that is used to help the client correct inaccurate thoughts and beliefs about a disaster, such as inflated perceptions of risk and danger, and to challenge and change a broad range of other distressing cognitions, such as self-blame related to how the client reacted to the event or for not having recovered from its effects, a pessimistic outlook on life, or a sense of complete loss of control over one's life.

3 RESEARCH ON TREATMENT FOR DISASTER

In the previous chapter, we argued from a theoretical perspective for the advantages of a transdiagnostic treatment for psychological symptoms people experience after a disaster. In this chapter, we present the research basis for such a treatment. Most treatments for postdisaster symptoms have been of two main types. The first type are preventative interventions that take a public health approach with the primary goal of reducing immediate psychological distress and the prevention of longer term problems such as posttraumatic stress disorder (PTSD) and depression. These interventions are offered early on in response to the disaster and (in the United States) are usually funded through Crisis Counseling Assistance and Training programs (CCPs) funded by the Federal Emergency Management Agency (FEMA). We will review the limited research available on these types of treatments.

The second type of treatments are delivered later in the disaster recovery phase and are targeted toward specific people who exhibit symptoms of a psychological disorder, usually PTSD. Most of the research on treatment after disasters is of this type. We will show that the research on these studies is of higher quality but does not address the full spectrum of psychological consequences that follow a disaster.

https://doi.org/10.1037/0000237-003
Treatment for Postdisaster Distress: A Transdiagnostic Approach, by J. L. Hamblen and K. T. Mueser

We conclude the chapter with a review of the development of and research on the transdiagnostic intervention we describe in this book, the Cognitive Behavior Therapy For Postdisaster Distress (CBT-PD) program. CBT-PD is of moderate intensity and is appropriate for delivery after the immediate, preventative treatment phase following a disaster, either before or after specific psychiatric disorders have developed. In fact, the CBT-PD program has been shown to be beneficial when delivered over a broad range of time after the immediate preventative phase that follows a disaster.

PREVENTATIVE TREATMENT APPROACHES

In the United States, after the president has formally declared a disaster, states can request FEMA funding to launch a CCP. These grants are intended to support community-based outreach, counseling, and other mental health services. An Immediate Services Program grant provides funding for the first 60 days, and then a Regular Services Program grant can extend that assistance for up to 9 months after the disaster declaration. Over the past 10 years, there have been more than 1,000 presidentially declared disasters (FEMA, 2020a) resulting in over $25 billion in public assistance funding from FEMA (FEMA, 2020b).

Research, however, is not formally allowed as part of a FEMA-funded mental health response. CCP performance is based on evaluations that are focused on program reach, perceived quality of services, and program consistency, but not on outcomes. For example, the FEMA CCP launched in response to the September 11, 2001, terrorist attacks was historic. With $155 million in federal funding for mental health, the State of New York launched Project Liberty. Knowing this was the single largest CCP to date, the state set out to carefully evaluate the program, providing the most comprehensive program evaluation data of CCPs thus far (Donahue et al., 2006). Questionnaires sent to CCP recipients documented that services were accessible, acceptable, and useful (Jackson et al., 2006), although no information was collected on whether the CCP services actually affected outcomes.

Since September 11, the Center for Mental Health Services, the agency that administers the FEMA funding, has developed a disaster toolkit (https://www.samhsa.gov/dtac/ccp-toolkit) that includes training materials on specific programs intended to prevent the development of mental health disorders. These public health approaches are by their very nature transdiagnostic and have the goal of decreasing the likelihood that symptoms will develop. As a result, these interventions are made available to a broad range of people early on after a disaster, they tend to be brief, and they are administered by nonprofessional staff.

Two programs are regularly offered as part of a CCP. In the immediate aftermath of the disaster, Psychological First Aid (PFA) is recommended first (Brymer et al., 2006). PFA is an evidence-informed modular approach for assisting people in the immediate aftermath of disasters and terrorism to reduce initial distress and to foster short- and long-term adaptive functioning. Then, in the first few weeks or months postdisaster, Skills for Psychological Recovery (SPR) is often offered (Berkowitz et al., 2010). SPR provides practical assistance to bolster disaster survivors' ability to cope. It is offered by paraprofessionals and can be delivered in a group or individually. Six core actions can be offered as part of SPR (Gathering Information and Prioritizing Assistance, Building Problem-Solving Skills, Promoting Positive Activity, Managing Reactions, Promoting Helpful Thinking, and Rebuilding Healthy Social Connections), with the idea that a survivor might meet as little as one time with a disaster response worker, or up to several times.

No randomized controlled trials (RCTs) have been conducted on either PFA or SPR; however, both have been used extensively. Some of the widely known disasters after which SPR has been used include the Indian Ocean tsunami in 2004; Hurricane Katrina in 2005; the *Deepwater Horizon* Gulf of Mexico oil spill in 2010; the 2011 earthquake in Japan that led to the Fukushima nuclear disaster; the Joplin tornado and Ferguson riots in Missouri in 2011 and 2014, respectively; the Flint, Michigan, water crisis that began in 2014; and the Camp wildfires in northern California in 2018 (P. J. Watson, personal communication, December 21, 2019).

Problem Management Plus (PM+) was developed by the World Health Organization (Dawson et al., 2015) as a preventative approach that can be broadly disseminated after a disaster. It is delivered by trained nonspecialists (ranging from licensed providers to volunteers), in five 90-minute sessions, either individually or in a group. PM+ includes psychoeducation, problem-solving, stress management, behavioral activation, and strategies to increase social support. Two promising RCTs of PM+ in people from a conflict-affected area of Pakistan have shown that those who received PM+ had less depression and anxiety 3 months after treatment than those who received enhanced usual care (Rahman et al., 2016, 2019).

Finally, in Australia, there is a new program called SOLAR (Skills fOr Life Adjustment and Resilience; Phoenix Australia, 2020). It too is a brief (five sessions) intervention for disaster survivors experiencing stress or adjustment problems to prevent of the onset of psychopathology. It is delivered by "coaches" who are front-line disaster workers, including case managers, volunteers, and nurses. SOLAR teaches skills for managing strong reactions, getting back into life, healthy living, managing healthy relationships, managing worry and rumination, and coming to terms with the disaster. In an open (noncontrolled) trial of 15 Australian bushfire survivors, participants showed large and significant decreases in psychological distress, PTSD symptoms, and impairment (O'Donnell et al., 2020).

The programs we have just discussed lend support to the idea that brief, transdiagnostic community responses offer a scalable, effective approach in the immediate aftermath of a disaster. However, they are all limited in that they are all delivered by nonprofessional staff and that they include more skills-based strategies to manage distress rather than treatments that make a concerted effort to ameliorate distress.

POSTTRAUMATIC STRESS DISORDER TREATMENTS FOR DISASTER

One very important reason for the limited research on postdisaster treatments is the inherently unpredictable nature of disasters, with each one requiring at least some services that must be uniquely tailored to meet the survivors' basic needs (e.g., medical, housing, food and clothing) and considerations of how to address psychological distress. The unexpected nature of disasters, and the urgent need to provide relief as soon as possible to large numbers of people in a particular geographic area, stands in stark contrast to most other psychological interventions, which are usually provided in established settings and serve known populations. Conducting research in specific settings and with well-characterized populations is easier because it allows for the extensive time usually required for planning, obtaining research funding, getting approval from local institutional review boards, hiring and training of research personnel in human subjects research, and training of clinicians. Although research on the treatment of psychological consequences of disaster can be conducted, substantial planning and resources are needed to overcome the challenges of mounting a research project in a timely fashion after such an event.

An additional impediment to conducting research on psychological interventions after a disaster is the need to coordinate the research with agencies and funding mechanisms aimed at addressing the numerous acute needs of the survivors. Such agencies may view research as cumbersome or a distraction from their primary mission of providing relief as soon as possible to survivors, and they may even discourage research on the most effective approaches to alleviating the psychological consequences of a disaster. As a consequence of these challenges, which also include restrictions on funding, the preponderance of research in this area has focused on the evaluation of treatments specifically focused on PTSD.

Trauma-focused therapy is recommended as the most effective treatment for PTSD in all of the most recent major clinical practice guidelines for PTSD (Hamblen et al., 2019). Only a limited number of RCTs have examined trauma-focused interventions targeting PTSD resulting from disaster. Three RCTs have evaluated traditional trauma-focused cognitive behavior therapy (CBT) interventions that included a combination of exposure plus cognitive restructuring delivered over eight to 12 weekly sessions and demonstrated positive effects. In the first study (N = 58), survivors of terrorism and civil conflict showed significant decreases in PTSD, depression, and social functioning compared with a waiting-list control group at posttreatment (Duffy et al., 2007). In the second study (N = 28), survivors of terrorist attacks in Thailand showed greater improvement in clinician-rated PTSD, and self-reported depression and complicated grief, than those in supportive counseling at posttreatment and at a 3-month follow-up (Bryant et al., 2011). In a third study, which focused on disaster workers (N = 31) who responded to the 2001 World Trade Center attacks, with full and partial PTSD, there were no differences between those receiving trauma-focused CBT or treatment as usual (TAU) at posttreatment. Among those who completed treatment (47% of the CBT group and 83% of the TAU group), however, survivors in the CBT group had significantly greater reductions in PTSD and depression than those in TAU (Difede et al., 2007), suggesting that, had participants remained in treatment, CBT would have been more effective.

In Turkey, Başoğlu and his colleagues developed control-focused behavioral treatment (CFBT) for survivors of the 1999 Marmara earthquake. Originally comprising eight to 10 sessions, CFBT was reduced to a single session so that it could be delivered more easily to a large number of survivors. The session focused on teaching people how to expose themselves to fear-evoking trauma cues (Başoğlu & Salcioglu, 2011). In the first RCT, 59 participants who received the single-session CFBT approximately 3 years after the earthquake showed greater decreases in clinician-assessed PTSD, depression, and improved functioning compared with a waiting-list control group at a 6-week follow-up; however, some survivors still had PTSD (Başoğlu et al., 2005). In an attempt to improve the effectiveness of the intervention, a second study was conducted with 31 survivors. In this study, survivors were randomized to one session of CFBT followed by a second session of simulated earthquake exposure or to repeated assessment. Participants who received the active treatment had significantly less severe PTSD symptoms, depression, and greater functioning at an 8-week follow-up, as assessed by self-report and interview, compared with those in the repeated-assessment control group; these gains were maintained 1 to 2 years posttreatment. Compared with the first study, in which a single session was used, the combined treatment achieved a greater reduction in PTSD symptoms (Başoğlu et al., 2007). In addition to the small sample sizes, another limitation of both of these trials is that the control groups received the treatment after the immediate posttreatment follow-up period, thus precluding a comparison of the two groups at the longer follow-up. This was especially problematic given that the control groups improved from pre- to posttreatment and may have continued to improve over the follow-up period.

Another trauma-focused intervention that has been used with disaster survivors with PTSD is narrative exposure therapy (NET), in which trauma survivors construct a detailed account of their lives with a focus on trauma across the lifespan (Schauer et al., 2005). The survivor's autobiographical account is recorded and corrected in subsequent readings. The therapist helps the survivor integrate details about their reactions to the trauma into a coherent narrative and to relive emotions when reading their account. NET varies in length but is often delivered in as few as four 60- to 90-minute sessions. Two small RCTs ($Ns \leq 30$) were conducted with survivors of the 2008 Sichuan earthquake in China. Approximately four sessions of NET delivered over the course of 2 weeks (Zang et al., 2013), or 1 to 2 days apart (Zang et al., 2014), resulted in significant decreases in self-reported PTSD symptoms and associated difficulties at posttreatment compared with those in a waiting-list control group. There was no long-term follow-up.

A number of open clinical trials of treatments for disaster-related PTSD have been conducted as well (i.e., noncontrolled studies). In these studies, survivors receive a treatment and are assessed before and after treatment, and often at follow-up as well, but there is no control group. These studies have generally reported improvements in PTSD symptoms over time, from pretreatment to posttreatment and follow-up. The majority of the treatments are also trauma-focused CBT interventions (Gillespie et al., 2002; Levitt et al., 2007), but there are also a few studies of eye-movement desensitization and reprocessing (EMDR; Konuk et al., 2006; Silver et al., 2005), and one that used yoga breathing (Descilo et al., 2010).

Noncontrolled studies provide a lower level of evidence for an intervention than RCTs because any improvement (or deterioration) that is observed could be due to something other than the treatment. For example, symptoms could improve over the natural passage of time, although some studies took place well past the time during which natural recovery would be seen. Another factor that could explain improvements in people who receive treatment other than the intervention itself is related to the naturally episodic course of PTSD over time. PTSD symptom severity and associated distress frequently fluctuate over time, with some periods associated with greater severity, impairment, and distress than other periods. Greater severity of PTSD symptoms and higher levels of distress may contribute to a greater willingness to seek treatment than when symptoms are more manageable, and thus some of the observed improvements in PTSD and distress could be due to the naturally fluctuating course of the disorder and the tendency of people's symptoms to improve somewhat on their own when they are at their worst. Thus, although their results are encouraging, they should be interpreted with caution.

In summary, among the seven RCTs, six reported significantly greater improvement in PTSD at posttreatment for the trauma-focused group than the control group. The one study that did not find support for trauma-focused PTSD treatment included participants with subsyndromal PTSD, which may suggest that PTSD treatment is not appropriate for disaster survivors who present with other primary symptoms. However, the majority of studies were conducted on relatively small sample sizes (i.e., 21–59 participants), and five out of seven had either no follow-up period or one that was less than 3 months. The other two studies had 1- to 2-year follow-up periods, but they pooled their data with the treatment group at follow-up. Finally, only one study (Bryant et al., 2011) included an active treatment comparator, which is a more rigorous test of the intervention.

HISTORY OF AND RESEARCH ON THE CBT-PD PROGRAM

For the reasons outlined previously, the CBT-PD program was designed to fill the gap in postdisaster interventions between brief, broad-based interventions aimed primarily at stress management and the prevention of postdisaster distress and treatments that narrowly focus on PTSD. The CBT-PD program is a transdiagnostic intervention that was designed to treat PTSD as well as the broad constellation of other symptoms that occur in the wake of a disaster. It was developed to be applicable to a wide range of clinical presentations, including people whose symptoms are of varying levels of severity, and that could be easily taught to community providers. CBT-PD is a time-limited cognitive behavioral treatment that focuses on helping clients challenge maladaptive beliefs and engage in more positive activities to reduce avoidance and improve mood.

The specific cognitive restructuring methods taught in CBT-PD have been used extensively with a broad range of trauma survivors with PTSD (Mueser et al., 2009), with rigorous research supporting its efficacy. To be specific, its approach to cognitive restructuring has been used to treat PTSD in people with severe mental illness (Mueser et al., 2008, 2015; Steel et al., 2017), borderline personality disorder (Bolton & Mueser, 2009; Kredlow et al., 2017), and addiction (McGovern et al., 2010, 2011, 2015). The approach has also been used successfully to treat PTSD in adolescents (Jankowski et al., 2011; Rosenberg et al., 2011) and in people in primary care (Prins et al., 2009). Table 3.1 provides a summary of research on the CBT-PD program.

September 11th Terrorist Attacks (2001)

The September 11th terrorist attacks are the deadliest attacks worldwide ("September 11 Attacks," 2020). Nearly 3,000 deaths occurred as a result, including 2,606 at the World Trade Center, 125 at the Pentagon, and 265 passengers killed in plane crashes ("September 11 Attacks," 2020). An additional 25,000 people suffered injuries. The rescue and recovery effort was prolonged, and the economic costs were estimated to be between $50 billion and $100 billion (Bram et al., 2002).

CBT-PD was first evaluated as part of Project Liberty, the CCP administered by the New York State Office of Mental Health after the World Trade Center attacks. The Office of Mental Health contracted with the National Center for Posttraumatic Stress Disorder to train clinicians in an intervention targeting disaster-related mental health problems (i.e., CBT-PD) and the University of Pittsburgh Grief and Loss program to train clinicians in an intervention to address traumatic grief (Donahue et al., 2006). These two interventions encompassed what was called their Adult Enhanced Services Program, an add-on to the basic CCP. As part of the response to that request, the program outcomes were evaluated.

Providers from 17 New York agencies were trained in CBT-PD over four 2-day trainings. Program evaluation data were obtained from 76 people who had received or were currently receiving either CBT-PD or the traumatic grief treatment through the Enhanced Services program. Participants responded to confidential telephone interviews approximately 18 and 24 months after the World Trade Center attacks, but the two assessment points did not necessarily correspond with pre- and posttreatment. There were significant improvements in self-reported symptoms of depression, grief, and functioning and marginal improvements in PTSD symptoms; however, the findings are difficult to interpret because the evaluation did not distinguish participation in one intervention from the other. In addition, because of the lack of a control group it was not possible to know whether improvements were attributable to the interventions (Donahue et al., 2006). What was clear was that

TABLE 3.1. Summary of CBT-PD Research Studies

Disaster	N	Treatment provided	When treatment was delivered	Assessment time points	Outcomes
September 11th World Trade Center attacks (2001)	76	CBT-PD or bereavement and grief treatment	1.5–2 years postdisaster	Participants were contacted approximately 18 and 24 months after the attacks.	Significant improvement in self-reported depression, grief, and functioning and moderate reduction in PTSD symptoms
Florida hurricanes (Charley, Frances, Ivan, Jeanne, 2004)	225	CBT-PD	1–2.5 years postdisaster	Pretreatment and post-treatment	Significant improvement in self-reported symptoms of postdisaster distress, PTSD, and depression. The pre–post effect size on the SPRINT-E was 1.57.
Hurricane Katrina (2005)	205	CBT-PD	1.5–2.5 years postdisaster	Referral, pretreatment, midtreatment, post-treatment and 5-month follow-up	Significant improvement in self-reported symptoms of postdisaster distress. The pre–post effect size on the SPRINT-E was 1.4.
Superstorm Sandy (2012)	342	CBT-PD	10 months–2 years postdisaster	Referral, pretreatment, midtreatment, post-treatment and 5-month follow-up	Significant improvement in self-reported symptoms of postdisaster distress. The pre–post effect size on the SPRINT-E was 1.4.

Note. CBT-PD = Cognitive Behavior Therapy for Postdisaster Distress; PTSD = posttraumatic stress disorder; SPRINT-E = Short Post-Traumatic Stress Disorder Rating Interview, Expanded Version.

more than 2 years after the attacks there were people who were still suffering who were willing to accept CBT-PD or a treatment for traumatic grief and who reported improvement across a range of postdisaster symptoms posttreatment.

The 2004 Florida Hurricanes

In 2004, Florida was hit with four powerful hurricanes in a 2-month time period: Hurricanes Charley, Frances, Ivan, and Jeanne. Although the number of deaths in Florida was low (9 direct deaths and 25 indirect deaths), the damage and destruction were significant (Pasch et al., 2011). Nine million people were evacuated from their homes; 8.5 million people lost power; and 13 hospitals, 16 fire stations, and 57 schools were destroyed (Brown et al., 2007).

As with the September 11th attacks, FEMA authorized CBT-PD as the sole enhanced service intervention for adults to be delivered through Project Recovery, Florida's CCP. Close to 100 providers were trained in CBT-PD over four 2-day trainings in the fall of 2005, approximately 1 year after the hurricanes, and weekly case consultation was made available. Data from 64 providers who agreed to complete surveys indicate that providers were overwhelmingly female (75%), White (73%), and held a master's degree or higher (73%). More than half of the providers reported at least "minimal" damage from the storms in their location.

Services were provided from September 2005 through March 2007. Data were available on 228 disaster survivors who provided informed consent to participate in Project Recovery. The exact number of adults who participated in the CBT-PD program was not known. Of the people who did participate, 75 (33%) completed therapy, which was defined as nine sessions or more. Fifty-eight of the 228 took part in at least two assessments. Significant and clinically meaningful improvement was observed for these disaster survivors with respect to postdisaster distress, PTSD, and depression. The overall pre–post effect size on the Short Post-Traumatic Stress Disorder Rating Interview, Expanded Version (Norris & Davidson, 2007), a measure of postdisaster distress, was 1.57, indicating a large effect. Survivors who received the most treatment also improved the most (Norris & Hamblen, 2007).

As part of the Project Recovery program evaluation, 29 providers were interviewed about their experiences delivering CBT-PD (Brown et al., 2007). The comments were overwhelmingly positive. Remarks like "This was a new format to me, but [I] didn't have any trouble with it. It was easy to follow" and "I thought [the CBT-PD program] was excellent" were common. However, some of the Project Recovery providers did not understand that they were being hired to deliver a particular intervention and did not think they should be forced to do so. For example, one provider said, "I think some providers thought that their training was being questioned[,] or they just felt threatened." Others seemed more open to it but struggled, saying it was not flexible enough to address the client's specific concerns, such as those related to housing, or that it should have allowed for up to 20 sessions. One important lesson learned from this first project involving CBT-PD was to establish clear expectations on the part of the providers during training on how to implement the program.

Hurricane Katrina (2005)

Hurricane Katrina was a Category 5 storm that made landfall in Florida and Louisiana in August 2005. It resulted in more than 1,800 deaths, 500,000 evacuations, and over $125 billion in damages ("Hurricane Katrina," 2020). Most of the loss of life and damage were a result of a failure in the levee system that led to severe flooding. New Orleans and the surrounding areas were hit particularly hard. One report stated that 80% of the city was flooded for weeks ("Effects of Hurricane Katrina," 2020). There were nearly 1,000 deaths in Louisiana as a result of drowning, injury, and heart conditions, with almost half of deaths occurring in people over age 74 (Plyer, 2016).

In response to Hurricane Katrina, the Baton Rouge Area Foundation launched a mental health initiative to provide free treatment to those affected by both Hurricane Katrina and Hurricane Rita called "InCourage" (Hamblen, Norris, Pietruszkiewicz, et al., 2009). The foundation selected CBT-PD as their treatment. Providers were hired with clear expectations that they would be delivering CBT-PD, and payment was based on submission of program evaluation forms. More than 100 local licensed providers were trained in CBT-PD approximately 1 year after Katrina. Ten team leaders with prior experience received additional training through weekly consultation on two cases. These leaders then provided weekly case consultation to the other providers throughout the entire program. At the same time, team leaders attended consultation calls with the treatment developers to discuss any issues that had arisen.

Over 14 months, 444 adult residents of greater Baton Rouge were referred to InCourage, and 205 (46% of referrals) enrolled. The majority were female, middle age (40–64), African American, and educated at the level of high school or some college. Most (90%) had been displaced by Hurricane Katrina and had experienced a broad array of stressors, including damage to their homes (84%), financial problems (83%), losing a family member (33%), and rescue or recovery work (25%). Of those who enrolled, 102 (50%) completed the program.

The evaluation used a quasi-experimental time series design. Although there was no control group, disaster survivors receiving CBT-PD were assessed at referral, pretreatment, intermediate treatment, posttreatment, and a 5-month follow-up to evaluate whether changes in symptoms had occurred. If changes were due to the treatment, one would expect more change from pretreatment to posttreatment than between referral and pretreatment or between posttreatment and follow-up. As Figure 3.1 shows, this is exactly what was found (Hamblen, Norris, et al., 2009). The CBT-PD treatment had a large effect, indicating significant clinical improvement, and the results were maintained at the 5-month follow-up. Improvement was seen for both postdisaster symptoms and coping skills, and White and African American participants improved equally.

FIGURE 3.1. Trend in SPRINT-E Means for the 66 Hurricane Katrina Participants Who Received CBT-PD and Provided Follow-Up Data

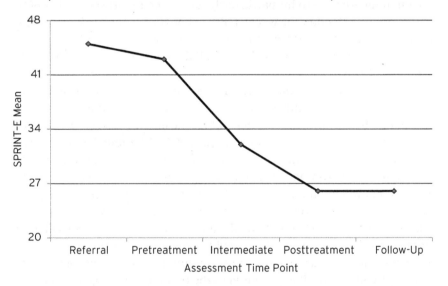

Note. SPRINT-E = Short Post-Traumatic Stress Disorder Rating Interview, Expanded Version; CBT-PD = Cognitive Behavior Therapy for Postdisaster Distress. From "Cognitive Behavioral Therapy for Postdisaster Distress: A Community Based Treatment Program for Survivors of Hurricane Katrina," by J. L. Hamblen, F. H. Norris, S. Pietruszkiewicz, L. Gibson, A. Naturale, and C. Louis, 2009, *Administration and Policy in Mental Health*, 36(3), p. 210 (https://doi.org/10.1007/s10488-009-0213-3). Copyright 2009 by Springer Nature. Adapted with permission.

Evaluation data from InCourage also allowed for a comparison of whether survivors with severe distress responded similarly to those with more moderate distress. This is important because it may be that those who are in the most distress need a more specific and intensive approach. As shown in Figure 3.2, the results were similar for participants who began treatment with severe as compared with moderate distress (Hamblen, Norris, et al., 2009). Those with more severe distress began treatment with higher scores but showed a response similar to those of people who began with more moderate symptoms.

FIGURE 3.2. Trends in SPRINT-E Means in the Primary Analysis Sample of Hurricane Katrina Survivors (*n* = 88) Who Received CBT-PD From Referral to Posttreatment Assessments

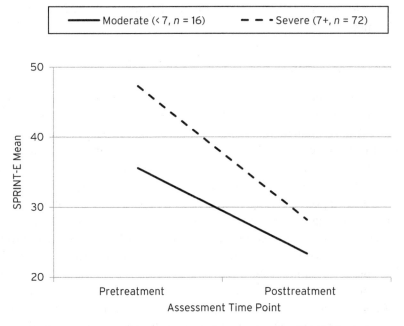

Note. Separate trends are shown for groups differing in the severity of their distress on the Short Post-Traumatic Stress Disorder Rating Interview, Expanded Version (SPRINT-E) at the point of referral. Moderate distress = fewer than seven intense reactions on the SPRINT-E (*n* = 16); severe distress = seven or more intense reactions on the SPRINT-E (*n* = 72). CBT-PD = Cognitive Behavior Therapy for Postdisaster Distress. From "Cognitive Behavioral Therapy for Postdisaster Distress: A Community Based Treatment Program for Survivors of Hurricane Katrina," by J. L. Hamblen, F. H. Norris, S. Pietruszkiewicz, L. Gibson, A. Naturale, and C. Louis, 2009, *Administration and Policy in Mental Health*, *36*(3), p. 211 (https://doi.org/10.1007/s10488-009-0213-3). Copyright 2009 by Springer Nature. Adapted with permission.

A subset of participants were mailed an anonymous survey at posttreatment to measure client satisfaction and therapeutic alliance; 77 participants responded (Hamblen, Norris, Gibson, & Lee, 2009). No fewer than 72% rated each primary component of the treatment as very or extremely helpful (i.e., breathing retraining, pleasant activity scheduling, and cognitive restructuring), and most had used each primary component no fewer than five times. Knowledge was also gained: Seventy-five percent could list at least three of the 5 Steps of Cognitive Restructuring, and 57% could name all five steps. The ratings of therapeutic alliance were also very high; 100% of respondents felt at ease with their therapist, 100% felt they liked each other, and 99% felt that the therapist understood them. All of the respondents said they would recommend InCourage to a friend. These results indicate that CBT-PD was effective at addressing postdisaster symptoms and concerns, was delivered with at least good fidelity, and that the participants felt CBT-PD addressed their concerns.

Superstorm Sandy (2012)

In 2012, Hurricane Sandy, often called "Superstorm Sandy," made landfall in the United States near Atlantic City, New Jersey, but affected 24 states in all. At least 71 deaths, the majority of which were in New York, resulted. It is estimated that Sandy caused $70 billion in damages ("Hurricane Sandy," 2020).

The Visiting Nurse Service of New York, funded by the American Red Cross, provided CBT-PD as part of their Disaster Distress Response Program, activated in response to Superstorm Sandy. Approximately 8 months after the hurricane, eight licensed providers were trained in CBT-PD. After the training, 342 adults enrolled in the program over 1.5 years. Survivors were again assessed at referral, pretreatment, intermediate treatment, posttreatment, and at a 5-month follow-up. Two hundred thirty adults (67%) completed the program, 202 (59%) provided data through posttreatment, and 111 (32%) provided 5-month follow-up data. The previous findings related to overall change and severity were replicated: Disaster survivors exhibited clinically significant improvements between pretreatment and intermediate treatment and, similar to Hamblen, Norris, Gibson, and Lee's (2009) study, the moderate and severe groups improved comparably (Hamblen et al., 2017).

In this evaluation the timing of how the treatment affected participant outcomes was also considered. The results suggest that timing is not a major concern. Disaster survivors benefited regardless of whether the treatment was initiated before the first year postdisaster or more than 2 years later (see Figure 3.3; Hamblen et al., 2017). No studies of CBT-PD have been

FIGURE 3.3. Trends in SPRINT-E Means in a Sample of Superstorm Sandy Survivors Who Received CBT-PD (*n* = 196) From Referral to Posttreatment Assessment

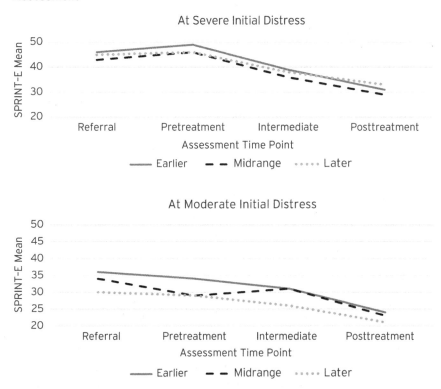

Note. SPRINT-E = Short Post-Traumatic Stress Disorder Rating Interview, Expanded Version; CBT-PD = Cognitive Behavior Therapy for Postdisaster Distress. Adapted from "Cognitive Behavioral Therapy for Postdisaster Distress: A Promising Transdiagnostic Approach to Treating Disaster Survivors," by J. L. Hamblen, F. H. Norris, K. A. Symon, and T. E. Bow, 2017, *Psychological Trauma: Theory, Research, Practice and Policy*, 9(Suppl. 1), p. 134 (https://doi.org/10.1037/tra0000221). Copyright 2017 by the American Psychological Association.

initiated sooner than 1 year postdisaster, which may be an indication of how difficult it is to launch a program in the immediate aftermath of disaster.

Other Disasters

In addition to these formal evaluations of CBT-PD there are two other disasters in which the program was a major part of an organized response. The Massachusetts Office for Victim Assistance trained 76 providers in CBT-PD to build capacity to provide treatment for survivors of the Boston Marathon bombing in 2013 and other disaster victims. A large in-person training and a recorded webinar were offered to local clinicians to build expertise and capacity to respond to a disaster. Providers were not required to deliver the intervention, and no evaluation was made. In addition, CBT-PD was used after the 2009 earthquake in L'Aquila, Italy, that killed at least 308 people ("2009 L'Aquila Earthquake," 2020). Several training workshops were provided, and the manual and workbook were subsequently translated into Italian and published (Hamblen et al., 2018a, 2018b). CBT-PD continues to be delivered after more recent earthquakes in that region of Italy.

Training

Training in the CBT-PD program has been relatively consistent across the different research studies, with the exception of clarifying provider expectations in the Project Recovery study (Norris & Hamblen, 2007). Most trainings consisted of an initial 2-day in-person session with 20 to 50 clinicians and two to four trainers. They began with a formal presentation on the mental health consequences of disaster, a treatment rationale for why a transdiagnostic treatment for postdisaster distress makes sense, and then a review of the evidence supporting the CBT-PD treatment program. Next, the trainers provided a step-by-step walk-through of each treatment session. The trainers would demonstrate new techniques and providers would then have an opportunity to engage in role-plays to practice using the skills. Worksheets were completed as group practice exercises and given as homework to be completed.

As part of the InCourage program offered after Hurricane Katrina, an evaluation of the training was conducted. One hundred four clinicians completed measures before and after training. Clinicians' attitudes about CBT significantly improved after the training, as did their ratings of how important CBT skills are and their ability to effectively teach those skills (Hamblen, Norris, Gibson, & Lee, 2009). Although none of the studies of the CBT-PD program included formal fidelity monitoring by an independent rater, as described above, clients who completed the evaluation of the InCourage program were able to name the major components of the CBT-PD program, suggesting that clinicians learned the skills well enough to convey them to their clients.

CONCLUSION

Despite the significant impact of disasters and the need for information about the most effective treatments for survivors' subsequent distress, research on disaster interventions is relatively limited. Statewide disaster mental health approaches have taken a transdiagnostic approach. Coping and skills-based interventions are offered broadly to people and focus on preventing the development of full-blown disorders. Program evaluation data provide information on utilization and satisfaction, but little is known about their effectiveness.

RCTs of PTSD suggest that trauma-focused interventions are effective in reducing symptoms as well as associated outcomes, such as depression, grief, and functioning levels; however, these studies have almost exclusively enrolled participants who met diagnostic criteria for PTSD. Whether the treatment would have been as effective for disaster survivors with other presenting problems remains unknown; in fact, the one study that included people with subsyndromal PTSD yielded null results. Thus, although treatment for PTSD is a good option for some people, it is not at all clear that it is the best option for others. In addition, even these more rigorous studies have significant limitations that restrict their generalizability.

By taking a transdiagnostic approach, CBT-PD can be offered to almost any disaster survivor experiencing distress. It fills a gap between what is offered as part of CCPs and traditional diagnosis-specific mental health treatment in the community. To date, CBT-PD has been delivered to hundreds of participants, with promising results. The program leads to a reduction in symptoms of PTSD, depression, and postdisaster distress as well as improvements in functioning and coping. It has successfully been implemented across a range of both natural disasters and terrorism and is appropriate for people with both moderate and intense symptoms. In the remaining chapters we review CBT-PD in more detail and discuss implementation challenges.

4 THE COGNITIVE BEHAVIOR THERAPY FOR POSTDISASTER DISTRESS PROGRAM

In this chapter, we provide a more in-depth description of the Cognitive Behavior Therapy for Postdisaster Distress (CBT-PD) program, including practical information about who is most likely to benefit from the program and where, when, and by whom it can be provided. We begin with a brief overview of the program and then address logistical issues, including broader challenges that arise when implementing it as part of a formal disaster mental health response. Next, we describe the core components of the program, including assessment, education about trauma and posttraumatic stress disorder (PTSD), breathing retraining, activity scheduling, and cognitive restructuring. We end with a vignette of a client who participated in CBT-PD to illustrate how the treatment can address the unique challenges people face after a disaster.

PROGRAM OVERVIEW

CBT-PD is a time-limited program designed to address the broad range of mental health problems that arise after exposure to a disaster or act of mass

https://doi.org/10.1037/0000237-004
Treatment for Postdisaster Distress: A Transdiagnostic Approach, by J. L. Hamblen and K. T. Mueser

violence, including PTSD and depression. Because CBT-PD is a transdiagnostic program it is appropriate for anyone experiencing persistent distress after a disaster. The program is delivered in eight to 12 individual 1-hour weekly therapy sessions, by a licensed clinician, typically at least 60 days after a disaster. Each of the four principles for treating PTSD and other post-disaster reactions (which we reviewed in Chapter 2) is fully integrated into the CBT-PD program, including (a) education about PTSD and other reactions to a traumatic event; (b) teaching skills to decrease physiological arousal; (c) increasing the client's involvement in rewarding and meaningful activities and reducing avoidance of safe trauma-related stimuli; and (d) challenging negative, inaccurate thinking that often follows a traumatic event. Homework assignments to practice specific skills taught in the program are collabora-tively set by the client and therapist at the end of each session and followed up during the next session.

After screening and assessment, the first two sessions of CBT-PD focus on providing *psychoeducation* about PTSD and related reactions after a disaster, teaching *breathing retraining* as a skill for reducing arousal, and encouraging *activity scheduling* (a type of behavioral activation) to reduce depression and avoidance of trauma-related stimuli. Information about the psychological effects of disasters, including PTSD, is taught in an interactive way to help clients relate the information to their own lives; this is bolstered by the use of educational handouts and worksheets. Breathing retraining is taught and practiced in the sessions, with the skill individually tailored to the client on the basis of their experience practicing it on their own. Activity sched-uling is initiated by having the client begin scheduling pleasant and personally meaningful events on a weekly basis. Both the breathing retraining skill and activity rescheduling are followed through on a regular basis over the course of CBT-PD.

Beginning in the third session, *cognitive restructuring* is introduced, and this remains the primary focus of the rest of the sessions. The long-term goal of cognitive restructuring is to help the client evaluate, challenge, and change inaccurate thoughts and beliefs that have emerged in the wake of the disaster and that underlie PTSD, depressive, and other distressing symp-toms. Cognitive restructuring is taught as a skill for dealing with negative feelings, and the initial emphasis of the teaching is on learning how to use it to deal with any negative feelings that may arise on a daily basis, no matter how minor. As clients gain proficiency in using cognitive restructuring, the focus gradually shifts to evaluating and changing trauma-related thoughts and feelings.

LOGISTICS OF IMPLEMENTING CBT-PD

CBT-PD can be delivered by individual providers in private practices, community mental health centers, other treatment settings, or as part of a more formal community or statewide disaster response. In each case there are logistical and implementation issues to consider.

Timing

There is no definitive answer about the optimal time to initiate CBT-PD; however, there are both clinical and administrative considerations. Clinically speaking, the CBT-PD program should be delivered at least 1 month after the disaster, although the optimal clinical timing is based on the specific circumstances of the disaster and the survivor. Clients need to be able to attend regular therapy sessions to benefit from the program, but this may be difficult to do if they are still actively dealing with the aftermath of the disaster. Survivors who are looking for housing, have numerous medical injuries, are caring for someone who was injured significantly, or have other major life issues that require attention (e.g., reenrolling children in school after a displacement) may be unable to commit the time to CBT-PD until their other needs have been attended to. For example, the displacement after Hurricane Katrina in 2005 was widespread ("Hurricane Katrina," 2020), and it took months for many people to resettle and begin to rebuild their lives. These disaster survivors needed support in the immediate weeks and months after the hurricane, such as the ones provided through Skills for Psychological Recovery (Berkowitz et al., 2010), but they would have been unlikely to benefit from CBT-PD early on. For different reasons, some survivors of the 2013 Boston Marathon bombing also needed more time to be ready for CBT-PD because they had lost limbs or had serious injuries that required time to heal. In contrast, although the World Trade Center attack in 2001 was a horrific event, it did not destroy people's homes, and those who survived did not typically suffer from permanent injuries, making them potentially suitable for CBT-PD sooner after the event.

After some disasters, crisis counseling programs that offer case management may be available. In these cases, initiating CBT-PD sooner, after the case manager has begun to meet regularly with the client to develop a recovery plan to address any unmet needs, may be possible. Provision of such supportive services can alleviate the client's most pressing concerns and free them up to begin focusing on their mental health issues.

In an administrative sense, initiating the CBT-PD program less than at least several months after a disaster may be difficult. For example, in the United States, if CBT-PD is delivered through a crisis counseling program that is funded by the Federal Emergency Management Agency, providing the program earlier than 60 days after a disaster usually is not possible because of the time required for states to obtain the necessary funding. In addition, even if timely funding for the program is available, delays related to the hiring and training of therapists can occur, depending on the number of survivors affected by the disaster and the availability of qualified clinicians.

Client Eligibility

Because CBT-PD is designed to address a broad range of psychological problems after a disaster, the eligibility requirements are minimal. It is appropriate for older adolescents and adults who, in addition to having experienced a disaster at least 1 month ago, report significant distress or interference in functioning related to the disaster and are willing and able to attend weekly sessions for about 3 months. As we describe in Chapter 5, the Short Post-Traumatic Stress Disorder Rating Interview, Expanded Version (SPRINT-E; Norris & Davidson, 2007) can be used to assess psychological distress and interference in functioning.

There are also relatively few exclusion criteria for participation in the CBT-PD program. If the initial screening indicates that the client has significant suicidal ideation, further assessment is necessary to determine whether there is imminent danger. In some cases, a safety plan can be established and then CBT-PD can proceed safely. The presence of thoughts about death and suicide should not preclude people from participating in CBT-PD given that the core elements of the program have been used to successfully and safely treat PTSD in clients with significant suicidal ideation (Kredlow et al., 2017).

When CBT-PD is offered as part of a formal program, clear policies should be provided about what to do when a client expresses suicidality at the initial screening. If the screen is conducted as part of a crisis counseling session by a paraprofessional (as opposed to a licensed provider), clear instructions should be in place that address how to refer the person for immediate psychiatric care. If the screen is conducted by a licensed provider, programs can establish a specific policy that outlines how providers should respond given that they have the training and experience to conduct more in-depth assessment and determine the safety of the client.

CBT-PD can be delivered to clients with serious psychiatric conditions (e.g., schizophrenia, bipolar disorder, major depression, borderline personality disorder, or substance use disorder), as long as they can attend the sessions and focus in the sessions. It is best if other mental health problems are being treated by another provider so that the therapist can focus on CBT-PD. Clients with an active substance use disorder need to be willing and able to attend weekly CBT-PD sessions when they are not under the influence. It is also important that clients with a substance use disorder indicate a willingness to practice the skills taught in the program on their own (i.e., complete the homework), when they have not used substances, in order to learn the skills and evaluate their impact on distressing symptoms. Clients with significant substance use problems that interfere with session attendance or skills practice may require more acute treatment of their substance use disorder before they can benefit from the CBT-PD program.

Clients with low cognitive ability can also benefit from the CBT-PD program (Mueser et al., 2018). This is important because people with lower cognitive functioning are more vulnerable to developing PTSD after a traumatic event (Bustamante et al., 2001; Seow et al., 2016). Clients with significant neuro-cognitive impairment may benefit from the involvement of a significant other/ support person (e.g., family member, friend) in CBT-PD who can help them review pertinent information and practice skills taught in the program (e.g., read handouts together, assist in completing worksheets). When a significant other or support person is involved in treatment it is useful for the therapist to regularly invite them into the closing minutes of the session with the client to review what was covered and explain the home practice assignment.

As we mentioned earlier, it is not uncommon for clients to be facing numerous life challenges as a result of the disaster. The CBT-PD program can help clients manage the stress associated with these different problems. For example, breathing retraining can help clients manage their anxiety, and cognitive restructuring can help them focus on challenging beliefs related to these stressors (e.g., "I won't be able to find a job"). Therapists do need to be cautious, though, to not spend all of their time in sessions helping clients solve their most pressing life problems and to ensure the majority of the time focuses on helping the client deal with the psychological impact of the disaster.

Setting

CBT-PD can be delivered in a range of settings. Most traditionally, it is delivered in a therapist's office. In cases where there is significant property damage and limited access to transportation, other public spaces have been used; for example, churches and community and recreational centers sometimes provide free private office space. CBT-PD can also be provided in a client's home, but certain potential challenges may arise, such as distractions due to the presence of children during sessions and a potential loss of confidentiality if others are present and there is no private space to meet. The therapist should discuss these issues in advance with clients to minimize distractions during the sessions themselves. When CBT-PD is being offered as part of a formal program, administrators must also consider the safety and security of the provider.

Length and Timing of Treatment

CBT-PD is designed to comprise between 10 and 12 sessions. It is important for clients to know at the outset that the program is time limited and to understand what the limits are in terms of length. In some cases, a program may have an upper limit, such as 10 sessions. This is typically done to enable therapists to see more clients and to keep costs down. If there is no externally imposed upper limit on the number of sessions, therapists might consider 16 sessions as a point at which there would be diminishing returns. Eight sessions could be considered a reasonable lower limit. New material is taught during the first four sessions, so eight sessions gives clients at least a few sessions to practice the skills they have just learned.

Sessions are typically 50 minutes long and are delivered on a weekly basis. The therapist and client may elect to lengthen the time between the last few sessions (e.g., meet once every 2 weeks) so that the client can have more opportunity to practice the skills on their own, without the support of the therapist. In practice, though, most clients prefer to stick to a schedule of weekly sessions, and even with that plan some cancellations or missed visits are common.

Involvement of Others in the Program

As we discussed in Chapter 1, social support is a protective factor that can lessen the severity of posttraumatic reactions to a disaster (Norris & Kaniasty, 1996). For some clients, especially those who have other major psychiatric challenges and more impaired functioning, such as a severe mental illness (e.g., bipolar disorder, schizophrenia, or recurrent major depression), including a significant other in aspects of the CBT-PD program can be helpful. Significant others can support the client's recovery in at least three different ways. First, by understanding and recognizing common posttraumatic reactions to disasters (e.g., PTSD symptoms and depression) in a loved one, the significant other can avoid reacting to those symptoms or misunderstanding the person, such as by blaming the person or themselves for the symptoms. By understanding that these are common psychological reactions to a disaster for which effective treatments exist, the significant other can support their loved one during their postdisaster symptoms. Second, because significant others know the client better than anyone else, they are in a unique position to understand and support the client's work toward their goals in the CBT-PD program (e.g., return to work, improved relationships, connection with a spiritual community) and their specific participation in the program. Third, significant others can play an important role in helping a loved one practice and use at home the skills taught in the CBT-PD program, in their natural living environment where they need them the most. This can include helping the client follow through on homework assignments and practicing the skills in the real world. To capitalize on the potential support of a significant other for the client's progress in the CBT-PD program, however, that person's involvement in the program needs to be explored and planned.

The therapist should first determine whether there are appropriate people to include in the program. If there are, the therapist should then discuss with potential clients whether this is something they are interested in and what that involvement might look like. Many clients' significant others appreciate learning about the nature and purposes of the CBT-PD program, as well as the nature of common posttraumatic reactions to a disaster, because this can help them better understand their loved one and how the program works. The therapist can arrange for the support person to meet briefly with them and the client toward the beginning of the program to receive an overview and discuss how they can be helpful.

There are several ways that information about postdisaster reactions can be shared with the significant other. The client can share the educational handouts with the significant other at home after they have reviewed them in sessions with the therapist, choosing whether or not to describe their own specific experiences. Alternatively, the therapist can directly provide the handout materials to the significant other (e.g., by mail or in person) and offer to answer any questions. Yet another approach is to invite the significant other to join toward the end of one or two of the psychoeducation sessions (e.g., the final 10–15 minutes) and to review some of the information about postdisaster reactions together with the therapist and client, including some of the client's experiences.

The most important role for the significant other is to facilitate the client's learning of the skills taught in the CBT-PD program by helping the client complete home practice assignments and reminding them to use the skills in appropriate situations. After learning some basic information about post-disaster reactions, the support person could receive information about the skills that are being taught by briefly joining the end of selected sessions. Specific homework assignments could be planned with the involvement of the significant other/support person with the purpose of helping the client understand and practice the skills as needed.

Last, when planning for termination of therapy, the possible role of the significant others as a support to the client to enable continued use of their newly acquired skills should be considered. Depending on the level of support desired, and the need for coordination between the therapist and client at the end of the program, part of a session could be devoted to including the significant other in the development of an aftercare plan. We have had success using this general approach to involving significant others in the treatment of PTSD in people with severe mental illnesses (Mueser et al., 2009).

Therapist Considerations

CBT-PD was designed to be delivered by licensed clinicians. Therapists who have experienced with cognitive behavior therapy (CBT) may learn CBT-PD more quickly, but those without this background have also successfully learned to deliver the program. Similarly, those with experience treating trauma or PTSD may find it easier to learn, although prior experience is not necessary. More information on training is covered in Chapter 12.

Case consultation is critical when providers are new to CBT and manualized treatments. Programs would benefit from identifying a supervisor who can provide ongoing support in delivering the intervention throughout the course of the disaster response program. For those with prior experience, peer supervision may be sufficient, providing an opportunity for them to come together and problem solve solutions around challenging cases.

CORE COMPONENTS OF THE CBT-PD PROGRAM

After a screening for postdisaster distress, confirmation of the client's eligibility for CBT-PD, and an explanation of the program, treatment begins in the first session by providing the client with a brief orientation to the program. This includes a clear explanation of the nature of the program, the rationale for the different treatment components, what will be expected of the client, and what the client can expect of the therapist. After this, also in the first session, psychoeducation is provided about common reactions to disaster, including PTSD and depression, which lets clients know they are not alone in having symptoms and that effective treatments for them do exist.

In the second session, breathing retraining is taught as a strategy to help clients reduce their physiological arousal and anxiety and improve their ability to focus. Activity scheduling is also initiated in the second session to help clients engage in more positive and meaningful activities in order to improve their mood and reduce avoidance of feared situations and stimuli. In subsequent sessions the therapist follows up on the client's ability to use the breathing retraining skill, conducts additional teaching as needed, and continues to facilitate weekly scheduling of activities.

In the third and fourth sessions, cognitive restructuring is introduced and taught as a skill to help deal with negative feelings by having clients examine the thoughts and beliefs underlying them; challenge the thoughts when they are inaccurate; and replace them with more accurate, balanced, and less distressing thoughts. The majority of the remaining sessions are devoted to helping clients learn and hone their cognitive restructuring skills and applying those skills to address negative, inaccurate thoughts and beliefs about the disaster that led to their symptoms. In the last session, an aftercare plan is established, and the therapist and client review the information and skills that have been covered in the program and discuss how to address new issues if they arise.

Table 4.1 summarizes the core components of the treatment and notes approximately when they occur. Before providing a more in-depth description of each component, we address the role of home assignments in CBT-PD and the monitoring of symptoms over the course of treatment.

Home Assignments

Like all CBT interventions, home assignments are an integral part of the CBT-PD program and are aimed at helping clients learn the information and

TABLE 4.1. Outline of CBT-PD Core Components, Estimated Time, and Session Numbers

Session number	Component	Approximate time (minutes)
1	Orientation to CBT-PD	10
1	Psychoeducation	45
2	Breathing retraining	10
2	Activity scheduling	25
3, 4 (plus one or two more sessions, as needed)	Cognitive restructuring (teaching)	80
5+	Cognitive restructuring (practicing)	Approximately 225
10 (or final session)	Treatment review and aftercare plan	45

Note. CBT-PD = Cognitive Behavior Therapy for Postdisaster Distress.

skills necessary to help them recover from the effects of the disaster on their lives. Home assignments are developed collaboratively by the therapist and client at the end of each session and are followed up at the beginning of the next session. Over the course of CBT-PD, clients are given handouts that summarize the material covered in each session and worksheets to complete that help them apply the information to their own lives (e.g., how to recognize and manage specific symptoms of PTSD) or use skills on their own (e.g., breathing retraining, cognitive restructuring). Handouts are generally reviewed during sessions, and some worksheets (or parts of worksheets) are completed in session to ensure the client knows how to use them. Assignments are then developed that involve the client finishing or completing additional worksheets on their own before the next session.

Home assignments are the primary vehicle for ensuring that clients can apply the information and skills taught in the CBT-PD program to their own lives. The review of assignments in each session, including a discussion of challenges experienced by clients as they try to use the skills, informs the teaching that occurs in each session. When clients do not follow up on home assignments, the therapist problem solves with the client to identify obstacles to completing assignments and solutions to overcoming them.

Monitoring Outcomes

Monitoring changes in the client's distress over the course of the CBT-PD program can provide valuable information about the effectiveness of the program and alert the clinician to the need to attend particular areas of distress. Therefore, a brief self-report measure of symptom distress (e.g., the SPRINT-E) is completed at the beginning of the first treatment session and every other session thereafter until the end of the program. The scores on the measure are shared and briefly discussed with the client so that changes in distress can be noted and potential problem areas identified. For example, if the client reports increased depression or avoidance, more attention could be focused on identifying relevant pleasant activities, or if the client reports significant distress related to intrusive memories of the disaster, the therapist could inquire about what the client is thinking about and then target these thoughts with cognitive restructuring. Information from the measure can also be used to identify when treatment should end and whether a referral may be indicated. In Chapter 11, we provide detailed information on how to decide when it is time to end treatment. More information on how to monitor outcomes is addressed in the next chapter, Chapter 5.

Orientation

An orientation to CBT-PD is provided after a person has indicated an interest in participating in the program and knows basic information about it, such as how long it takes. As a part of the initial engagement of the client, they may also know some of what is covered in the program, such as education about trauma and common reactions and skills for dealing with anxiety and stress. This information may have been covered in previous meetings with the therapist that could have happened 1 or more weeks ago, or potentially addressed by another clinician if the client was referred to CBT-PD by another provider. Thus, at the point when the orientation is provided the client may already have a basic understanding of the program.

The purpose of the orientation is to more fully explain how CBT-PD works, the nature of the program, and why it is expected to be effective. This typically involves helping the client understand more about how their postdisaster symptoms developed and how the CBT-PD program will address those symptoms. During the orientation the therapist also sets positive expectations about what the client will do during the program (e.g., consistent attendance, completion of home assignments), as well as what the therapist will do (e.g., teach information and skills, provide handouts and worksheets).

At the beginning of the orientation to CBT-PD clients are given an overview of the program and a description of its four main components (education, breathing retraining, behavioral activation/activity scheduling, cognitive restructuring; see Handout 1 in Appendix B on the American Psychological Association website at http://pubs.apa.org/books/supp/hamblen). Clients are told how each component is expected to work and why it is expected to work. They are also told that the CBT-PD program has been shown to be effective for people who have experienced a range of disasters and that those clients have gone on to lead productive and happy lives. Setting positive expectations for treatment effectiveness instills hope, improves engagement, and has been shown to contribute to better outcomes (Addis & Jacobson, 2000; Feeny et al., 2009).

Psychoeducation

Psychoeducation—the process of explaining psychiatric symptoms (or common reactions) to clients with the goal of helping them relate these symptoms to their own experiences—is formally introduced in the first session, although the therapist is encouraged to continue to provide education about symptoms throughout the entire program. It is an essential component of treatment and serves several critical functions. Most important, explaining to clients about specific common reactions to a disaster, such as the symptoms of PTSD, normalizes their reactions and lets them know that others experience similar symptoms. The fact that many other people have the same experiences after a traumatic event, and that they are in a treatment program specifically designed to treat postdisaster symptoms, also increases clients' hope, motivation to actively participate in the CBT-PD program, and confidence in the provider's ability to help them.

The specific content covered during psychoeducation includes information about common reactions to trauma, PTSD symptoms, substance use, sleep problems and nightmares, and impairment in functioning (including work, relationships, and health). The therapist begins by explaining each of the symptoms and reactions and then asks the client if they have experienced the symptom and, if they have, to provide some examples. This gives the therapist an opportunity to learn more about the client's personal experiences with symptoms and the relative importance of the symptoms to the client. For example, a woman might be having trouble sleeping but report she is not bothered by that because it is not influencing her relationships or ability to work. On the other hand, she might also indicate feeling irritable and on edge, which she sees as more problematic because it is affecting her relationship with her son. The therapist can take the opportunity in these discussions to explain again to this woman how the various CBT-PD components will help her deal with these issues. For example, the therapist might point out that the breathing retraining might help the client feel more focused and calm around her son and explain how scheduling pleasant activities can be used to plan fun things to do with her son.

Standardized educational handouts are used to guide the teaching. The client can share these handouts with significant others/support people if desired. Sharing the materials can result in increased social support because loved ones can gain a better understanding of the client's experiences and the steps they will be taking to address them. The client is also given worksheets to record their specific postdisaster symptoms and reactions. These worksheets can be completed during sessions, as home assignments, or a combination of both. Tips for managing symptoms are included in the handouts so that clients can begin coping with the symptoms even before they move onto the main components of the CBT-PD program.

Breathing Retraining

Breathing retraining is introduced in the second session of CBT-PD as a skill for reducing physiological arousal and anxiety. It is offered early on because it is easy to teach and clients can experience some immediate relief while learning other skills that take more time to practice. Teaching involves brief instruction and then about 10 minutes of in-session practice for clients to develop an understanding of how to use the technique.

Clients are then encouraged to practice the breathing exercise regularly on their own to enhance their expertise in using the skill. It is important that clients initially practice breathing retraining at times when they are not extremely anxious or stressed in order to develop competence in it. Within a few days or weeks, most clients become comfortable and practiced with it and are able to begin using it when they are feeling anxious, on edge, or uncomfortably overaroused. The therapist checks in with the client at the beginning of the remaining sessions to determine whether the client has mastered breathing retraining and is applying it in situations where it could be helpful. If the client is having trouble, the therapist makes suggestions for how to improve the effectiveness of the skill and/or proposes other situations for which the breathing might be useful.

Clients are taught breathing retraining not only to help them manage anxious arousal but also to help them focus and relax throughout the day. There is a growing appreciation for the benefits of being able to focus on the present rather than becoming distracted or overwhelmed by what is going on around you. Breathing retraining, like mindfulness or meditation, can be used to help clients focus on the present and become aware of their breathing and surroundings rather than bombarded by their thoughts and feelings. The ability to focus attention can also help clients later, when they are first learning cognitive restructuring. Rather than getting anxious when examining their thinking, clients can use breathing retraining to help them relax and focus their attention on the task at hand.

Activity Scheduling

CBT-PD facilitates the reengagement of clients back into their usual routines through the systematic use of behavioral activation/activity scheduling, which is introduced in the second session. Like breathing retraining, activity scheduling is a skill that is relatively simple to teach and can have an immediate impact on the client's quality of life. Activity scheduling involves helping people identify previously enjoyed activities (or new activities) that they are currently avoiding and make formal plans to participate in those activities. Each week, the therapist and the client identify five pleasant activities and schedule them on the client's calendar.

Engaging in pleasant activities results in positive feelings; however, after a disaster a person can become depressed and develop low expectations for how rewarding these activities will be. Therapists can ask clients to predict how enjoyable an activity will be and then, immediately after the activity, evaluate how enjoyable it actually was. People often think that an activity will be much less enjoyable than it actually is, and this discrepancy between the person's prediction and the actual pleasure experienced can be used to gently challenge negative expectations and beliefs a client may have about their life since the traumatic event.

Clients may also avoid certain pleasurable activities because they are afraid of the activity itself. For example, a client who was present at a shooting at a nightclub or movie theater may avoid public places for fear of being shot at again. Using pleasant activity scheduling (sometimes along with cognitive restructuring), therapists can help clients reengage in activities they have been avoiding and learn that they are safe and enjoyable.

A third way behavioral activation can be effective is by helping clients engage in more rewarding or personally meaningful activities. These activities may not be pleasant in and of themselves, but they can be rewarding. For example, going back to work may not be fun, but it can be incredibly important and satisfying. Similarly, few people enjoy doing chores, but completing tasks such as laundry and grocery shopping is critical to functioning, and failure to do so results in feelings of inadequacy and hopelessness.

Throughout the CBT-PD program the therapist monitors the client's weekly activity scheduling and makes adjustments as needed. The therapist helps the client identify the activities that will help them meet their specific goals. For example, a client who wants to improve their relationships should schedule activities that involve being with other important people in their life, whereas a client who wants to stop feeling guilty and depressed might schedule a range of new activities, looking to identify the ones that are most enjoyable. A client who is depressed and withdrawn might need to focus on scheduling a time to take a shower or do the dishes.

Cognitive Restructuring

Cognitive restructuring is taught as a skill for dealing with negative feelings; it is the primary approach to identifying and changing trauma-related schemas that underlie PTSD and other postdisaster symptoms. It is taught over two sessions, and the remaining five or more sessions are spent helping clients use the skill to challenge negative, inaccurate, and upsetting beliefs, including those that are related to the disaster. Clients are introduced to the *thought–feeling–behavior triad* to explain how thoughts, feelings, and behaviors are connected. Examples are used to demonstrate the connection. For example, if you *think* you are in danger, you may *feel* afraid, and choose to *stay inside* where you feel safe, even if a more objective evaluation of the situation indicates there is little or no danger. The therapist uses additional examples to show how inaccurate thinking can lead to inaccurate conclusions, resulting in negative feelings and maladaptive behavior.

Problematic Thinking Styles are then introduced and defined to the client as common but inaccurate ways people have of reaching distressing conclusions, such as catastrophizing or engaging in black-and-white thinking. Different problematic thinking styles are reviewed, and examples from the client's life are explored, followed by a discussion of why each style is inaccurate (and thus problematic). Clients learn to recognize when their feelings of distress are related to engaging in one of these thinking styles and how to use specific strategies to correct their thinking and reduce their distress. Through home assignments, clients begin monitoring upsetting situations and their associated thoughts and feelings. They then identify which problematic thinking style applies and come up with a more helpful thought.

Once the client has mastered how to identify and avoid problematic thinking styles (usually in one to two sessions), they are then taught the 5 Steps of Cognitive Restructuring. Building on the problematic thinking styles discussions, the client again starts by *recognizing* (Step 1) an upsetting situation, *identifies* (Step 2) the thoughts or beliefs underlying the negative feelings, and *evaluates* (Step 3) whether they reflect a problematic thinking style. Then the client *assesses* (Step 4) whether the thought is accurate and, if it is inaccurate, *changes* (Step 5) the thought. Clients first learn cognitive restructuring by using the skill to deal with any negative feelings and, as they become more skillful, their attention is turned to trauma-related thoughts and beliefs. The therapist helps the client identify core beliefs that are underlying distressing feelings, such as "The world is an unsafe place" or "I am incompetent." These core beliefs come up repeatedly, and by working through different situations related to the same underlying belief (e.g., "Movie theaters are unsafe," "The subway is unsafe," "The football stadium is unsafe") clients learn to connect their reactions to a specific situation to the larger underlying belief.

If the underlying thought associated with the negative feeling is deemed to be accurate, the client is taught to develop an Action Plan to address the problem. The therapist uses brainstorming and problem-solving techniques to help the client determine the best approach to handling the situation. For example, a client who is fearful after hearing that a Category 5 hurricane is headed their way may determine that their belief that they are not safe staying in their home is accurate. In this case, the therapist helps the client think through what steps they need to take to prepare to evacuate as well as strategies for managing their anxiety (e.g., breathing retraining). Action Plans can also be used when the client determines that their thought is not supported by the evidence but still feels negative emotions associated with the situation. For example, a client who concludes that it is safe to fly but still feels afraid may develop an Action Plan that includes using their breathing exercises on the plane, inviting a friend to accompany them on the plane, or even exposure therapy (e.g., sitting on an empty plane) before the trip.

Treatment Review and Aftercare Plan

An individual course of the CBT-PD program ends with a review of the information and different skills that have been taught: psychoeducation, breathing retraining, behavioral activation/activity scheduling, and cognitive restructuring. The therapist engages in a discussion with the client about each of these areas: how they have worked for the client, which ones were most helpful, and how they will use them in the future. The therapist should encourage the client to think about current or upcoming situations that might be difficult and either complete a cognitive restructuring worksheet in advance for how to handle it or discuss what other supports the client has in place for managing those situations.

The therapist should also share with the client how their scores on the SPRINT-E (or other assessment) have changed over the course of therapy. The therapist should encourage clients who have shown modest or minimal improvement to continue to use the skills they have learned in the program and see how things go. We know from most skills-based treatments that clients continue to show improvement after the therapy has ended because they are continuing to use and refine their skills. Even clients who have shown a significant response to treatment should be given the message that, with continued attention to the skills, they can expect continued improvement. If after a few months clients are still struggling, a referral to another provider for a more specific treatment may be warranted.

CASE VIGNETTE

We present here a case vignette of an older woman who participated in CBT-PD after Hurricane Katrina in 2005 to illustrate how the program can address a range of issues that arise postdisaster.[1] Dolores was a separated

---

[1]This case vignette, and all others in later chapters, is a composite case in which details from several different clients have been combined to protect their confidentiality.

65-year-old licensed practical nurse who was working at a local hospital before the hurricane. She had two daughters; her elder daughter, age 40, had passed away from cancer 3 months before Katrina, and her younger daughter, age 37, was single, unemployed, and had an 8-year-old son with special needs. Dolores's daughter and grandson were living with her in her home in New Orleans when the hurricane struck. Her mother lived in a nursing home nearby.

Dolores initially chose not to evacuate because she did not want to be separated from her mother. The nursing home had told her it was not safe to move their patients, and Dolores wanted to be close in case her mother needed her. As the water level started to rise, Dolores realized that she had made a mistake and was in trouble. Miraculously, her husband came by and helped the family get to the roof. They were all ultimately airlifted to the University of New Orleans. From there, they made several stops before relocating to a cramped one-bedroom apartment in Baton Rouge. Her mother was not as lucky: She drowned in her bed in the nursing home.

Dolores was depressed. She had not gotten over the loss of her elder daughter and was now grieving the loss of her mother. Her younger daughter and grandson were again living with her, and she felt like they were on her nerves all the time. She had given them the bedroom, and she was sleeping on the couch in the living room, but this meant she had no privacy. Although Dolores initially thought about trying to find a new job as a nurse, she decided to retire instead, feeling like she did not have the energy to start over. This resulted in financial issues, exacerbated by the fact that the family had lost all their possessions.

Dolores's husband had been trying to reunite with her since he helped them evacuate, which was something she had wanted before the hurricane. But now she felt numb and indifferent toward him (a common symptom of PTSD). She also found that she had turned into a worrier. She worried about everything and second-guessed all of her decisions, and she was very scared that another hurricane would hit and that this time none of them would survive. At the start of treatment, her score on the SPRINT-E was a 49, a score indicative of severe symptomatology and probably PTSD.

Psychoeducation

Dolores had many PTSD symptoms. She had intrusive thoughts about Hurricane Katrina that were brought on by stories on the news, bad weather, and any type of memory of her mother. She also had significant trouble sleeping and was taking sleeping pills to get through the night. She did not exhibit much avoidance, although she never went out when the weather was bad. Dolores did not trust the weather reports, even when the weather looked okay. She stayed inside listening to the news in case there was an announcement to evacuate. She found that she was irritable and had less patience with her grandson, and she lacked the ability to concentrate, which was interfering with her ability to read, something she used to greatly enjoy.

Dolores also identified with common reactions to trauma. She was anxious about storms and fearful that something bad was going to happen. She was afraid to be away from the house because her daughter and grandson might need her. She reported tremendous guilt over the loss of her mother and believed she should have taken her from the nursing home herself as soon as people were encouraged to evacuate. Dolores was depressed and found little pleasure in things that used to be enjoyable. She also was furious with her current situation: After working and saving her whole life, she found herself trapped in a small apartment, with little money and no job.

Breathing Retraining

Dolores immediately took to the breathing retraining. As a nurse, she understood how the body works and felt a sense of calm and quiet when she practiced her breathing. At the beginning, Dolores was able to use the breathing techniques only when she was alone and could concentrate but, with practice, she was able to use them even when in public, taking a few slow exhalations to avoid becoming overwhelmed. She found the breathing particularly useful at home when she would get frustrated with her daughter and grandson.

Activity Scheduling

Activity scheduling was an important part of Dolores's treatment. One focus of her activities was to help her get connected with her new community. Activities included going to several different churches until she found one that she liked. She then focused on getting involved in church activities that got her out of the house and connected with friends. A second focus was on finding hobbies that Dolores could do to bring more pleasure into her life. This included some solitary things, such as taking a walk and reading a book, as well as activities she could do with her daughter and grandson, such as playing board games and going to the park. As she began reporting feeling better, the therapist also helped her focus on repairing her relationship with her husband. Going on dates became regular, pleasant activities scheduled into her week. Once Dolores reconnected with friends and family, she began to experience more joy.

Cognitive Restructuring

In the cognitive restructuring sessions several of Dolores's core beliefs related to the hurricane were challenged. First and foremost, Dolores felt guilty over the death of her mother. The therapist helped Dolores challenge the thought that it was her fault that her mother had died in the nursing home. Over the course of the therapy Dolores was able to recognize that even if she had been able to take her mother out of the nursery home before the storm, her death was due to a natural disaster and the negligence of the nursing home administration. As with most core beliefs, Dolores's thoughts that she should have done something different resurfaced around other situations as well. The therapist also helped Dolores challenge guilt related to her feelings that she should be doing a better job caring for her daughter and grandson and that she should be "over" the hurricane by now.

The second core belief that the therapist helped Dolores work through was that something else bad was going to happen. Although Dolores was mostly concerned about another hurricane or flood occurring, given that her daughter and mother had passed away she was also fearful that someone else would get sick or die, that someone would be injured, or that some other misfortune might occur. She also did not trust herself to make the "right" decisions and was afraid that this would result in harm to her family. Dolores was eventually able to replace these catastrophic thoughts with more accurate and realistic ones.

Outcome

At the end of treatment, Dolores reported feeling "like myself again." Her post-treatment SPRINT-E score was 25 (a drop of 24 points, indicating a significant reduction in distress). Although she did not go back to work, she felt satisfied with her life. She even began volunteering at a hospital where she would talk and visit with elderly patients. She was active in her church community, was enjoying rebuilding her relationship with her husband, and felt less angry about her circumstances in regard to her daughter and grandson. Although she was still grieving the loss of her elder daughter and mother, she said that she was more focused on remembering the good times and no longer felt like her mother's death was her fault. Although she continued to report some fears about the consequences of future storms, once she was able to put an evacuation plan together she felt more comfortable being away from home even when the weather was unsettled.

CONCLUSION

CBT-PD is a transdiagnostic treatment used to target postdisaster distress. Unlike treatments that target only PTSD, it is specifically designed to address a range of reactions that are common after a disaster. Built on the core principles of PTSD treatment, CBT-PD incorporates strategies appropriate for people with PTSD as well as those with other psychiatric symptoms or who are just having difficulty adjusting to the aftermath of disaster. CBT-PD is a flexible treatment that provides therapists and clients with the ability to tailor the treatment to fit the clients' needs. It can be delivered by individual practitioners or as part of a formal disaster mental health program.

PART II THE TREATMENT PROGRAM

5

SCREENING AND ASSESSMENT

Although the Cognitive Behavior Therapy for Postdisaster Distress (CBT-PD) program is based on a transdiagnostic approach, screening and assessment are still vital to identifying those disaster survivors who are in need of, and could benefit most from, treatment. Screening and assessment can also inform providers about how to tailor CBT-PD and evaluate its effectiveness with individual clients. Nevertheless, screening and assessment for the CBT-PD program can be minimized in order to make it feasible to deliver in postdisaster settings and to avoid establishing formal psychiatric diagnoses, which some disaster survivors may experience as stigmatizing. A single measure can be used to determine a person's need for treatment and to monitor outcomes over the course of CBT-PD. In this chapter, we describe methods for screening and assessing people for the CBT-PD program. We also review other relevant outcome measures that individual providers may choose to evaluate the effects of the program on their clients.

https://doi.org/10.1037/0000237-005
Treatment for Postdisaster Distress: A Transdiagnostic Approach, by J. L. Hamblen and K. T. Mueser

SCREENING

As we discussed in Chapter 1, many people experience some psychological symptoms after an event, but only a small proportion of them ever receive care. There are several potential reasons for this. First, some people recover naturally on their own. Second, early on in the aftermath of disaster other priorities take precedence. People may be displaced, injured, or focusing on needed house repairs. They may not have time to attend therapy sessions or even the time to figure out where to go. Third, disaster survivors may not think that they need help and expect that they will feel better over time. To some extent this is true, especially within the first few weeks after a disaster. In the longer term, however, natural recovery becomes less and less likely. Screening is needed to determine who needs help, when that help should be provided, and what level of help is indicated.

The primary aim of screening is to identify people with significant levels of distress who could benefit from treatment. Screening instruments should be brief and easy to administer. Questions should be phrased in plain language with easy-to-use response scales. In addition, when the screening measure is to be administered by staff at a crisis counseling program or large community clinic, it should be easy to score so that nonspecialists can accurately and quickly score it and make referrals when appropriate.

Postdisaster Distress Screening Measures

Several screening measures are available to gauge postdisaster distress. In the sections that follow, we describe the one most commonly used as part of the CBT-PD program and then another that has been used in several disaster studies.

Short Post-Traumatic Stress Disorder Rating Interview, Expanded Version

The Short Post-Traumatic Stress Disorder Rating Interview, Expanded Version (SPRINT-E; Norris & Davidson, 2007), can be used to identify disaster survivors who might benefit from CBT-PD. It has been used extensively across occurrences of natural disasters and terrorism and was developed specifically for use as a screen for postdisaster distress (Norris et al., 2006; see Appendix A on the American Psychological Association website at http://pubs.apa.org/books/supp/hamblen). The SPRINT-E contains 12 questions, including four that correspond to common types of PTSD symptoms (intrusive thoughts, avoidance of trauma-related stimuli, emotional numbing, and overarousal) as well as questions that tap other areas, such as depression, physical health, drinking and smoking, and psychosocial functioning. Two additional questions ask how distressed, overall, the person feels and how concerned they are about whether they will overcome their problems without assistance. A final item that assesses suicidality is also included but is not used in the overall scoring. The SPRINT-E is a self-report measure, although it can also be administered verbally, as an interview. It assesses reactions over the past month.

Each item on the SPRINT-E is rated on a 5-point scale: 1 = *not at all*, 2 = *a little bit*, 3 = *moderately*, 4 = *quite a bit*, and 5 = *very much*. "Intense" reactions to the disaster are defined as scores of 4 or 5, with the number of items rated as "intense" used to summarize overall distress and need for treatment. Treatment should be offered to people who score at least a 3 (i.e., three or more items scored as intense or higher; Norris et al., 2006). A score of 3 or more is indicative of a possible disorder while 7 or more is indicative of a probable disorder. The SPRINT-E can also be scored on a continuous scale, with full score range of 11 to 55, to evaluate changes over time. The measure has three subscales: Distress, Functioning, and Coping.

The SPRINT-E can be administered over the phone or in person. In some cases, programs have elected to have the SPRINT-E administered as part of a help center call line. Anyone who calls seeking information about disaster mental health resources can be screened, and then the CBT-PD program and other resources can be discussed. Other programs have trained nonlicensed crisis counselors to administer the SPRINT-E. The items should be read to the respondent exactly as written; administrators should not try to explain the meaning. Alternatively, individual practitioners can use it as a screen before initiating treatment.

The 12th item on the SPRINT-E is a screen for suicide. It should always be administered, although it is not scored as part of the instrument. The item asks, "Is there any possibility that you might hurt or kill yourself?" A "yes" response should be followed up by an immediate referral for psychiatric intervention. The person may still be appropriate to participate in the CBT-PD program, but further assessment is needed to determine imminent danger.

Kessler Psychological Distress Scale

The Kessler Psychological Distress Scale (K6; Kessler et al., 2003) is another option to consider that screens for nonspecific distress. The first item asks respondents to rate how frequently they experience psychological distress (e.g., nervousness or hopelessness) in the past 30 days on a scale that ranges from 0 (*none of the time*) to 4 (*all of the time*). The six items are then summed. Scores of 13 to 24 are indicative of a probable disorder, scores of

8 to 12 are considered mild to moderate disorder, and scores of 0 to 7 are considered noncases. Additional items ask whether those symptoms are more or less intense or frequent than the previous month and inquire about the respondent's ability to work and their physical health. Although the K6 was not designed specifically for administration after a disaster or traumatic event, it has been used to identify people who need psychological treatment after several disasters, including Hurricane Katrina (Kessler et al., 2008) and the 2011 Tōhoku earthquake and tsunami in Japan (Matsuoka et al., 2011).

Disorder-Specific Screening Measures

Some programs or providers may also want to screen potential clients for specific disorders in addition to postdisaster distress. There are several well-validated screens to consider, many of which have been used with disaster survivors.

Posttraumatic Stress Disorder

A very brief screen for PTSD is the Primary Care PTSD Screen for *DSM-5* (PC–PTSD–5; Prins et al., 2016). Its initial question assesses whether the respondent has been exposed to a traumatic event and, for those who answer affirmatively, is followed by five additional yes/no questions about how that experience has affected them over the past month. A cutoff score of 3 (out of 5) is used to identify probable PTSD (Prins et al., 2016). Clinicians can be fairly confident that people who score lower than 3 do not have PTSD. The PC–PTSD–5 has been validated with survivors of the World Trade Center attacks (Boscarino et al., 2011).

A second PTSD screen with good reliability and validity is the Trauma Screening Questionnaire (TSQ; Brewin et al., 2002), a 10-item instrument that was designed for use with survivors of all types of traumatic events. It assesses five PTSD symptoms of reexperiencing the traumatic event and five symptoms of hyperarousal. Respondents are asked to endorse, on a yes/no scale, whether they have experienced each symptom at least twice in the past week. A score of 6 or more is considered a positive screen for PTSD. The TSQ has been used after several disasters, including a rail crash (Brewin et al., 2002), the London Underground bombings (Brewin et al., 2008), and Hurricane Katrina (McLaughlin et al., 2011). Data from repeated screenings done after the London bombing suggest that the TSQ is good at identifying people with PTSD who definitely need help, although some of the people in the study who screened positive were experiencing considerable distress but did not meet diagnostic criteria for PTSD (Brewin et al., 2010).

There are several other self-report measures of PTSD that correspond one to one with PTSD as outlined in the fifth edition of the *Diagnostic and Statistical Manual of Mental Disorders* (*DSM-5*; American Psychiatric Association, 2013). These measures are longer, but they also have better diagnostic accuracy. One of the most common and well-validated of these is the 20-item PTSD Checklist for *DSM-5* (Weathers et al., 2013). People rate, on a scale that ranges from 0 (*not at all*) to 4 (*extremely*), how frequently each PTSD symptom occurred in the past month. A provisional PTSD diagnosis can be made by treating each item rated 2 ("moderately") or higher as a symptom endorsed and then by following the *DSM-5* diagnostic rule, which requires at least one reexperiencing symptom (Questions 1–5), one avoidance symptom (Questions 6 and 7), two symptoms of alterations in cognition and mood (Questions 8–14), and two hyperarousal symptoms (Questions 15–20). A score of 31–33 on this instrument appears to be a reasonable cutoff for determining PTSD (Bovin et al., 2015).

Another common, well-validated, self-report PTSD measure is the 24-item Posttraumatic Diagnostic Scale for *DSM-5* (PDS-5; Foa et al., 2016). The PDS-5 begins with a two-item trauma screen and continues to 20 questions that assess the presence and severity of each of the *DSM-5* PTSD symptoms, which respondents rate on a 5-point scale that ranges from 0 (*not at all*) to 4 (*6 or more times a week/severe*). The scale ends with four items that assess symptom interference and distress as well as onset and duration. A cutoff score of 28 is recommended for a probable diagnosis.

Depression

The Patient Health Questionnaire 9 (PHQ-9; Kroenke et al., 2001) is a commonly used and well-validated screen for depression. The PHQ-9 includes nine questions that correspond to each of the diagnostic criteria for depression, with items rated on a scale that ranges from 0 (*not at all*) to 3 (*nearly every day*). Major depressive disorder is indicated if five or more symptoms have been present at least "more than half the days" in the past 2 weeks, and one of the symptoms endorsed is depressed mood, or anhedonia. PHQ-9 scores of 5, 10, 15, and 20 represent mild, moderate, moderately severe, and severe depression, respectively. The ninth item also serves as a screen for suicidality.

DIAGNOSIS

The transdiagnostic CBT-PD program was designed for people experiencing high levels of postdisaster distress or functional impairment, irrespective of the presence of specific psychiatric disorders. The primary information clinicians require to determine who might benefit from the program is whether the person is experiencing enough distress to warrant intervention; however, there is still value in evaluating the effect of the program on specific disorders, especially PTSD.

Diagnostic interviews can be administered to establish diagnoses, or self-report measures can be given as an indication of a probable diagnosis. Some providers may choose to use a more specific assessment because of the additional information it provides, which can be used to tailor CBT-PD to the specific problems the client has. For example, clients who have significant symptoms of depression could benefit from an increased emphasis on activity scheduling, whereas cognitive restructuring could be used to challenge assumptions about substance use in clients who have been using alcohol to cope with PTSD symptoms.

If clinicians are most interested in PTSD, the gold standard diagnostic interview for PTSD is the Clinician-Administered PTSD Scale for *DSM-5* (CAPS-5; Weathers et al., 2014). It can be used to determine both diagnostic status and symptom severity. In addition to assessing the 20 *DSM-5* PTSD symptoms, questions target the onset and duration of symptoms, subjective distress, impact of symptoms on social and occupational functioning, improvement in symptoms since a previous CAPS-5 administration, overall response validity, overall PTSD severity, and specifications for the dissociative subtype (e.g., depersonalization and derealization). The CAPS-5 is an update to the extensively validated CAPS-IV (Weathers et al., 2001). It has strong reliability and diagnostic correspondence with a diagnosis based on the CAPS for *DSM-IV* (Weathers et al., 2018).

INDIVIDUALIZED ASSESSMENT IN CBT-PD

Standardized measures provide valuable information for therapists to determine which people are most in need of the CBT-PD program and to learn about their specific symptoms and reactions; however, more individualized assessment is also conducted during the first session. This can help the therapist develop a more complete understanding of the client's experience in the disaster as well as important background information about their family, occupation, or other current issues.

Individualized assessment begins by asking the client to briefly describe their exposure to the disaster, how it affected them, and their symptoms. This discussion is used to begin exploration of the person's goals for treatment.

For example, at the beginning of Session 1, the therapist can ask the client to briefly describe their experience in the disaster:

THERAPIST: Before we get started with the CBT-PD program, it would be helpful if I could learn a little bit about your experience in the disaster and how it is currently affecting you. Can you tell me what happened to you, and how it has been affecting you?

CLIENT: I don't really like talking about it. What do you want to know?

THERAPIST: Can you briefly tell me what you experienced and who else was with you? We can go into more detail later, but for now, just the big picture.

CLIENT: Oh, okay. Well, it all happened really fast. There had been warnings of fires for a few days, but they weren't really anywhere near us. Then all of a sudden, we got word to evacuate. We had to flee from our house. My husband, our two boys, and the dog got in the car and left. We just left everything behind. I think we were out of the house in like 5 minutes. Driving away, it was like a movie set; everything was on fire and we couldn't see in front of us.

THERAPIST: What was that like for you?

CLIENT: Terrifying. The kids were crying and the dog was barking. I tried to keep everyone quiet because I knew my husband needed to concentrate.

THERAPIST: Then what happened? Where did you go?

CLIENT: All of a sudden we just came out on the other side of it. We couldn't go back to the house for a couple of days, though, so we stayed with some friends.

THERAPIST: And then were you able to go home, or was the house damaged?

CLIENT: Surprisingly, the house was fine. The fire didn't make it all the way up the hill to our house.

THERAPIST: That sounds pretty scary. So how are you doing now?

CLIENT: Well, I feel like I should be relieved. Nothing happened to us in the end. But I can't stop worrying. I have my "getaway bags" packed in case we have to flee again at the last minute, but even when there are no fire warnings I keep worrying about other bad things that could happen.

THERAPIST: And how has the worrying been affecting your life?

CLIENT: Well, I know my husband is super-annoyed with me. We've been fighting a lot. He is mad that I don't seem to be able to leave it in the past. Even when we get a babysitter and go out, I end up talking about my fears, and that ruins things.

THERAPIST: What would you say are the main things you would like to get out of participating in this program? It sounds like having less conflict with your husband might be one of your goals?

CLIENT: I would like to be able to focus on the present. To enjoy playing with my kids or being with my husband, rather than just thinking about the past or worrying about future events.

THERAPIST: So, it sounds like a goal is to stop worrying so much, and that if you could do that then you would be able to enjoy your family more, and they would enjoy you more too.

CLIENT: Yes.

THERAPIST: So tell me, if you were more able to focus on the present, and were not so worried about bad things happening, what kinds of things might you be doing with your family that you're not currently doing?

CLIENT: Well, I used to volunteer at the kids' school. I would help out in the classroom. That would be nice to do again. I miss seeing them in that setting, but I get anxious when I leave home. I would also like to do things together as a family. Even when I am home, I know I am not as much fun. I mean, we have a pool, and we used to barbeque and invite friends over. I miss that.

In this example, the therapist elicits enough information about the disaster to have an understanding of the client's experience and to begin to determine how the disaster is affecting them now and what the client's therapy-related goals are.

The therapist continues to learn about the impact of the disaster as part of the psychoeducation discussions. The therapist may even have enough information from this brief discussion about the event to begin to tailor the intervention to the client and make it more relevant. For instance, in the description above it appears that anxiety and relationship issues may be primary, and more time can be spent on these topics. During psycho-education the therapist might also want to explore whether the client blames herself for not having left the house sooner. As each symptom is discussed, the therapist asks the client if they have been experiencing that symptom and, if so, to give an example. In this way the client slowly provides more detail about how the disaster is currently affecting them, and the therapist can begin to get a better understanding of the client's treatment goals.

Session 1 closes with a case formulation: The therapist summarizes for the client their understanding of what the client experienced, the client's current symptoms, and their treatment goals. If the client feels the therapist has overlooked or missed anything important, there is an opportunity to provide more information. The session ends with the therapist explaining how the treatment can help the client meet their treatment goals.

THERAPIST: Based on what you told me, you and your family had a close call with the wildfires. You had to suddenly evacuate, which was really scary because for a little while you didn't know if you would make it out safely.

CLIENT: That's right. We told the kids everything was fine, but then it wasn't. We should have left sooner. I can't believe we put them through that.

THERAPIST: And now you are having a hard time relaxing. You feel like something else bad might happen and that you need to be prepared?

CLIENT: Yes.

THERAPIST: It also sounds like your fears have impaired your relationship with your husband and the boys. And you said that one of your treatment goals is to stop worrying so that you can start enjoying your family again.

CLIENT: That would be great.

THERAPIST: Just to make sure I understand it all, have you noticed other changes in functioning, like with work or self-care?

CLIENT: I was not working before, but as I said, I have stopped volunteering, so I guess a little bit. And I would say I'm definitely not taking as good care of myself, but that doesn't bother me as much as the other stuff we've talked about.

THERAPIST: Well, there are a couple of different ways that this treatment can help. First, in the next session I will teach you a breathing technique that can help you relax and stop the racing thoughts you are having.

CLIENT: Okay.

THERAPIST: We will also pick some activities you can do with your family so that you can get back to the way things were before the fire.

CLIENT: I really haven't done much recently because I am so wound up I just don't think I'd enjoy anything.

THERAPIST: I understand. That's a common experience other people often have after a traumatic event. The breathing exercises should help a little with that. But at the same time we will also work on helping you examine your beliefs that something bad is going to happen. It sounds like this is one of the things that keeps you wound up?

CLIENT: Yes.

THERAPIST: It also sounds like you feel a little guilty, as though it were your fault that your kids went through this. Is that right?

CLIENT: Yes, I do.

THERAPIST: In this program I will work with you to help you examine these kinds of upsetting thoughts, and when they are inaccurate, to replace them with more accurate and less upsetting thoughts. If you could stop feeling worried and responsible for what happened, do you think you would feel better?

CLIENT: Definitely.

OUTCOMES MONITORING AND MEASUREMENT-BASED CARE

Evaluating clients at the beginning and end of treatment can help determine whether a program worked, but symptom rating scales can also be used throughout the course of a treatment program to inform clinical decision making, an approach often referred to as *measurement-based care*. Routine assessment over the course of treatment, and discussion about progress or obstacles, can improve the therapeutic relationship and pinpoint areas in need of special attention. Furthermore, measurement-based care is associated with better treatment outcomes because it enables the therapist to refine and tailor treatment to the individual client while providing an ongoing source of feedback about the effectiveness of those targeted efforts (Fortney et al., 2017).

In order to monitor response to the CBT-PD program, we recommend that clients rate their symptoms at the beginning and end of treatment as well as every other session. Clients should complete the SPRINT-E (or a suitable alternative scale) in the waiting room before the session begins or, if that is not feasible, at the start of the session. For clients who have trouble reading, the therapist can administer it verbally at the start of the session. Furthermore, in some cases (e.g., with clients who may not be fluent in the therapist's spoken language) reading the questions to the client may be preferable. The therapist should explain to the client why they are being asked to complete the rating scale and how the measure will be used in treatment:

THERAPIST: I'd like to ask you to fill out this brief questionnaire at the beginning of our meeting today. You'll notice it is the same one I used to understand whether this treatment program would be a good fit for you. I'll be asking you to fill it out every other time we meet together.

CLIENT: Okay. But I don't think it will change much.

THERAPIST: Well, that is one of the things we will want to keep an eye on. Each time you complete it we will review your answers together. This will help us to see how you are progressing in the treatment and if there are any specific issues that we should be spending more time on.

CLIENT: All right, if you think it will help.

It is best if the self-report measure is scored immediately by the therapist and then the results are shared and discussed with the client. This can be done in a variety of ways. The therapist might just review the items and ask about any scores that seem higher than the others. In addition, the therapist might choose to focus on the overall total score and either provide feedback on progress that has been made or normalize minimal improvement and set expectations for recovery.

For example, in terms of using the SPRINT-E to identify a particular area on which to focus, the therapist might say something along the following lines:

> I see that you indicated that you are having the most trouble just handling stressful events? Can you give me an example in the last week of a time you felt you had a hard time coping? Perhaps we can use that situation in the session today when we work through a "5 Steps of Cognitive Restructuring" Worksheet.

Reviewing individual items that indicate little change over time can also be useful in identifying areas where further attention is needed. For example, if there is improvement in all of the symptoms except numbing, the therapist might want to spend some additional time identifying pleasant activities that focus on interpersonal relationships.

THERAPIST: You are making good progress, but I notice that you are still reporting that you have trouble experiencing feelings. Is that right?

CLIENT: Yes. It is still really hard to feel joy. Especially with my husband. I just feel like he is waiting for me to just snap out of it.

THERAPIST: Let's take a look at the pleasant activities you have been scheduling. Some activities are going to be better at targeting numbing symptoms that others.

CLIENT: Okay. For the past few weeks I've been running and gardening. Those are things I had stopped doing and I have found that I have started to enjoy them again.

THERAPIST: That is great. And I want you to keep doing them, especially since they are making you happy. But it is best if we can keep adding to the list. Can you think of an activity you could do with your husband?

CLIENT: Well, we used to like to go out to dinner. But lately I don't feel up to it.

THERAPIST: Remember, that is how you felt about running and gardening. . . . But once you started it, you found out you liked it. Do you think you could schedule a dinner date?

CLIENT: Yes, I could try that.

THERAPIST: Great!

Rating scales can also be used to identify areas to target in the treatment. For example, a disaster survivor may indicate on a rating scale that they have been having problems sleeping. Cognitive restructuring could then be used to target maladaptive beliefs that the person is at risk during the night because they cannot monitor the weather forecast to determine whether a thunderstorm might turn into a hurricane. They may also be used to determine whether more sessions are required or if the therapist should try a different treatment altogether.

In addition, the therapist can summarize the questionnaire results and either graph the scores over time or just keep a note of the total score at each measurement point. If things are improving, the therapist might say "Ah, we are seeing another decrease in your scores on this measure of postdisaster distress. What do you think has been helping you with your improvement?"

For clients in whom little or no improvement is seen, the therapist might take an approach like the following one:

> I notice that your symptoms did not improve much from two sessions ago. There could be a couple of different reasons for that. It is common for it to take a few sessions before people begin to improve in this program. And sometimes people will improve some, be stable for a period of time, and then improve more. This is because you are still learning the skills and getting better at using them. But let's also take a closer look at your "5 Steps of Cognitive Restructuring" Worksheets. There may be a place where you are getting stuck. And, if not, I have some other methods you can try that might work better for you.

At the end of treatment, the changes in the client's SPRINT-E scores from the first session to the last should be discussed. A review of the improvements the client has experienced can serve as a starting place to talk about how the program went, and particular areas on which the client might need to focus after treatment ends. In Chapter 11, we discuss more extensively this and other details about the last session.

CONCLUSION

Assessment is an essential part of the CBT-PD program. At the beginning, the SPRINT-E (or another measure of symptom distress and impairment) can be used to identify people who can benefit from the CBT-PD program. At a program level, crisis counseling programs may elect to screen all disaster survivors who are showing some signs of distress or functional impairment in order to identify those who need psychotherapy. At an individual level, therapists may screen individual clients presenting for treatment to determine whether they might benefit from the CBT-PD program. Screening not only identifies people who need psychological services but also provides the therapist with an overall assessment of the severity of the client's symptoms and reactions to the disaster.

Individualized assessment occurs next, after the client has been found to have sufficient distress or functional impairment to be suited for CBT-PD. Through discussions with the client about their experience with the disaster, their symptoms, and their treatment goals, the therapist begins to develop a case formulation about what is causing the client the most distress and what they would like to see change in their life. The therapist continues to gather information about the client through the psychoeducation that is offered in the first session. Once treatment has been initiated, the therapist uses the SPRINT-E (or another measure) to monitor outcomes over the course of the treatment by administering it every other session. Scores on the SPRINT-E and changes over time are routinely discussed with the client, and information gleaned from it is used to inform the delivery of the CBT-PD program, including a focus on specific areas in which less progress has been made. The incorporation of this systematic tracking of progress in the CBT-PD program with the SPRINT-E, called "measurement-based care," allows greater precision and individualization of treatment to the client's specific needs, thereby optimizing outcomes.

6

BEGINNING TREATMENT

Engagement and Psychoeducation

In this chapter, we describe the first steps of the Cognitive Behavior Therapy for Postdisaster Distress (CBT-PD) program. The goals of the first therapy session are twofold. First, the therapist seeks to motivate and solidify the client's engagement in treatment by providing an overview of the program and beginning psychoeducation about disasters and posttraumatic stress disorder (PTSD). Second, the therapist works to get enough information about the client's background and current functioning in order to formulate a case conceptualization. This session begins with a brief review of the client's experience with the disaster (see Chapter 5), followed by an explanation of the rationale for the program and an overview of it. Psychoeducation on postdisaster distress (which includes information about PTSD and related conditions) is then used to help the client understand their reactions and how the treatment will help them manage those reactions. The information elicited is then shared back to the client in a cohesive case formulation and treatment plan.

https://doi.org/10.1037/0000237-006
Treatment for Postdisaster Distress: A Transdiagnostic Approach, by J. L. Hamblen and K. T. Mueser

ENGAGEMENT

An essential part of engaging clients in care is the treatment rationale. When people understand how a program will work for them, they become interested and motivated to participate in it. In providing the rationale for the CBT-PD program there are several areas to cover. First, it is important to let the client know that the program has been used after many other disasters, including both natural disasters and terrorism, and that it has been shown to be helpful to those survivors. Learning that it has worked for others can increase its credibility and create expectations of recovery. The following is an example of how a therapist might explain things to the client in the first session:

THERAPIST: This program helps relieve symptoms commonly experienced after a disaster. It has been used with survivors following many events, including the September 11th terrorist attacks, Hurricane Katrina, and the Boston Marathon bombings. The program is intended for people like you who have experienced a disaster and have distress related to the event. Many people who have participated in this program have reported that they feel better and have improved functioning. It works for people with both moderate and severe symptoms, and it can continue to work even years after the disaster has ended.

CLIENT: I hope so. Nothing has worked so far.

THERAPIST: Let me tell you more about how the program works, and then I can answer any questions you might have.

CLIENT: Okay, that sounds good.

Second, it is important to explain the components of the CBT-PD program and how each one is expected to help. The client is given Handout 1 at the end of the session for review (see Appendix B on the American Psychological Association [APA] website at http://pubs.apa.org/books/supp/hamblen). This information helps the client understand how and why the program works, which can increase the client's engagement in treatment, facilitating retention and increasing follow-through on home practice assignments between sessions.

THERAPIST: The program that we will be doing can be thought of as skills training. If you've ever been in psychotherapy before, you might find this program is somewhat different. The sessions will be very structured. I'll be asking you a lot of questions and teaching you new skills, which I'll ask you to practice between sessions. We will also be focusing primarily on coping with the disaster you experienced, although you may also find that the skills you learn here are helpful in dealing with other difficult experiences you have had in your life.

The program is divided into four main parts: education, breathing retraining, activity scheduling, and changing problematic thoughts and feelings. In the education part you will learn about symptoms that are common after a disaster, including the symptoms of PTSD. Being aware of these symptoms is an important step toward being able to recognize and cope with them more effectively.

In the second part of the program, we will work to build resiliency skills, and you will learn some immediate ways of coping with anxiety or other distressing feelings. I will teach you a technique called "breathing retraining," which is very effective at reducing feelings of anxiety, as well as symptoms of physical tension and feeling overstimulated or "hyper." Purposefully slowing down your breathing not only helps you to relax but also sends a message to your brain that you are safe. This is an easy skill to learn that you can begin using right away.

We will also consider ways of increasing the number of fun or pleasurable activities in your life in the third part of the program. After a traumatic event, it is very easy to forget to do things that once were associated with joy in your life. Getting yourself to start doing enjoyable activities is one basic way to start yourself on the path to feeling better.

The last part of the program focuses on changing problematic thoughts and feelings and is called "cognitive restructuring." "Cognitive restructuring" refers to a set of skills you will learn to evaluate the thoughts that may be causing you distress and to replace them with more balanced, less distressing thoughts. Part of what causes the distress you have been feeling are these catastrophic and negative thoughts about the world. Finding ways to examine and change those thoughts so they are more accurate can decrease distress. A simple example is if you tell yourself the plane you are on is going to crash you feel very afraid, but if you tell yourself there are thousands of flights a day with no crashes you will probably feel less distressed. The idea isn't to lie to yourself but to find more balanced and accurate ways of thinking. Does that make sense?

CLIENT: I guess so. It sounds sort of complicated.

THERAPIST: I can understand why you might feel that way. But we will take it slow and break it down so that it is easier to learn.

CLIENT: Okay. I like the idea of learning new skills.

THERAPIST: Finally, it can be helpful to talk briefly about how therapy sessions are structured and the use of worksheets and handouts.

Although not formally part of the treatment rationale, setting expectations and explaining the importance of following the structure can help clients understand that they are being given a treatment that has been specifically designed to teach them skills in a particular way that has been shown to work for other people. It also provides a good opportunity to set expectations about the number of treatment sessions and the importance of the client practicing the skills they are learning outside of the sessions.

THERAPIST: We will meet today for about an hour. I will ask you about your experiences during the disaster and begin to learn about your symptoms. After today, we will meet together for seven to nine more sessions (N.B.: This can vary depending on whether the therapist can determine the number of sessions or if there is a limit that is set by a formalized program), which will run for 55 minutes each. One of the things that we know from working with people who have experienced traumatic events is that it can sometimes be difficult to concentrate. In this program we will do several things to help you remember the skills and information that we have covered. First, I will give you handouts that review the concepts we cover in the sessions. Second, I will start each session with a review of what we discussed previously and end each session with a review of what we covered in that hour. This way, you do not have to worry about missing or forgetting something important that we have talked about. Finally, I will give you worksheets so that you can practice the skills you'll be learning. It is important that you bring the worksheets to each session. We will use them in the sessions together to work on different problems you may be having. When the program is over you will keep your worksheets. You can refer to them in case new or similar issues come up. The handouts also contain other helpful tips for dealing with upsetting feelings.

CLIENT: It looks like there are a lot of worksheets, but I do like the idea of having the workbook to refer back to.

THERAPIST: There are a lot of worksheets! But we will go over them together.

PSYCHOEDUCATION

In CBT-PD, psychoeducation covers the symptoms of PTSD, common reactions to trauma, alcohol and substance use, sleep problems and nightmares, and problems in functioning. The goal is to cover all of the material in Session 1, spending more time on the symptoms that the client reports and less time on those that appear less relevant. The client is given handouts (see Handouts 2–6 in Appendix B on the APA website at http://pubs.apa.org/books/supp/hamblen) that describe the symptoms and provides tips for how to begin to cope with them. Worksheets are a specific type of handout on which the client records their own information. In the psychoeducation section of the treatment program clients complete worksheets to help them identify their specific symptoms, determine which symptoms are the most frequent and upsetting, and consider how those symptoms are currently affecting them (see Handouts 7–17 in Appendix B on the APA website at http://pubs.apa.org/books/supp/hamblen).

Psychoeducation should be delivered in a didactic manner. Information about each symptom is provided and followed by a brief discussion of the client's experiences with that symptom. In this way the therapist can be assured that the client understands the material that is being reviewed, and the therapist can begin to get a feel for the relevance of each symptom. The handouts and worksheets can either be referred to during the session, to clarify the material being presented, or clients can review them at home after the session. Therapists should definitely review with clients the various PTSD symptoms and common reactions to trauma. If the therapist runs out of time during the session they can instruct the client to review the rest of the symptoms for homework. Then, at the beginning of the next session, the therapist can review the information to ensure the client comprehends it and provide more information about any symptoms the client may not fully understand or on those that seem particularly relevant.

If the therapist has concerns about reading ability, they should continue the psychoeducation at the start of Session 2. Clients can also be encouraged to share the handouts with a supportive person, such as a spouse or other significant person. This can help in two ways. First, the person might be able to help the client understand the material. Teaching what you have learned to someone else can be an effective learning strategy. Second, it might also help the support person have a greater appreciation for what the client is going through and a better understanding of how to help them.

Posttraumatic Stress Disorder

Psychoeducation begins with a discussion of PTSD (see Handout 2 in Appendix B on the APA website at http://pubs.apa.org/books/supp/hamblen), the most common disorder after a disaster. The therapist explains what PTSD is and the four symptom clusters associated with it.

THERAPIST: I want to begin by telling you what posttraumatic stress disorder is and the types of symptoms that occur in the disorder.

CLIENT: Okay.

THERAPIST: PTSD can develop after someone has been through a life-threatening event like combat, sexual or physical assault, a serious car accident, or a disaster like the one you experienced. Not everyone who experiences a life-threatening event develops PTSD, but most people have at least some symptoms. There are four types of symptoms that make up PTSD.

If PTSD has not been formally diagnosed, the therapist should point this out to the client so that they do not incorrectly assume they have PTSD.

THERAPIST: To be diagnosed with PTSD, a trained professional has to ask you a specific set of questions as part of a clinical diagnostic interview. We did not go through the interview together, so I do not know for sure whether you meet criteria for PTSD.

CLIENT: So I don't have PTSD?

THERAPIST: I won't be able to diagnose you with or without PTSD. But we can still see whether you are experiencing any PTSD symptoms. It is common for people to experience some PTSD symptoms after a traumatic event, even if they do not meet the criteria for a diagnosis of PTSD. This program is designed to help people with PTSD symptoms, and other common symptoms after a disaster, whether or not they have a diagnosis of PTSD.

Intrusive Symptoms

The first cluster of PTSD symptoms comprises the *intrusive symptoms*. These are symptoms that have as their common element an unwanted recollection or reexperiencing of the trauma. Unwanted memories, nightmares, flashbacks, and emotional and physiological upset at traumatic reminders are all intrusive symptoms.

THERAPIST: The first set of symptoms is called "intrusive symptoms." You may have intense, unwanted memories of the disaster that you are unable to get rid of. These memories may seem to come from out of the blue, or a reminder of the event may trigger them—such as hearing hurricane warnings on the news if you were in a hurricane, or learning about a terrorist attack if you survived September 11th. These memories often cause emotional reactions, such as feeling afraid, anxious, or angry, and physical reactions such, as sweating, shaking, a racing heart, or shortness of breath. Flashbacks are particularly vivid reexperiencing symptoms that feel so real that it seems like the disaster is happening again. Nightmares are another common way people reexperience a traumatic event. Do you experience any upsetting memories of the disaster?

CLIENT: I don't tend to have a lot of thoughts about the hurricane itself. I have nightmares that are really upsetting in which my parents get hurt or die. I also tend to have lots of thoughts, over and over, about what *could have* happened to my parents.

THERAPIST: How often do the nightmares occur?

CLIENT: At first it was several times a week, but now it's probably once a week or less. But when I have them I get really freaked out.

THERAPIST: What happens when you wake up?

CLIENT: I'm all sweaty, and I can't fall back asleep.

THERAPIST: Okay, and how often do you have thoughts about what "could have" happened to your parents, and how upsetting are the thoughts?

CLIENT: I would say that the thoughts still happen multiple times a day. Usually they happen when I'm reminded of the hurricane somehow. They haunt me and make it hard to focus on other things. They also get me to thinking about how this is all my fault.

THERAPIST: Okay, we'll definitely want to target these kinds of intrusive thoughts in the treatment.

Avoidance Symptoms

The second cluster of PTSD symptoms are avoidance symptoms. People avoid distress by actively staying away from disaster-related reminders (called "triggers"). This can include avoiding other people, places, and situations, and is sometimes called *behavioral avoidance*. Often, they believe it is important to avoid these situations not only to prevent the negative feelings associated with reminders of the traumatic event but also to keep safe. For example, someone who experienced a mass shooting may avoid crowds not only because being in a crowd reminds them of the shooting but also because they are afraid that being in a crowd increases the chances that they will be hurt. A similar symptom is *emotional avoidance*, in which people try to avoid their feelings about the trauma, often by engaging in some form of distraction like working, keeping busy, or sometimes by using substances.

THERAPIST: The second set of symptoms that make up PTSD are avoidance symptoms. You may find that you work hard at avoiding memories and reminders of the shooting as a way of managing your distress. It is very common to avoid situations that remind you of a traumatic event, such as where it occurred. Another type of avoidance involves trying to push away upsetting thoughts, feelings, and memories. On some level, this may serve as an adaptive response to a trauma as you try to move on with your life; however, if avoidance gets too extreme it can get in the way of your everyday life. Since the shooting, what situations have you been avoiding?

CLIENT: Well, I obviously don't go to concerts anymore.

THERAPIST: What is keeping you from going?

CLIENT: Even just thinking about going to a concert brings back memories.

THERAPIST: I understand. That is an intrusive symptom like we just talked about. Thinking about concerts brings back memories.

CLIENT: Right; so why would I want to go to a concert if I am going to spend the whole time just thinking about that night in my head?

THERAPIST: So you avoid going to concerts now as a way to keep from thinking about it?

CLIENT: Yes. I stay away from anything that reminds me of it. Country music, people who were there with me that night, news stories about mass violence—actually, crowds in general.

THERAPIST: Those are all good examples of avoidance symptoms and will be something we will focus on in our work together. Another way people avoid is by trying not to think about the event. They may refuse to talk about the disaster, or they may engage in other activities to prevent the thoughts from intruding. For example, people may work all the time, use substances, or just try and keep busy. Do you find yourself trying to avoid your upset feelings?

CLIENT: I think so. I have stopped reading because when I read my mind wanders and I find that I start thinking about concert. It is better if I just keep busy.

THERAPIST: Yes, that is a type of avoidance because you are trying not to feel your feelings.

Negative Alterations in Cognitions and Mood

The third cluster of PTSD symptoms are *negative alterations in cognition and mood*. These symptoms are related to having negative thoughts about oneself or the world. People may feel that the world is unsafe or that they (or someone else) is bad. They may also blame themselves for the trauma, or for how they responded to that trauma, or they may simply feel "down," or negative. Numbing symptoms, including a difficulty experiencing positive emotions or a lack of pleasure in previously enjoyed activities, are also part of this cluster.

THERAPIST: After a traumatic event, some people feel bad about themselves and the world. They may experience guilt or shame, or just feel numb. You may feel distant or detached from other people, even those you are close to, or lose interest in activities you used to enjoy. Have you had any of these reactions since the tornado?

CLIENT: Of course! If I had gotten my family to the basement sooner, my father would still be with us.

THERAPIST: So you blame yourself for his death? How are things with your wife? Do you still feel close to her?

CLIENT: She says it's not my fault, that he should have headed downstairs when he heard the sirens, but I still should have checked on him. She tries to console me, but I don't feel anything when she hugs me or holds my hand. She wants to go out and do things together, but I just don't feel like it.

THERAPIST: Yes, those are the kind of symptoms I'm talking about. You feel bad, and detached from people you care about, and you aren't interested in doing things with your wife that you used to enjoy. Those symptoms are very common, especially after a traumatic event in which someone you loved was killed. We will be working together on ways you can start reconnecting with your wife again.

Alterations in Arousal and Reactivity

The last cluster of symptoms include *trauma-related arousal and physical reactivity*. People with PTSD are often in a heightened state of arousal or alertness, on guard and jumpy. Many people describe sitting with their backs to the wall so they can scan the room for danger and nothing can surprise them from behind. They may check the exits in case they need to escape or check their locks multiple times to make sure they are safe. Irritability, insomnia, and difficulties with concentration are also symptoms in this cluster.

THERAPIST: The final set of reactions involves feeling keyed up and jumpy. It is common for people to startle easily, be overly watchful and on edge, and have trouble sleeping or concentrating. Since the wildfires, have you noticed that it is hard for you to settle down, relax, or sleep? Do you find that you are more irritable or overly alert?

CLIENT: I feel like I have to always be prepared to evacuate. You know, there was almost no warning. One minute everything was fine, and then the winds changed and the house was filled with smoke. At night I'm always listening for the sound of burning embers. An extra few minutes could be the difference between life and death. I can't sleep. My concentration is shot.

THERAPIST: That all makes sense. It's like your body is in overdrive, ready to race to the car again if you need to evacuate. I'll be teaching you a skill, called "breathing retraining," that can help with reducing some of these overarousal symptoms. Later on, we'll also work together to examine more closely some of your thoughts about the disaster that are keeping you wound up and on edge.

Common Reactions to Trauma

After reviewing PTSD symptoms, the therapist should discuss with the client common negative emotional reactions to trauma, including four common emotional reactions: (a) fear and anxiety, (b) anger and irritability, (c) sadness and depression, and (d) guilt and shame (see Handout 3 in Appendix B on the APA website at http://pubs.apa.org/books/supp/hamblen). These reactions are described not as symptoms but as common negative feelings, which makes them easier for clients to talk about. A review and discussion of these reactions both normalizes their presence after a traumatic event and serves as the foundation for teaching cognitive restructuring later in the treatment.

Fear and Anxiety

Fear and anxiety are normal reactions to experiences that are life threatening, that cause physical or emotional harm, or that endanger one's physical safety or emotional well-being. In moments of danger, people's bodies are hardwired to respond in ways that promote survival, which can include feeling an acute sense of alarm, focusing attention on the source of the threat, and mobilizing the body to flee or fight. In this sense, fear is an adaptive reaction when one is faced with a dangerous situation. Unfortunately, after a trauma people's internal alarm systems can become hypersensitive or can be easily triggered by events that are not actually dangerous. These reactions can get in the way of daily living. Chronic fear and anxiety can be distracting; impair concentration; cause feelings of tension, agitation, and jumpiness; and can even make people less able to discern real danger. Consider, for example, a house alarm that goes off all the time: Aside from the unbearable noise, the repeated false alarms will eventually decrease people's ability to distinguish them from real danger.

THERAPIST: In addition to the specific symptoms that make up PTSD, there are other common reactions people experience after living through traumatic events. Although each person responds in his or her own unique way, you may find that you have experienced many of these reactions. Do you feel fearful, tense, or anxious? Do you find that you feel unsafe or threatened in situations that did not previously make you afraid?

CLIENT: I really hate crowds. I get almost panicky if I am in a situation where I think I might not be able to get away.

THERAPIST: Like what?

CLIENT: Like, if I am in a restaurant, I need to be able to see the door. That way, I could see if someone comes in with a gun. Sometimes I even check to see if there is a backdoor, just in case. My kids wanted me to take them to the 4th-of-July parade. I couldn't go, and in the end I didn't let them go either. If something happened you could be trapped in the crowd. It's not safe.

THERAPIST:　So since the nightclub shooting you have felt less safe out in public, especially in situations where it could be hard to escape?

Anger and Irritability

Anger is an understandable and normal reaction to perceived injustice, violation, abuse, unfair treatment, or loss of control. It is common for people to have persistent anger even after the threat is gone and they are no longer in danger. This anger not only is emotionally uncomfortable and disruptive to relationships, but also chronic anger and hostility are risk factors for a variety of problems, including violent behavior, interpersonal problems, and health conditions, such as high blood pressure and heart disease.

THERAPIST:　Have you noticed that you are more irritable or feel more anger since the World Trade Center attacks?

CLIENT:　I find myself snapping at my wife and kids all the time these days, which of course makes me feel even worse.

THERAPIST:　Does the anger ever get directed inward, at yourself?

CLIENT:　Yeah, a lot. I get angry at myself for having such a hard time with all this and still not being able to move on. It doesn't seem like everyone else is as messed up as I am. Why can't I just move on? It's been a year!

THERAPIST:　Those are common thoughts and feelings for people to have after this type of experience. Hopefully this program will help you move on while also helping you deal with the painful feelings you're having.

Sadness and Depression

Sadness and depression occur naturally in response to loss. After a disaster, a sense of loss can stem from the death of a friend or loved one, loss of property or job, or loss of one's previous way of life. Sadness and depression can also be related to a felt loss of innocence, religious faith, or faith in fellow human beings.

THERAPIST:　In what ways do you feel like you have experienced a loss?

CLIENT:　I've lost everything: my house, my job, my friends. My husband was killed in Iraq, and the hurricane destroyed the few things of his that the army returned. I looked for them, but I couldn't find them. We had to move back in with my parents, and they live in another state so I don't even have my friends.

THERAPIST: Are your parents a source of support?

CLIENT: Oh, definitely. But it's different. I'm not standing on my own two feet. It's like I have to start from scratch again, and I don't know if I can.

THERAPIST: It sounds like at times it can all feel pretty overwhelming. How are you doing right now?

CLIENT: I'm okay. I'm actually somewhat hopeful that this program can help me.

THERAPIST: I think it can help. But everyone has ups and downs. And if at some point you start feeling hopeless and have thoughts of hurting yourself, I'd like you to let me know so I can help you. Okay?

CLIENT: I can do that.

Guilt and Shame

Guilt and shame are common, highly distressing emotions that people often feel in the wake of a disaster. Not only are they painful emotions in and of themselves, but research suggests that they also can complicate recovery from other problems, such as depression and anxiety. Guilt and shame may be brought on by thoughts about things the client did or did not do during the trauma itself, before the trauma, or afterward. Some people feel guilty because they are having a hard time coping after the disaster. Others feel guilty that they lived when someone else died, or if their losses or injuries are not as severe as someone else's.

THERAPIST: You mentioned before that you think you are responsible for your father's death. Is that correct?

CLIENT: Yes, when the tornado sirens went off I ran to the girls' bedroom to get the kids. My wife was out of town, so the plan was for me to get them. My father, who lives with us, told us he would be fine getting to the basement on his own. He was in his 70s and in good health. But instead of coming to the basement, he went looking for the dog. That was supposed to be my job if my wife was around to get the girls. Anyway, I got the girls, and when we got to the basement he wasn't there.

I should have gone to look for him, but I didn't want to leave the girls alone. If I had, I could have convinced him to leave the dog. A tree fell on the house where he was looking.

THERAPIST: Oh, I am terribly sorry. That's awful! So, just to make sure I understand, though—you had a plan in place in case of a tornado?

CLIENT: Yes.

THERAPIST: And you followed the plan, but your father did not?

CLIENT: Yes, but I should never have left him on his own.

THERAPIST: I understand. These kinds of thoughts are common after an event such as this. We're going to be spending some time together in this program examining this and related thoughts and evaluating just how accurate they are. If they are not accurate, we'll also work on helping you come up with more balanced and accurate thoughts, which are usually less distressing.

Other Reactions to Trauma

People often experience reactions in addition to the four common types of reactions to trauma. If time allows, or if there is an indication that a person may be experiencing one of these reactions, the therapist should include them in the psychoeducation.

Substance Use

In the aftermath of a disaster, some people increase their use of alcohol or other substances (see Handout 4 in Appendix B on the APA website at http://pubs. apa.org/books/supp/hamblen). Substance use may be a way to avoid thinking about what happened or a means of diminishing strong negative feelings like anxiety, sadness, guilt, or anger. Increased substance use (or relapse) is most common in people with a history of alcohol or drug problems. It is important to determine whether substance use is a relevant issue for clients.

THERAPIST: Tell me whether your use of substances—alcohol, marijuana, prescriptions—has changed since the disaster. Are you drinking more than you used to? Are substances interfering in any way with your ability to work or get along with others? Have others expressed concern over your use?

CLIENT: I used to have a problem with alcohol, but I had been sober for years. Since the floods, I've picked up a drink now and again. I go to bars, so I don't worry my wife. She doesn't know about it.

THERAPIST: How often and how much are you drinking?

CLIENT: Not much. I've probably gone out to bars three or four times in the past few months. Each time, I've only had two beers. I've limited it intentionally. Still, I'm worried that I'll slip back into drinking regularly. I had completely stopped before the floods.

THERAPIST: It sounds like even though you feel your drinking is controlled you are still worried. Do you think you could stop again now that you have started in this treatment? The skills you will be learning should help you cope with the stress that is causing you to drink.

CLIENT: Maybe. I think so.

THERAPIST: Okay, good. I'll continue to check in with you about your drinking, and some of the skills you will learn should help you cope so maybe you won't feel the need to continue to drink. But if you find that you can't stop, let's talk over your options, which might include telling you wife or getting some counseling specific to the drinking.

Sleep Problems and Nightmares

People who have experienced a disaster often report sleep problems, including difficulty falling asleep and waking up frequently during the night (see Handout 5 in Appendix B on the APA website at http://pubs.apa.org/books/supp/hamblen). These problems may be related to fear and anxiety or to increased physical arousal. Hypersomnia, or sleeping too much, is another sleep problem people sometimes experience after a disaster. This can also be related to feelings of sadness and depression, as well as to attempts to avoid thinking about what happened. Sleep problems can be exacerbated by the use of alcohol or drugs in response to a traumatic event. Nightmares are also common.

THERAPIST: You mentioned that you've been having some sleeping problems since the industrial fire. I'd like to hear more about that.

CLIENT: I've never been a great sleeper, but it's gotten worse since the fire at work. I mostly have trouble with getting to sleep and with waking up too early. I toss and turn at night—I worry about everything.

THERAPIST: How much sleep do you actually get?

CLIENT: I usually toss and turn for an hour or more before falling asleep about midnight. Then I sleep until about 4:30 or 5:00 a.m., when I wake before my alarm and can't get back to sleep.

THERAPIST: There are some simple things you can do that might help your sleep, like limiting your use of caffeine. But if that doesn't help, there are good strategies for improving sleep that I can recommend. In the longer term, over the course of this program we may be able to address some of the things you are worried about and that are keeping you up, which may improve your sleep.

CLIENT: That would be a relief.

Impairment in Functioning

Symptoms like anxiety, depression, guilt, and anger can have a negative impact on relationships. They can also interfere with a person's ability to function at work or school, and in some cases they can exacerbate health concerns. For clients who have had a hard time relating to the way the disaster is making them feel, a discussion about how the disaster has interfered with functioning can be especially helpful. A conversation about functioning is also important because it can elicit goals on which the client wants to work (see Handout 6 in Appendix B on the APA website at http://pubs.apa.org/books/supp/hamblen).

THERAPIST: In what areas have you been having difficulty functioning? In your relationships, at work, in your health, or in your eating habits?

CLIENT: Work is okay. I'm not as productive as before, but I'm getting by. But I definitely don't feel like I'm a good mom right now. I cry all the time, and I never feel like playing with my son.

THERAPIST: Do you feed him dinner? Give him a bath? Take him to school?

CLIENT: Yeah, I do all that stuff. But that's it.

THERAPIST: Okay, so that is an area you would like to work on. We can definitely do that.

CASE FORMULATION

At the end of the first session the therapist provides a case formulation for the client. Although some types of case formulations are very detailed and mechanistic, we have found that in CBT-PD the most practical case formulation links the clients' negative feelings, avoidance, and problems in functioning with their thoughts and beliefs about the disaster. The case formulation is based on the therapist's working hypothesis about what is causing and maintaining the clients' symptoms and provides the therapist with a starting place for how to tailor the treatment to address these causes. It should include the origin of the problem (i.e., the disaster), a summary of the symptoms and problems caused by the disaster, and a description of what is maintaining those problems (i.e., the underlying core beliefs). The case formulation is then shared with the client to communicate to them that the therapist has an understanding of the problem and a plan to address it and for the client to correct any misunderstandings.

THERAPIST: From what you have said, it sounds like it was terrifying being in the classroom with your students while the shooter was loose in the school. Let me check in with you about my understanding of how the shooting has affected you. You were afraid for your life and for the lives of your students. You felt helpless, especially because one of your students was bleeding and you didn't know if she would live. You feel guilty that you were not able to keep her safe. Since the shooting, you have not been able to go back to work, and you find it hard to leave your house because you feel unsafe. You are worried that your husband is getting frustrated with you because it is taking you so long to get better, but you can't seem to get the shooting out of your mind. Do I have that right?

In this example, the maintaining factors are core beliefs of inadequacy or shame (i.e., that the client should have been able to protect the student, go back to work, and get over it sooner) as well as a new belief that the world is an unsafe place.

PRACTICE EXERCISES

At the end of the session, time should be taken to assign practice exercises. The therapist should give the client the handouts that are referred to in the session (Handouts 2–6) and review which worksheets need to be completed before the next session (Handouts 7–17). If certain areas have been identified as more relevant, the therapist can encourage the client to focus on those topics. In many cases, having the client identify a time when they can plan to work on the assignment can be helpful. At the beginning of the next session, the therapist should review the assignment.

Any assignments that are incomplete should be finished together before moving to the next topic.

CONCLUSION

Session 1 is the foundation for the therapy. It begins with a rationale, to solidify the client's engagement in the treatment program and to set clear expectations for the length and focus of the program. Although the therapist does not directly ask the client to describe in detail the disaster, through the individualized assessment and psychoeducation they are able to get a relatively full picture of what happened and the current impact of the disaster on the client's life. There is a significant amount of information to cover in this first session, and we caution therapists against taking too long getting through the material. Although there is clear value in the psychoeducation, it also delays the onset of components that have additional therapeutic value. In addition, because there are multiple opportunities over the course of the program to reinforce or reteach psychoeducation, it is preferable to move through it quickly and come back to any issues that are unclear as they arise. Session 1 ends with a case formulation that communicates to the client that the therapist has a good understanding of their concerns and a plan for how to focus the treatment to address those concerns.

7

RESILIENCY SKILLS

Whereas the first treatment session in the Cognitive Behavior Therapy for Postdisaster Distress (CBT-PD) program is intended to help ensure the client's engagement in treatment and to provide and gather information that helps focus and tailor the treatment to the client's needs, the next session is intended to provide the client with more immediate symptom relief. *Breathing retraining* is a very simple skill that can be used to help the client manage their anxiety as they begin to address their disaster-related symptoms. In addition, slowing down one's breathing can reduce the overarousal symptoms of posttraumatic stress disorder (PTSD) and more broadly facilitate relaxation, focused attention, and the ability to tolerate negative emotions. *Activity scheduling* is also introduced in the second session, to reduce the client's depression and avoidance behaviors by increasing the number and quality of their positive and meaningful experiences. Both of these skills are conceptualized as resiliency skills because their benefits extend beyond symptom relief to improved quality of life, and both can play an important role in helping people recover from the devastating effects of a disaster. These are taught early in CBT-PD and then practiced and reviewed with the client throughout the program.

https://doi.org/10.1037/0000237-007
Treatment for Postdisaster Distress: A Transdiagnostic Approach, by J. L. Hamblen and K. T. Mueser

BREATHING RETRAINING

Breathing retraining can generally be taught in about 15 to 20 minutes. It is introduced early on to provide clients with an easy-to-learn skill they can immediately use to help manage their anxiety and reduce overarousal symptoms. The therapist provides a rationale for the skill, demonstrates how to do it, and develops a plan with the client to practice the skill between sessions. A handout is used to facilitate the teaching of breathing that reviews the instructions and provides space for the client to track when they used the breathing techniques and how it went (see Handouts 18 and 19 in Appendix B on the American Psychological Association website at http://pubs.apa.org/books/supp/hamblen).

When people are anxious or hyperalert, their quickened respiration increases the flow of blood to the brain; breathing retraining is intended to reduce the amount of oxygen in the brain, thereby decreasing physiological arousal and the associated anxiety. People who have been through traumatic experiences can feel frightened in situations where there is no impending danger. They may be in a state of perpetual fight or flight, constantly alert to any signs of a possible threat, which is maintained by their shallow breathing and hyperventilation. Slowing down one's breathing sends a message to the brain that the person is safe. Situations can then be reappraised as being safe or neutral. Slowing down one's breathing can also be useful in helping people focus their attention and tolerate negative affect. The following hypothetical exchange is an example of how to provide the rationale for breathing retraining:

THERAPIST: It is very common for people who have experienced a disaster to have symptoms of physical tension and anxiety. Breathing retraining is a particular style of breathing that can help reduce physical tension and anxious feelings. I want to teach you this now, so you can begin using it right away.

CLIENT: Okay.

THERAPIST: What happens to your body when you are upset and panicky?

CLIENT: I get tense and it's hard to breathe.

THERAPIST: Exactly. That's what happens to most people. It's our body's way of preparing for fight or flight. If you are in trouble, you need to be able to get away, so our breathing speeds up, sending more oxygen through our bodies. But what if running away or fighting back isn't indicated by the situation? A message is being sent to your brain that is saying you are in danger, but you're not. Then this overly aroused state just makes you feel panicky.

CLIENT: Yes. That happens to me a lot.

THERAPIST: Right. As we were talking about last week, these overarousal symptoms are very common after a disaster, and are part of what defines PTSD. Often, people try to calm down when they feel uncomfortably hyperalert or anxiety by taking a deep breath. Do you ever try that?

CLIENT: Yes. I try and breathe deeply, but it doesn't always help.

THERAPIST: Right. That's because breathing deeply usually continues to send extra oxygen to your brain, which is a signal that you are in danger. Instead, you need to slow your breathing down.

CLIENT: How?

THERAPIST: By taking a normal breath in and then exhaling slowly. You can also say a soothing word to yourself, like "relax" or "exhale," when you are breathing out. Can you think of a good word you might like to say to yourself?

CLIENT: I'll try "relax."

THERAPIST: Okay; let's try the breathing together. We will take a bunch of breaths together, and I'll walk you through the skill. You can do it with your eyes open or closed. I will close my eyes, though, because that is the most comfortable way for me to use the skill. The idea is we will be taking a normal breath, but then let it out much more slowly than usual. Any questions?

CLIENT: Nope, sounds pretty straightforward to me.

THERAPIST: Let's begin by taking a normal breath in through your nose, hold it for a second (*pause*), and now exhale slowly (*pause*), and r-e-e-e-e-l-a-a-a-x (*pause*). (N.B.: Do this seven to 10 more times until the person seems to have mastered the skill. Each time, slow it down a bit more. Then, before the last breath, announce that it is the last one.) And, last breath, breathe in (*pause*), and out. Now, open your eyes. How was that?

CLIENT: Good. At first it was hard to match my breathing with your counting, though.

THERAPIST: Yeah, that can happen when it is being led by someone else. But were you able to slow your breathing in the end?

CLIENT: Yes.

THERAPIST: And how do you feel?

CLIENT: Actually, more relaxed. I didn't really think I would notice anything. But I was a little nervous about the session today, and now I am feeling calmer.

THERAPIST: Great! With practice, you should be able to get to that same relaxed state even faster.

During the teaching of breathing retraining, some clients may say that they prefer to use another type of breathing technique or mindfulness strategy. The CBT-PD program focuses on breathing retraining because of its established effectiveness in decreasing both anxiety and physiological arousal. However, other techniques can be added to breathing retraining, or used as an alternative if the client has difficulty learning or benefiting from the breathing retraining technique. When clients bring up the issue of using an alternative relaxation technique we recommend the therapist first show interest in understanding a little more about the technique the client is describing and then encourage the client to try learning and practicing the breathing retraining technique because it may be another useful strategy they can use to cope with their anxiety or overarousal. As the client gains some familiarity and experience with breathing retraining, the therapist can explore with them whether combining the technique with other relaxation skills the client already knows, or using breathing retraining instead, further improves their ability to alleviate anxiety and hyperarousal.

Home Assignments for Breathing Retraining

To become proficient in breathing retraining, the skill needs to be practiced regularly. At first, it is important for clients to practice the breathing when they are feeling relatively calm and are not especially anxious, so they can focus on learning the skill. This can be explained as follows:

THERAPIST: Now that you have been introduced to the skill of breathing retraining, let's talk about when you might practice using it. Can you think of a quiet time that might work?

CLIENT: I think I can do it at night, before I go to bed.

THERAPIST: That's a good time to do it. Is there another time that you can think of?

CLIENT: When I am not running around?

THERAPIST: Yes; for now we are looking for another time when you practice when you aren't distracted or anxious and can focus.

CLIENT: I guess on the three mornings a week when the kids are at day care, I could maybe find time. I usually take that time to run errands, but I should be able to fit it in.

THERAPIST: That sounds good. For now I would like you to practice the breathing at least once a day. Practicing when your kids are at day care is a good option, and you can also practice when you are going to bed at night. The goal is for you to learn the skill so that later you will be able to use it at times when you are anxious. The instructions for the breathing are included on Handout 18, and on Handout 19 there is a space to record when you did the breathing and how it went.

In a few weeks, after the client has mastered the skill, the therapist can help them learn to use the breathing in other situations, such as when they feel overly alert or anxious. The therapist should acknowledge that the client has learned the skill and then suggest other opportunities to use the breathing:

THERAPIST: Now that you are able to use the breathing exercise when you are calm, let's begin to consider when you might be able to use the skill when you are feeling tense, overstimulated, or anxious. The breathing can help counteract negative thoughts and feelings that occur during periods of stress. What are some of the situations in which you feel stressed, or when some of the symptoms we've talked about tend to be worst?

CLIENT: I guess when I am picking up the kids at day care. I get anxious around all the other mothers and all the activity.

THERAPIST: Can you tell me more about that? What happens specifically to you around the pickup time?

CLIENT: I start feeling stressed just driving over there. I know I have to go inside, and there are usually other moms around. They want to chat and I get nervous and I say stupid things, which only makes me feel more nervous.

THERAPIST: That sounds like a good time to use the skill. Do you think you could try using the breathing retraining right before you get out of the car?

CLIENT: I think so.

THERAPIST: That would be great. As you get better and better at the skill, you'll also learn how to monitor your breathing in different situations, such as when you're talking with the other moms. You'll begin to notice when your breathing is getting shorter and faster, and that can be your signal to slow it down.

CLIENT: That would be nice.

THERAPIST: I agree. So, to recap, for this week the goal is for you to start using the breathing retraining skill at times when you feel anxious or tense or just want to focus and relax. For now, you have identified pickup from day care as one time when you want to use the breathing. But really any time you begin to notice you are becoming anxious, that should be a clue to try and breathing. Does that make sense?

CLIENT: Yep, I think I got it.

THERAPIST: Great! I will check in with you about it next week.

Following Up on Breathing Retraining

At the beginning of each of the next several sessions, the therapist should check in with the client about how the breathing retraining practice has been going. In the beginning, the therapist should focus on whether the client is practicing it daily and how it is working. The therapist can refer to Handout 19 to see how often the client has practiced, how they felt when using the exercise, and note whether there are issues with it they would like to discuss. If the client has forgotten to bring their handout to the session, or has not filled it out, the therapist can ask questions to explore how practice is going, such as "When are you using the breathing?" "How do you feel when you use the breathing?" and "Are there any problems that you have noticed?" If the client is having trouble the therapist can teach the exercise again. The therapist can also explore any problems the client may be having and make adjustments, such as not counting as long when exhaling, not holding the breath as long, or adding a pleasant image to accompany the exhalation.

Once the client has learned the skill, the check-in about the practice of breathing retraining shifts to helping the client use the skill in situations in which they are anxious or overly aroused. After helping the client identify these situations, the therapist should check in with the client about how breathing retraining has been working by asking questions such as "Have you found that you can use the breathing in the moments when you feel anxious or only later when the situation has resolved itself?" and "How does the breathing help with your focus?"

ACTIVITY SCHEDULING

Activity scheduling is a primary component of behavioral activation. As we discussed in Chapter 2, the theory underlying behavioral activation is that stressful events disrupt people's usual engagement in pleasant or rewarding activities, leading to the loss of reinforcement, which in turn results in depression (Lewinsohn, 1974). Behavioral activation is also effective in targeting the avoidance associated with PTSD. In CBT-PD, the therapist helps the client identify activities that are pleasurable and that help reduce avoidance, including personally meaningful activities the person may have avoided since the disaster. For example, whereas for a client who is avoiding social interaction reading a book is pleasurable, a preferred, helpful activity might be going for a walk with a friend. A long list of possible activities is included in Handout 21 ("Pleasant Activities List"; in Appendix B on the APA website at http://pubs.apa.org/books/supp/hamblen). The therapist and client can review the list together and consider which activities the client would like to schedule. More information about how to select activities is provided a little later in this section.

As with all the CBT-PD treatment components, activity scheduling begins by providing the client the rationale for how it works. Clients experiencing significant depression may be skeptical that something as simple as scheduling pleasant and meaningful activities may reduce their depression. People with significant PTSD avoidance symptoms may be reluctant to try engaging in activities that may bring up memories of their traumatic experience; therefore, a strong rationale needs to be provided to help encourage clients to engage in activities that are easier to avoid then perform.

Using the Thought–Feeling–Behavior Triangle (see Figure 7.1), the therapist teaches the client how feeling depressed can result from either too many negative experiences (i.e., behaviors) or from negative thoughts and that they can improve their mood by either engaging in more positive behaviors or by learning to appraise the situation differently. Engaging in more rewarding

FIGURE 7.1. The Thought-Feeling-Behavior Triangle

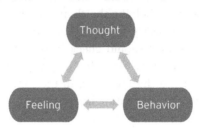

Note. The Thought-Feeling-Behavior Triangle illustrates how thoughts, feelings, and behaviors are all interconnected and can influence one another. For example, someone who survived a terrorist bomb explosion in a mall might later react to an invitation to go to a concert with a friend with the *thought* "Crowded places are unsafe—they are easy targets for terrorist attacks," which would lead to *feeling* afraid, which would then result in the *behavior* of avoidance and turning down the friend's invitation.

behaviors is accomplished through activity scheduling. This information is also reviewed in Handout 20 in Appendix B on the APA website at http://pubs.apa.org/books/supp/hamblen.

THERAPIST: As we discussed in the last session, sadness and depression are frequent reactions to disaster. It is common for people to feel down or low after a traumatic event. Depression results from having more negative experiences than positive ones. Pleasant experiences tend to generate positive emotions, whereas negative experiences tend to generate distressing emotions. So, if you want to improve your mood, you need to increase positive experiences and decrease negative ones. Does that make sense?

CLIENT: I guess so. But I really don't feel like it these days. When I feel better I plan to start doing things again.

THERAPIST: The problem is that in order to feel better you have to start *doing* things first. When people are depressed they often try hard to change their feelings, but it turns out that's really difficult to do. Look here at this diagram. Thoughts, feelings, and behaviors are connected. So far, you have tried to tell yourself to feel better, but that hasn't worked. Right?

CLIENT: Right.

THERAPIST: But you can also change your feelings by changing your thoughts or behaviors. Today we are going to work on changing behaviors in order to change your feelings. Changing behaviors can also change how you think about things. Doing positive things results in both feeling better and in more positive thinking. So, we'll work on beginning to change your behaviors in this session. Then, in the next session, we will start working on evaluating your thinking and changing that when it isn't accurate. So, in order to feel better, you must first put yourself into more positive situations.

CLIENT: I'm not sure I am up for that.

THERAPIST: That's understandable. When people are depressed they stop doing things that can make them feel better, like spending time with friends and family or pursuing hobbies. They may also skip work or not perform as well at work because they're not trying as hard. This can have negative consequences, which can make them feel even worse. Is that something you can relate to?

CLIENT: Definitely. My wife has been on me to go to our kids' school activities.

THERAPIST: Like what?

CLIENT: Most recently, it was a school concert. But I didn't feel like it, so I didn't go.

THERAPIST: And then what happened?

CLIENT: I ended up feeling guilty about it, and my wife was clearly pissed at me.

THERAPIST: Exactly. You avoided the school event because you didn't feel up to it, and you probably thought it wouldn't be much fun anyway, but instead you ended up feeling even worse. And the bigger problem is that you didn't try going to the concert, which you might have found more enjoyable than you thought it would be.

CLIENT: That makes sense.

After the therapist explains the purpose of activity scheduling, the next part is to help the client identify activities that are both rewarding and may help improve their situation. Some activities are fun but may be less personally meaningful or rewarding, like going to the movies. Other activities may be difficult but are very meaningful, like agreeing to go to marriage counseling. Activities may also be selected because they may help clients meet a personal goal or because they target avoidance behaviors that may be interfering in their life. The therapist should help the client carefully consider these issues when selecting activities. The activities that are chosen typically cover a range of these issues: Some are just fun, some are personally rewarding or help the client meet a goal, and some target avoidance.

There are lots of ways to help clients come up with activities. Included in the book is a long list of activities the therapist can review with the client (see Handout 21). Many of the activities are simple things that are free and relatively easy to accomplish, like going for a walk or calling a friend.

THERAPIST: So, the goal is to find things that you can do that will make you feel better.

CLIENT: Okay.

THERAPIST: Do you have any ideas of things you would like to try or things you used to do but have stopped doing?

CLIENT: Not really.

THERAPIST: No problem. Let's take a look at this list and see if there are some activities on it you think you could do and that would be pleasurable. (*Review the list provided in Handout 21*). Is there anything on this list that you think would be fun?

CLIENT: I used to do woodworking. I actually started a bench for the front hall. I was building it in the garage, but it got ruined when the house flooded.

THERAPIST: Did you enjoy working on the bench?

CLIENT: Yeah. We wanted a bench but couldn't find one that was the right size for the spot we had. It felt good to build it myself.

THERAPIST: Do you think you could start over?

CLIENT: Maybe. Before when I thought about it, it just reminded me of the hurricane. But now I guess I see it differently.

THERAPIST: How so?

CLIENT: Well, it's just that now I'm making a choice to do something that at least used to be fun. I don't want to let the hurricane control me anymore.

THERAPIST: Okay, so do you think you could give it a try? And if it does bring back bad memories, we can actually begin working on those over the next few sessions.

CLIENT: That sounds good.

THERAPIST: Do you have what you need to get started?

CLIENT: Not really. But I like going to the lumber yard.

THERAPIST: Perfect. That can be one of your first activities.

Another way to identify activities is to help the client consider what areas of their life they would like to work on and then come up with activities in those areas. After a disaster there is often a lot of loss, and clients can feel as if they have nothing to live for or that life has lost meaning. By helping the client explore relevant life areas and personal values, activities can be identified that will help in those areas (see Handout 22 in Appendix B on the APA website at http://pubs.apa.org/books/supp/hamblen). For example, if the client wants to work on improving family relationships, then finding an activity they can do with their son/daughter, father/mother, or significant other is a good idea. This could include reading to their child at night or going out to dinner with their spouse. Other areas to explore are other social relationships (e.g., eating lunch with a coworker, going to a movie), intimate relationships (e.g., saying "I love you," holding hands), education/training (e.g., taking an online course), employment/career (e.g., asking if there is a new project they could work on), hobbies/recreation (e.g., attending a yoga class), volunteer work/charity/political activity (e.g., volunteering at a school event), physical/health-related activities (e.g., cooking a healthy meal), spirituality (e.g., going to a church service or group), and psychological/emotional-related issues (e.g., talking with a friend or therapist; Lejuez et al., 2011). Once the client has identified an area on which they want to focus, the therapist can help them brainstorm activities that will help them make improvements in that area. The therapist can use Handout 22 to help the client identify personally meaningful areas or, if the therapist is already aware of a personally meaningful area, lead a discussion:

THERAPIST: Now, one thing to keep in mind is that some activities can serve more than one purpose. They can make you feel good, but they can also focus on an area of your life you want to work on.

CLIENT: Okay.

THERAPIST: So, one of the activities you identified was shooting hoops. But, you also previously told me that you have been feeling guilty about not spending time with your family. Would your son enjoy playing basketball with you?

CLIENT: Definitely.

THERAPIST: Would that also be enjoyable for you?

CLIENT: Yeah. As long as it was just in the driveway.

THERAPIST: That's a great start. So how about we modify the activity to say shooting hoops with your son at home?

CLIENT: Yeah, I could do that.

Finally, if the therapist has identified avoidance of any people, places, or situations related to the disaster, they can use activity scheduling to target the avoidance. For example, for a client who was at the 2017 Harvest Music Festival shooting, a large country music festival in Las Vegas where a man began shooting into the crowd from above ("2017 Las Vegas Shooting," 2020), listening to country music on their iPod at home might be a good first step. Then a later goal may be going to a local music festival or to a restaurant with live music.

An important part of scheduling activities is to help the client actually plan when they are going to do the activity and anything else that might be required to do it. People who are depressed often put off doing things because they don't feel like it at the moment. Planned activities should be put on a calendar, and some thought should go into any preparation needed to participate in it (e.g., call a friend, make a reservation, check the movie listings). Handout 23 (in Appendix B on the APA website at http://pubs. apa.org/books/supp/hamblen) provides a place to identify and schedule activities. If the client uses a calendar on their smartphone, the therapist should have them enter their activities on that. A reminder can even be set to prompt the client to engage in an activity. Clients are also asked to rate the activity on how enjoyable it was and how important it was.

THERAPIST: Okay, so now that we have some activities picked out let's spend a few minutes thinking about when you are actually going to be able to do these activities.

CLIENT: Well, some of them I can just do when I have some free time. Like I can go for a walk whenever.

THERAPIST: Yes, but what we find is that people are much more likely to do an activity if they plan for it and then actually schedule when they will do it. For example, you picked reading and going for walk. It's easier to read a book if you already have a book picked out. And it is easier to go for a walk if you have that scheduled and have thought about where you'll walk. So, what book are you planning to read?

CLIENT: Well, I got a book as a gift that is on my bedside table. I was going to read that.

THERAPIST: Okay. And when would be good times to you to read it?

CLIENT: I don't know. I used to read before bed, but I stopped. I could try that again.

THERAPIST: Okay, so what night do you want to read before bed?

CLIENT: I think I will try every night for at least 15 minutes.

THERAPIST: That sounds great, but to start with, how about just a few nights?

CLIENT: Okay, how about Sunday and maybe Thursday?

THERAPIST: All right. And what about your walk? When do you think would be good times to take a walk?

CLIENT: Hmm; I don't really like walking alone. I would rather walk with a friend.

THERAPIST: Is there someone you could call?

CLIENT: Yes. I have a friend who goes for long walks with her dog on the weekends. I think I could call her.

THERAPIST: So it's Wednesday now. Can you call her today or tomorrow so you can set it up for this weekend?

CLIENT: Yes.

THERAPIST: Now let's take a moment to review how Handout 23 works. Each week you will list the five activities you have planned in the first column. You had reading on Sunday night as one activity, reading on Thursday night as a second activity, and going for a walk with a friend as a third activity. You will need to schedule two more activities for this week.

CLIENT: Okay.

THERAPIST: Then in the next column you write down the day or date you plan to do the activity. Right now you have activities scheduled for Sunday night, Thursday night, and the weekend.

CLIENT: Yes, that's right.

THERAPIST: Then, after you do the activity I want you to rate on a scale from 0 to 10 how enjoyable the activity was and how rewarding it was. You can also write down any observations you had when doing it, like if it was more fun than you expected, or if it was hard to get started, or why you didn't do the activity. Any questions?

CLIENT: Nope, I got it.

Home Assignments for Activity Scheduling

Clients should be encouraged to engage in five activities each week. They should begin with activities that are relatively easy so that they can experience success and get in the habit of planning and engaging in the activities. Each week in which there has been good follow-through on the scheduled activities there should be an increase in the meaningfulness of some of the activities, or in the effort required to engage in some of the activities.

THERAPIST: Okay, now that we have identified some areas of your life you want to work on and some possible activities, let's pick five activities you can do between this week and next week. Let's start with activities that are relatively easy to accomplish.

CLIENT: Okay, well, I want to work on being a better mother. I feel like I have been really impatient with my daughter, and I never want to play when she asks.

THERAPIST: That seems like a good goal. So, within that area, what are some things you think you could do that would be fun for both of you?

CLIENT: Well, my daughter always wants to use my nail polish. Maybe we could do like a spa thing and paint each other's nails?

THERAPIST: That sounds like a good one. Do you already have nail polish, or do you need to buy some?

CLIENT: I have some light colors, but nothing she would like.

THERAPIST: Hmm, maybe you could also add picking out and buying nail polish to your list? Would you and your daughter enjoy that?

CLIENT: Actually, yes.

THERAPIST: Okay, let's pick a few more things and then we will pull out the Pleasant Activities Log Worksheet [Handout 23] and find some times when you can do them.

CLIENT: Okay.

THERAPIST: That's great. I'm really looking forward to seeing how it goes. Over the next few weeks we will identify more activities for you to do, including ones that are increasingly pleasurable and rewarding.

Following Up on Activity Scheduling

At the start of each of the next sessions the therapist checks in with the client to assess how the activity scheduling is going. The therapist should review the Pleasant Activities Log for the past week and determine whether the client did the activity, and how they felt while doing it, and then plan with them the activities they will do for the following week. If an activity was missed, it is important to determine why it was missed and make a new plan if it is still a desired activity. If the activity was avoided because it was too hard or ambitious, the therapist can help the client break it down into smaller, more manageable steps. If the client says they did not have enough time, then the therapist can help problem solve around whether there are some less valued activities that could be skipped to free up time or whether a less time consuming activity could be substituted. Perhaps the client wanted to do the activity but needed help, like a ride to the store. In this case, the therapist can help the client problem solve how to find a ride. If the client engaged in the activity but it wasn't enjoyable, the therapist can explore why they didn't enjoy it. Did they enjoy it a little, but not as much as they thought they would, or was it truly not enjoyable at all? On the basis of the experience, the therapist can consider with the client whether to keep the activity on the list and try it again or drop it from the list.

THERAPIST: How did the activity scheduling go last week? Can I see your activity log?

CLIENT: I did some things, but not others.

THERAPIST: Let's start with what you did.

CLIENT: Okay. I took a bath, and I bought myself new shoes.

THERAPIST: And how did it feel? I see you gave the bath an "8" for how enjoyable and a "7" for how important it was.

CLIENT: Yes, the bath was relaxing. I haven't taken a bath in years, and it felt good to prioritize my own needs so I gave that a 7 for importance. And I love the shoes! I gave that a 9 for enjoyable, but only a 3 for importance because I didn't really need them.

THERAPIST: That's great! And what about the things you didn't do? What got in the way?

CLIENT: Well, one required coordination with other people. I was supposed to go to lunch with a friend, but I never called her. I just got busy and ran out of time.

THERAPIST: Is it still something you think would be enjoyable?

CLIENT: Yes.

THERAPIST: So what can you do differently this week to make it happen?

CLIENT: Well, it's been so long since we have talked that every time I thought of calling I just didn't feel like I had the energy. But maybe I could set it up by email or even text. That wouldn't require a conversation. And then we could catch up in person.

THERAPIST: That sounds like a good plan. What about the other activities? What happened there?

CLIENT: Well I chickened out on asking my boss if I could go to the training. I just got worried she would say no.

THERAPIST: Would it help to do a brief role-play of it? I could pretend to be your boss, and you could ask me?

CLIENT: Yeah, that might help.

THERAPIST: Okay. Let's do that after we finish reviewing what you did last week. What about your last activity? What happened there?

CLIENT: I was going to try and go to a yoga class. But I never found one.

THERAPIST: Perhaps we should break this goal down a bit since it seems a little more complicated than it did at first. First you need to find out about where yoga classes are available, and then you can schedule a class. How can you find out who offers yoga classes?

CLIENT: There is a woman at work who I think goes to yoga classes. I could ask her.

THERAPIST: That sounds good. When will you see her next?

CLIENT: I see her every day. I could ask her tomorrow.

THERAPIST: Okay.

In the beginning, the focus is on helping the client engage in the activities. Over time, though, the therapist should help the client identify activities that will bring increasing reward and that target any disaster-related avoidance that may be present. Activity scheduling is a powerful tool that can help clients feel better and help them make substantial progress toward meeting their individualized treatment goals.

CONCLUSION

In this chapter, we have reviewed two resiliency skills that are taught to clients, usually in the second session of CBT-PD. Breathing retraining is a simple but important skill that can have an immediate impact on how clients are feeling. Clients should be encouraged to practice breathing retraining at least once a day in situations in which they are not feeling stressed or anxious so they can master the skill under optimal learning conditions. Over the following sessions, their breathing retraining practice is reviewed, obstacles to using it are problem solved, and minor adaptations to the skill are made to accommodate the client's needs and preferences. As the client gains mastery over the skill, they are helped to begin using it in more stressful situations to reduce anxiety or overarousal symptoms.

Activity scheduling is also a relatively straightforward skill to teach that can have a major impact on clients' emotions and behaviors; however, it also takes more motivation on the part of the client to follow through on planned activities and therefore requires more attention by the therapist. Each week the therapist must attend to how the activity scheduling is going and ensure that the client is identifying and engaging in rewarding activities, including potentially meaningful activities that have been avoided since the disaster. As the therapy progresses and the attention shifts to the cognitive restructuring, the therapist needs to ensure that the client does not overlook continued work on these skills.

8
COGNITIVE RESTRUCTURING 1
Problematic Thinking Styles

Cognitive restructuring (CR) serves as the foundation of the Cognitive Behavior Therapy for Postdisaster Distress (CBT-PD) program. Once CR has been taught, the remainder of the program focuses on helping clients identify and challenge their thoughts and beliefs related to the disaster, including core beliefs (or schemas) that underlie their posttraumatic reactions. CR is typically taught over the course of the third and fourth therapy sessions. The first CR session begins with the therapist helping the client learn about the connection between thoughts and feelings. The therapist teaches the client how to recognize four specific feeling states—fear and anxiety, sadness and depression, guilt and shame, and anger—and their associated inaccurate or negative thoughts. Worksheets are provided to help clients identify disaster-related cognitions for each feeling state and to track their negative feelings and thoughts.

Building on the concept that inaccurate or negative thoughts lead to negative feelings, in the second half of the third session the concept of *Problematic Thinking Styles* is introduced. Problematic Thinking Styles are common but inaccurate ways people have of reaching conclusions that lead

https://doi.org/10.1037/0000237-008
Treatment for Postdisaster Distress: A Transdiagnostic Approach, by J. L. Hamblen and K. T. Mueser

to distressing feelings; they are sometimes referred to as *cognitive distortions* in cognitive behavior therapy programs. Clients are taught to examine upsetting thoughts to see if those thoughts correspond to a specific Problematic Thinking Style. Strategies for coming up with more accurate thoughts to replace thoughts related to each Problematic Thinking Style are then offered and incorporated into the worksheets. At the end of the first CR session, clients should grasp the fundamental idea that they can change their negative feelings by examining their thoughts and understanding that changing them when they are inaccurate leads to a reduction in distress.

ESTABLISHING THE CONNECTION BETWEEN THOUGHTS AND FEELINGS

The idea that thoughts, feelings, and behaviors are connected is initially introduced in Session 2, during the activity scheduling part of the CBT-PD program (see Chapter 7). In that session, clients are taught that their behaviors influence their feelings and that by engaging in more rewarding behaviors they will feel better. In Session 3, clients are introduced to CR and learn to focus on examining and correcting their thoughts to make them more accurate as another means to change feelings.

The teaching of CR begins with a discussion of the relationship between thoughts and feelings and an explanation of how people's life experiences, including traumatic experiences such as surviving a disaster, can have a major impact on their thinking. Most important, the therapist seeks to establish that what people think in a situation has an important effect on how they feel in that situation and that not all thoughts that people may have in a situation are equally accurate. This sets the stage for teaching the client how to examine their thoughts when they are feeling upset, how to recognize common Problematic Thinking Styles, and how to change their thinking when it starts to become inaccurate. An example is typically used to illustrate the importance of how thinking influences feelings:

THERAPIST: One of the most important things to understand about upsetting feelings is that they are usually linked to our thoughts about a particular situation or event. So, what we think when something happens determines, in large part, what we feel in that situation. For example, imagine that you're walking down the street and you see a friend, but they don't say hello to you. You sort of nod and smile, but they just keep walking. How would you feel if that happened?

CLIENT: I think I would feel hurt. Maybe a little foolish, too, if someone saw me.

THERAPIST: Right. A lot of people say they would feel hurt. Now, what did you just say to yourself about *why* your friend didn't say hello?

CLIENT: I guess that they were mad at me for some reason.

THERAPIST: Okay, so if you thought "My friend is mad at me and that's why she didn't respond to me," you'd feel hurt. Now, do you think someone else in that same situation might think something different?

CLIENT: Well, my friends say I am overly sensitive. One of them might have thought "That person is a real jerk."

THERAPIST: Great, let's use that. So, if your friend thought "That person is a jerk," how might they then feel?

CLIENT: Angry, I guess.

THERAPIST: Right. If someone thought their friend heard them say "Hello" but chose not to respond because he didn't care or thought he had something better to do, she might feel angry at him and think he's a jerk. And how might the person act the next time they saw their friend?

CLIENT: Maybe a little cooler than usual? Who wants to be friends with a jerk?

THERAPIST: Right! Not only would thinking her friend is a jerk make her feel angry, but it might also influence her behavior towards him—make her a little less friendly.

CLIENT: True.

THERAPIST: Now, what if I told you that your friend had just received some really bad news or that your friend was talking on a cell phone. Would that change how you felt about the situation?

CLIENT: Yeah, I think so. I wouldn't be hurt if I thought my friend was just in a bad mood about something else or if they didn't even notice me because they were on the phone.

THERAPIST: Exactly, and see—you are already connecting thoughts and feelings. If you think your friend is mad, you feel hurt. If you think your friend is being a jerk, you feel angry. And, if you think your friend is distracted in some way, you feel what?

CLIENT: I don't know, nothing. It's no big deal, then. I just feel fine.

THERAPIST: Great. So that is an example of how thoughts and feelings are connected. A lot of different thoughts are possible in this situation, and different feelings are connected with each different thought.

Some clients may need a second example before they fully understand that thinking influences feelings. In this case, it can be helpful to use an example that elicits fear rather than feeling bad or angry. A useful example is to ask the client to imagine that they are home alone in a first-floor apartment or house, sleeping, when they are awoken by a noise outside. If they think the noise is someone trying to break in, then they would likely say they feel afraid. They might stay up all night, listening for more sounds, or even call the police. However, if they thought it was just their cat, which they let out earlier, or a trash can being knocked over by an animal, they would probably be annoyed, but not afraid, and they would go back to sleep.

Once the client understands that thoughts lead to feelings, the therapist helps them see that not all thoughts are equally accurate. The therapist can illustrate to the client that at the time the situation is occurring the thought seems to be almost automatic, but that just because the client may *think* these things does not make them true.

THERAPIST: So, let's go back to the friend example for a moment. Initially, you said if your friend didn't acknowledge you, then you would feel hurt.

CLIENT: That's right.

THERAPIST: But then when I said what if they hadn't seen you when you walked by, you said you would feel fine.

CLIENT: Yes.

THERAPIST: So which thought is right?

CLIENT: Well, I guess I wouldn't necessarily know right away.

THERAPIST: Correct. And what about the loud noise example? Should you think it is someone trying to break in, or just the cat?

CLIENT: Again, I guess I wouldn't really know until later.

THERAPIST: That's right. So we have these automatic negative thoughts that we may not even really be aware of, and we don't actually know if they are accurate. All we know is that they make us feel bad.

CLIENT: I never thought about it that way.

Clients typically understand easily that thoughts and feelings are connected, but some will resist the idea that their thoughts might not be accurate. This resistance often stems from a fear that if they let their guard down they may be putting themselves or loved ones at risk. At this point in the teaching of CR it is not critical to change a client's thoughts or to even challenge their thinking. What is important is that the client can see how their appraisal of a situation changes how they feel in that situation. Once that has been established, the therapist helps the client to understand why some people are more prone to having these automatic negative thoughts than others.

THERAPIST: Why do you think that one person might have the thought "My friend is mad at me" or "There's someone trying to break in," while another might think "My friend didn't notice me" or "An animal must have knocked over my trash can again?"

CLIENT: I'm not sure. I just know I always think the worst because it seems like the worst things really happen to me.

THERAPIST: That's right. People tend to have different thoughts because they have had different previous experiences. And people who have been through a disaster or other traumatic experiences often have more negative thoughts than those who have not had those experiences. But the truth is that, in the moment, you can't really know if your friend saw you or if there was an intruder. It is our previous experiences that cause us to form automatic negative thoughts.

The therapist labels the thoughts as "automatic" because they appear to occur instantaneously and often are not based on facts. In the walking-down-the-street example, the person sees their friend fail to respond to them, which they "automatically" interpret as ignoring them, and they instantly feel bad. Or they wake to a loud noise and feel afraid. The thought that their friend might be mad or that there is an intruder is immediate (or automatic) and typically does not involve any consideration or active thinking. As a result, people often have to learn how to identify specific thoughts underlying their negative feelings.

THE GUIDE TO THOUGHTS AND FEELINGS

When teaching people how to identify the thoughts underlying negative feelings, the therapist focuses on four broad negative feeling states that are common reactions to a disaster: (a) fear and anxiety, (b) sadness and depression, (c) guilt and shame, and (d) anger. Clients are taught to recognize the types of thinking that are associated with each of these feeling states. Handout 24, the Guide to Thought and Feelings (see Appendix B on the American Psychological Association website at http://pubs.apa.org/books/supp/hamblen), provides clients with information and questions to help them identify the automatic thoughts that are most commonly associated with each of the four feeling states. It can be used to help clients who are able to identify a negative feeling, but not the underlying thought, determine what their automatic thought is.

The handout explains that each of the four major negative feeling states is associated with a broad type of thought. Thus, feelings of fear or anxiety are related to thoughts of possible harm or danger, feelings of depression or sadness are related to thoughts of having lost something, guilt and shame feelings are related to thoughts of having done something wrong, and angry feelings are related to thoughts of having been wronged in some way or things being unfair. For example, if a client feels angry but, when asked about the specific thought related to the anger, can only say "I'm just pissed off" or "This sucks," the Guide to Thoughts and Feelings poses the question, "What is unfair about the situation?" The answer "FEMA (the Federal Emergency Management Agency) should pay for my repairs" is the specific thought that underlies the anger. The handout can help clients who can identify their thoughts, but not their feelings, to identify the emotions underlying their negative thoughts. They can locate on the handout a thought close to the one they have and then learn which feeling is most related to that type of thinking.

THERAPIST: We have talked a lot about the fact that people who have experienced a disaster or trauma often experience four different major types of upsetting emotions: fear and anxiety, sadness and depression, guilt and shame, and anger. There are lots of other negative emotions that are important, but most of them fit into one of these four major categories.

CLIENT: Okay.

THERAPIST: The first step to being able to change our thinking patterns is to be able to identify what we are thinking. The Guide to Thoughts and Feelings (Handout 24) lists the four feeling states and the thoughts that are typically related to those thoughts. Let's review how this handout can be used. For example, when you feel afraid, it's usually because you think that you're in danger and are concerned that something bad is going to happen. Can you think of a time recently that you felt afraid? What were you thinking?

CLIENT: Hmm. I was afraid last night. It was raining hard, and the lights flickered.

THERAPIST: And what were you thinking at that moment?

CLIENT: Oh, no, here we go again.

THERAPIST: Can you be more specific? See here on the handout, ask yourself what bad thing did you expect to happen?

CLIENT: Oh, I see. Well, I thought the house might flood again and we would have to quickly evacuate. I couldn't go to bed until the rain lightened up.

THERAPIST: Okay, so when you thought "My house might flood," you felt scared.

CLIENT: Yes.

THERAPIST: What about a recent time you felt sad? When people feel sad, they are often thinking about a loss.

CLIENT: Um, I was sad last weekend. My daughter had a class assignment to write about a family heirloom. She asked me if we had any. I reminded her that I had an antique doll that was my grandmother's that I had passed down to her. But the doll is gone now. We had to throw it away after the hurricane. It was ruined in the flood.

THERAPIST: That's a good example. In the case of Hurricane Harvey, the flooding was as bad as the storm itself. A lot of people lost treasured possessions. So, what do you think you were thinking when you were reminded about the doll?

CLIENT: I guess that I had lost a lot of important things.

THERAPIST: Sure, that makes sense. But what does it mean to you that you lost these things?

CLIENT: That nothing will be the same again. That I won't ever be happy again.

THERAPIST: Right. Often, feeling sad or depressed isn't just about the loss of something, but also about the belief that things will never be better again. Now let's consider guilt and shame. When people feel guilt or shame they tend to think that they have done something wrong or that there is something wrong with them. Have you felt guilt or shame recently?

CLIENT: All the time. I just feel like everything is my fault. I am bringing down my whole family because I can't just get over what happened.

THERAPIST: Okay, so let's see if we can identify the specific thought. What do you think is your fault?

CLIENT: It's my fault that my family is having a hard time. If I could just forget about the hurricane, everyone would feel better.

THERAPIST: That is exactly the type of thought we will want to examine more closely in the next few sessions. You think you are making them feel bad, but we will consider whether there are other ways to look at the situation. Okay, let's consider anger. Have there been times when you were angry? If so, what were you thinking?

CLIENT: I am also angry all the time.

THERAPIST: And what are you thinking when you are angry?

CLIENT: Just how unfair it all is. We almost died. We lost everything. The insurance company refuses to help. FEMA is doing nothing. My husband lost his job. We have no place to live. It's a lot!

THERAPIST: Yes, there is a lot to be upset about. It sounds like the primary thought is that "It's unfair that I am in this situation." Is that accurate?

CLIENT: Yes. We don't deserve this.

THERAPIST: Right. And that's the thought that makes you feel angry. So, over the next few sessions we will be examining the thoughts that are related to your most distressing feelings and evaluating them to determine how accurate and helpful they are. When the thoughts are inaccurate or not helpful, we'll work on identifying a more accurate or more balanced way of looking at the situation, which can reduce the upsetting feeling.

PROBLEMATIC THINKING STYLES

Once clients have learned to identify their negative thoughts, they can immediately work on changing them. Problematic Thinking Styles are introduced as a way to identify extreme patterns of thinking that typically result in a person feeling negatively. If a client can recognize they are using one of these thinking styles, they can often use that information to help them come up with a more balanced, accurate thought. For example, *Catastrophizing* and *All-or-Nothing Thinking* (also called *black-and-white thinking*) are two common Problematic Thinking Styles. If clients are able to recognize that they engage in these types of thinking, they are acknowledging a tendency to base their thinking on broad beliefs about the world rather than on evidence. For each type of thinking style there are suggested strategies for modifying the thought. The therapist should review Handout 25, Problematic Thinking Styles (in Appendix B on the APA website at http://pubs. apa.org/books/supp/hamblen), with the client to familiarize them with the different inaccurate ways of thinking and explore whether the client can identify specific examples of when they might have engaged in each one.

THERAPIST: I'd like to review something called "Problematic Thinking Styles," or common inaccurate patterns of thinking that people often have in their reactions to everyday events, to see if you identify with any of them. Everyone engages in these thinking styles sometimes. However, people with traumatic experiences may use these thinking styles more than others, which can contribute to their negative feelings. Let's review each Problematic Thinking Style and see why each one is inaccurate in some way.

CLIENT: Okay.

THERAPIST: The first one is "All-or-Nothing Thinking." All-or-Nothing Thinking, or "black-and-white thinking," is when you see a situation in absolute terms; that is, everything is either all one way or all another way, with nothing in the middle. For example, if you made a minor mistake but thought you were a failure, that would be an example. Or if you think the world is either completely safe or totally dangerous when in reality there are some situations that are safer than others—that is All-or-Nothing Thinking. Can you think of any examples in your own life of using All-or-Nothing Thinking?

CLIENT: Well, what about thinking the police can't be trusted. Is that All-or-Nothing Thinking?

THERAPIST: Yes, that's a good example. So, when you notice that you are using that type of thinking, try to find the gray area. I know that you told me that after the school shooting some of the police officers were put on administrative leave for not following proper protocol. So does that mean no police can be trusted? Ever? Did any police help?

CLIENT: For sure a lot of the force actually saved lives. But when I am upset, I start thinking I can't trust any of them.

THERAPIST: Perfect! So you can see how you have automatic thoughts about police that are inaccurate and unhelpful. When you catch yourself using this kind of black-and-white thinking, then you need to remind yourself of the gray areas.

CLIENT: I can try.

THERAPIST: So, rather than telling yourself, "The police can't be trusted," what is a more accurate and balanced thought that takes into account the new information you just shared, that police can save lives?

CLIENT: I don't know. I guess "Some police can be trusted," or maybe even "Most police are good."

THERAPIST: Perfect. Either of those thoughts are less distressing than telling yourself that no police can be trusted. And, I think you would agree the new thought is more accurate too. Replacing negative thoughts with more accurate thoughts is called "cognitive restructuring." This is what we will be doing for the majority of our remaining sessions. Okay, let's review the next thinking style, "Catastrophizing." This type of thought occurs when you focus on the most extreme negative consequences. This leads to heightened fear and anxiety. Most catastrophic thoughts are triggered by "What if" thoughts, such as "What if there is another disaster?" or "What if I will never have a home again?" Can you think of a time you used Catastrophizing?

CLIENT: All the time. I always think the worst is going to happen.

THERAPIST: Can you give me an example?

CLIENT: Like, on the way over here I was running late, and I thought "My session is going to be canceled, and then I won't be able to function all week." These sessions are really helping me, and I don't know what I would do if you canceled one.

THERAPIST: Well, I think that is two catastrophic thoughts! First, that I would cancel just because you were a little late, and second that if the session was canceled you wouldn't be able to function. When you notice you are Catastrophizing, try to change the pattern by asking yourself "What would be the most likely outcome if the event were to happen?" So, in this case, what do you think is the most likely outcome of running late?

CLIENT: I guess that I might just have a shorter session. I mean, if you have another client after me you might not be able to give me the whole hour, but you wouldn't have to cancel.

THERAPIST: Right. So, less bad. The thought "My session will be canceled" is more extreme and distressing then the thought "My session might be cut short." Now, what if you had been so late that we did need to reschedule. What do you think would have happened then? Could you really not function for a week?

CLIENT: I don't know. Maybe not.

THERAPIST: Well, what did you do before we started meeting?

CLIENT: I was upset a lot of the time.

THERAPIST: But you were working, right?

CLIENT: Yes. I guess, I mean I think I could work even if I missed the session, but I feel like we are making progress, and I didn't want to miss a session.

THERAPIST: Sure, but remember, thoughts and feelings are connected. Having the catastrophic thought that you won't be able to function makes you feel anxious and upset. Telling yourself that the most likely outcome is that it might slow down your progress but that you could still function is more accurate and less distressing, right?

CLIENT: Definitely.

Home Assignments

In this session clients have learned to recognize and identify automatic negative thoughts, determine if they fall into one of the Problematic Thinking Styles. For homework, clients begin to work on changing these negative thoughts. Clients are given Handout 26, the Problematic Thinking Styles Log Worksheet (in Appendix B on the APA website at http://pubs.apa.org/books/supp/hamblen), and asked to monitor their upsetting situations and come up with more helpful thoughts. Clients ideally will do this for every upsetting situation that occurs between the time they are given the assignment and the next treatment session. The therapist should use the in-session examples to demonstrate how to complete the worksheet.

THERAPIST: Between this session and the next I want you to begin using the skill we have just been reviewing. Let's take a look at the Problematic Thinking Styles Log, and I will show you what I mean.

CLIENT: Okay.

THERAPIST: Remember, we reviewed two situations where automatic negative thoughts led to bad feelings.

CLIENT: Uh-huh.

THERAPIST: The first was the situation of a friend walking by and not acknowledging you. So, you would write that here in the first column. You can see it is already filled in as an example.

CLIENT: Yes.

THERAPIST: And then you said you might feel bad in that situation. On the worksheet it says "guilt" because that is one of the four feelings we focus on.

CLIENT: Okay.

THERAPIST: And the associated thought was "I did something to make my friend mad."

CLIENT: Yes.

THERAPIST: Now, let's consider whether there is a Problematic Thinking Style that might apply. Looking over Handout 25, what do you think?

CLIENT: I'd say Self-Blame.

THERAPIST: Right. The person is blaming themselves even though they have no idea if they did anything wrong. Then, you can see that in the last column you would write a more helpful thought. Together we came up with that "your friend might have not seen you" or "they could be distracted." So that goes in the last column. Does that make sense?

CLIENT: Yes. I get it.

THERAPIST: All right. So, between this session and next week, I want you to try and fill in a row for every upsetting situation that occurs. Aim for at least one a day. Does that sound doable?

CLIENT: Yes. I think I can do that. Okay.

THERAPIST: Any questions?

CLIENT: What if there isn't one?

THERAPIST: Well, that would be nice! But, if that happens, you can try and come up with examples from the past.

CLIENT: Okay, I can do that.

Reviewing the Problematic Thinking Styles Log

At the start of the next session the therapist should carefully review the client's completed Problematic Thinking Styles Log. The therapist should look closely to make sure that client has been able to identify specific feelings and thoughts and list those feelings and thoughts in the appropriate columns. The therapist should point out errors and help the client correct their responses. When possible, the therapist should refer to the Guide to Thoughts and Feelings (Handout 24) for assistance. It is best if the client can use that worksheet instead of relying on the therapist for corrections because this helps the client become more self-sufficient. Next, the therapist should look at whether the client has been able to identify a Problematic Thinking Style and come up with a more helpful thought. Again, the therapist should refer to Handout 25 (Problematic Thinking Styles) when needed.

THERAPIST: How did it go completing the Problematic Thinking Styles Log? Let's take a look. [See Exhibit 8.1.]

CLIENT: Okay, I guess. I wrote down a few things.

THERAPIST: This is a good start. I see you identified three situations. Let's review the first one. It looks like your boss asked to meet with you and that you felt scared.

CLIENT: Yeah. I had no idea what I had done wrong.

THERAPIST: Okay, "scared" is definitely a feeling. But I think you will find it easier in the long run if you try and stick to feelings from the Guide to Thoughts and Feelings. Looking at the guide, which of the four feelings is closest to feeling scared?

CLIENT: Fear and anxiety. But also some anger and shame.

THERAPIST: Let's stick with fear and anxiety for a moment since it sounds like that is the strongest feeling. It is very common to have more than one feeling come up in a situation, though. In those cases I would add a separate line for each feeling. So, on the log you would have one row for fear and anxiety, another for shame, and then a third for anger. Let's stick with fear and anxiety. One of the feelings you experienced was anxiety, and the thought was "I'm in trouble." It can be helpful if you try and determine a more specific thought. Looking at the guide again, it suggests you ask yourself, "What bad thing did you expect to happen?"

EXHIBIT 8.1. Sample of a Client's Completed Problematic Thinking Styles Log Worksheet

Problematic Thinking Styles Log				
Upsetting situation	Feeling	Thought	Problematic Thinking Style	More helpful thought
1. Boss asked to meet with me	Scared	I'm in trouble	Catastrophizing	I might not be in trouble
2. Wife upset I did not do dishes	Unappreciated	Wife doesn't appreciate how hard I work	Overgeneralization	My wife did thank me for mowing the lawn
3. Kids won't stop fighting	They are driving me crazy	Why can't they just get along?	All-or-Nothing Thinking	They get along sometimes

CLIENT: That I would be fired.

THERAPIST: Okay, let's write that instead. Now, let's look at the Problematic Thinking Style. You put "Catastrophizing." Do you think that still fits?

CLIENT: Definitely.

THERAPIST: And so, looking at the Problematic Thinking Styles handout (Handout 25), if you catastrophize then you should consider the most likely outcome. What usually happens when your boss asks to speak to you?

CLIENT: He usually just wants to ask me for more information or to explain something.

THERAPIST: Okay, so the more accurate thought might be "My boss might just want some more information?"

CLIENT: Yes.

THERAPIST: Okay, so we can write that more specific thought now, rather than just saying you might not be in trouble. Is this making sense?

CLIENT: Yes.

THERAPIST: Now let's consider anger. What was the thought related to the anger?

CLIENT: That it's not fair.

THERAPIST: Again, can you be more specific? What's not fair?

CLIENT: That I am always the one getting in trouble.

THERAPIST: Okay, let's put down that thought: "It's not fair that I am always the one to get in trouble." Do you mean that others don't get in trouble?

CLIENT: That's how it seems, yeah.

THERAPIST: Okay, so should we add "It's not fair that I am always the one to get in trouble and no one else does"?

CLIENT: Yes.

THERAPIST: And is there a Problematic Thinking Style that seems to apply here?

CLIENT: Maybe "All-or-Nothing"?

THERAPIST: All right, if you are using All-or-Nothing Thinking, can you find a gray area? Are you really the only one to get in trouble? Has anyone else been in trouble?

CLIENT: No; there have been other people who have been spoken to.

THERAPIST: So what is a more accurate thought then?

CLIENT: Maybe that "No one likes to be in trouble"?

THERAPIST: Okay, that is still an upsetting thought. But it seems less upsetting than feeling like you are the only one.

CLIENT: Yeah, I'd agree with that.

THERAPIST: Now let's work on shame. What is the thought related to the shame?

CLIENT: I don't know. I just feel like I am always getting in trouble and messing things up.

THERAPIST: So again, looking at the guide, when you ask yourself "What's wrong with me," what are you thinking?

CLIENT: I guess just that. I think there is something wrong with me that I keep getting in trouble at work.

THERAPIST: Okay, so for shame we might add the thought "There is something wrong with me."

CLIENT: Okay.

THERAPIST: And how about a Problematic Thinking Style?

CLIENT: I'm not sure. Maybe "Overgeneralization"?

THERAPIST: In what way?

CLIENT: Well, because I get in trouble at work I overgeneralize and make it a bigger thing. Like, because I have this one specific problem, I blow it up and think it is true all the time.

THERAPIST: Okay, and does thinking about an example that does not fit the pattern help? What is an example where you did something right or where you feel good about yourself?

CLIENT: Well, I help out my mom, who is sick. And I am good with my kids. So those things don't fit the pattern.

THERAPIST: And does that help you come up with a more helpful thought then that there is something wrong with you?

CLIENT: Well, I guess I could say "I'm having problems at work." I mean, that is true.

THERAPIST: Okay. And does that change how you feel?

CLIENT: A little. There are lots of reasons why I am struggling at work. I have a lot going on. But it doesn't mean that there is something wrong with me.

THERAPIST: Okay, I'd say you are getting this.

In this example you can see one common problem clients have, which is when a situation results in more than one feeling. Using the Guide to Thoughts and Feelings, the therapist helped the client identify deeper emotions, such as shame. To have the most success with CR, clients must target their core beliefs. Reviewing each feeling listed in the Guide to Thoughts and Feelings can help ensure that key thoughts are not missed.

Depending on how well the therapist believes the client is comprehending the material, they may want to ask the client to make corrections as a homework assignment. For example, the therapist might ask the client to try and break down "unappreciated," which is the next feeling the client identified on their log (see Exhibit 8.1) into more than one of the four negative feeling states, such as a combination of sadness and anger, just as they did in the previous dialogue example. Allowing them to correct "unappreciated" on their own will help the therapist determine their level of understanding. The therapist might also point out that the client did a good job evaluating the Problematic Thinking Styles to generate a more helpful thought. The client identified "Overgeneralization" and then came up with a new thought that included an example of a time when he was not unappreciated.

If, however, the therapist has concerns that the client does not understand the skill, then they should continue to review the worksheet with the client. For example, on the basis of the Problematic Thinking Styles Log that was completed for homework, the therapist might want to point out that "They are driving me crazy," in the log entry for "Kids won't stop fighting," is not a feeling. The client should be encouraged to use the Guide to Thoughts and Feelings to see if there are any thoughts listed on the guide that come close to "Why can't they just get along?" and then see if the associated feeling makes sense. Perhaps "This situation is unfair" feels closest, in which case the feeling would be anger.

CONCLUSION

In this chapter we have described how the third and fourth CBT-PD sessions are devoted to the therapist teaching the client a skill to help them recognize and change Problematic Thinking Styles, or ways of thinking that lead to inaccurate or unhelpful conclusions. Clients work on recognizing recent times when they experienced each of the four common negative feeling states and then on identifying the specific thought related to the feeling. They then learn to recognize Problematic Thinking Styles and connect them to those thoughts as a way to help them come up with more accurate and helpful thoughts. Over the week that follows each of these sessions, clients are assigned homework to practice recognizing Problematic Thinking Styles that arise in upsetting situations, and replacing them with more accurate and helpful thoughts, using the Problematic Thinking Styles Log. Thus, as in the previous sessions (i.e., Sessions 1 and 2), clients have added a new skill to their repertoire to help them manage their negative feelings.

9

COGNITIVE RESTRUCTURING 2

The 5 Steps of Cognitive Restructuring

Somewhere between the fourth and fifth sessions, clients in the Cognitive Behavior Therapy for Postdisaster Distress (CBT-PD) program are taught the 5 Steps of Cognitive Restructuring, a skill that builds on the Problematic Thinking Styles taught in the previous one to two sessions. As with Problematic Thinking Styles, the 5 Steps of Cognitive Restructuring are a means of dealing with negative feelings, and clients learn how to use the steps to cope with any upsetting feelings they experience, regardless of their relationship to the disaster. Over time, and with practice, the skill is also used to help them examine, challenge, and change inaccurate, trauma-related thoughts and beliefs that underlie their posttraumatic reactions to the disaster.

The first three steps of the 5 Steps of Cognitive Restructuring skill are based on the Problematic Thinking Styles skill and include (1) recognizing the upsetting situation, (2) identifying the negative feeling, and (3) identifying the upsetting thought related to the feeling to determine whether it is a Problematic Thinking Style. In Steps 4 and 5, however, the 5 Steps of Cognitive Restructuring skill departs from the Problematic Thinking Styles. In Step 4, clients learn how to more actively assess the evidence supporting and not supporting their upsetting thought, including the possibility that the

https://doi.org/10.1037/0000237-009
Treatment for Postdisaster Distress: A Transdiagnostic Approach, by J. L. Hamblen and K. T. Mueser

thought is accurate. Then, in Step 5, the client learns how to take action to change the upsetting thought, depending on whether it is or is not accurate. If a close examination of the evidence supporting the thought in Step 4 reveals that it is inaccurate, then in Step 5 the client identifies a more balanced and accurate thought for the situation, similar to when using the Problematic Thinking Styles skill. If, however, a close examination of the evidence supports the accuracy of the upsetting thought, then the client is taught how to develop an Action Plan to deal with the situation and the negative feelings associated with it. For example, if a woman was worried because she was expecting a check from the Federal Emergency Management Agency to help with groceries, but it had not yet arrived more than a week after her case manager had told her it would, in the last step of the 5 Steps of Cognitive Restructuring she might develop an Action Plan to follow up and find out what happened to the check.

There are two advantages of the 5 Steps of Cognitive Restructuring over the Problematic Thinking Styles as skills for helping clients evaluate their thoughts. First, the 5 Steps of Cognitive Restructuring skill delves more deeply into teaching the client how to examine the evidence supporting upsetting thoughts, including how to identify inaccurate beliefs or schemas that may underlie the upsetting thoughts. Second, whereas the Problematic Thinking Styles skill is useful primarily for dealing with negative feelings that are based on inaccurate or distorted thoughts, the 5 Steps of Cognitive Restructuring can be used to deal with any negative feelings, regardless of whether the associated thought is accurate. Furthermore, the 5 Steps of Cognitive Restructuring prompt the person to take action in upsetting situations in which the underlying thought is accurate in order to rectify or modify the problem at hand.

INITIAL TEACHING OF THE 5 STEPS OF COGNITIVE RESTRUCTURING

Once the client has learned the basics of how to use the Problematic Thinking Styles skill to identify, challenge, and change upsetting thoughts related to negative feelings, the therapist can move on to helping them challenge these thoughts (see Handout 27, 5 Steps of Cognitive Restructuring Instructions, in Appendix B on the American Psychological Association [APA] website at http://pubs.apa.org/books/supp/hamblen). The client uses a new worksheet, called the 5 Steps of Cognitive Restructuring Worksheet (Handout 28 in Appendix B at http://pubs.apa.org/books/supp/hamblen), to challenge their cognitions. Building on the first three steps from the Problematic

Thinking Styles Log Worksheet (Handout 26 [http://pubs.apa.org/books/supp/hamblen], on which the client has described the upsetting situation, identified the negative feeling, and pinpointed the underlying thought), the new worksheet adds two more steps: (1) evaluating the evidence supporting the thought and (2) making a decision about whether to modify the thought or formulate an Action Plan.

In teaching the 5 Steps of Cognitive Restructuring the therapist should try to begin with a situation for which they believe they will be able to help the client successfully challenge the underlying distressing thought. In this way, the client both learns the skill and is reinforced to use that skill by experiencing a decrease in distress related to replacing the inaccurate thought with the more accurate one. Over the first few sessions, the therapist should be on the lookout for situations that are distressing to the client that appear to be related to inaccurate thinking. For example, if the client described a particular situation during the review of the Problematic Thinking Styles, that might be a good choice because the client has already shown some openness to the idea that their thought might not be accurate. Here is an example of how a therapist teaches the 5 Steps of Cognitive Restructuring (see Figure 9.1 at the end of this example).

THERAPIST: Now that we have moved on to cognitive restructuring, you are going to use a new worksheet, the 5 Steps of Cognitive Restructuring. Let's take a look at one of these worksheets. You'll notice it is just an expanded version of the Problematic Thinking Styles Log. In **Step 1**, you write down the upsetting **situation**. Earlier you mentioned that you had gotten upset when you heard there was a hurricane watch. How about if we work through that situation as an example of how the skill works?

CLIENT: Okay.

THERAPIST: Great. So go ahead and fill that in for Step 1.

CLIENT: Okay, I'll write "Hearing a hurricane watch on the radio." (*Writes item on worksheet*)

THERAPIST: Good. Now in **Step 2**, you want to identify the upsetting **feeling** you had in the situation. Remember, sometimes a person feels more than one emotion in a situation. That's okay. But we want to focus on the strongest or most upsetting feeling first. Which feeling was the strongest the last time this happened to you?

CLIENT: Okay, so of the four feelings on the worksheet, I think fear and anxiety were my strongest feelings.

THERAPIST: All right, go ahead and circle that. (*Client circles fear/anxiety on the worksheet*) Now, in **Step 3**, you want to identify your **thoughts** about the situation. Using the Guide to Thoughts and Feelings, which is Handout 24 (in Appendix B on the APA website at http://pubs.apa.org/books/supp/hamblen), we can see that when you feel fear and anxiety you are usually expecting something bad to happen. What bad thing might you have been thinking in that situation?

CLIENT: That I might not be able to evacuate to a safe place in time.

THERAPIST: Okay, so you would write that here, under "Step 3." (*Client writes this on the worksheet*) Are there any other thoughts?

CLIENT: That other people might also not be able to evacuate safely.

THERAPIST: Okay, so write that one, too. (*Client writes this on the worksheet*) Of those two thoughts, which is most strongly related to feeling fear and anxiety?

CLIENT: The first one.

THERAPIST: Okay, so then circle that first thought that "I might not be able to evacuate to a safe place in time." (*Client circles*) Good. And is there a Problematic Thinking Style that might fit this thought?

CLIENT: Catastrophizing?

THERAPIST: Yes, it certainly could be Catastrophizing. So circle that here. (*Client circles catastrophizing on the worksheet*)

The process of challenging negative thoughts involves helping clients consider both the evidence that supports their thought as well as the evidence against it. Learning why clients hold the beliefs they do can be essential to helping them challenge those thoughts. In addition, trying to understand the basis for a client's thoughts, and not jumping in and challenging them straight away, creates a more collaborative and less adversarial role for the therapist. Instead of directly confronting the client with evidence against their thinking and actively trying to get them to change it, in Step 4 the therapist gently guides the client through the process of closely examining their thoughts by adopting a more Socratic method of asking questions. At first these questions are aimed at understanding the client's perceptions of the evidence supporting their distressing thought, and then they consider possible evidence against the thought. All of the evidence both for and against the thought is written down on Handout 28 under "Step 4."

Most clients have no problem identifying evidence to support their thinking. The therapist does not need to probe deeply here. The therapist should also resist the temptation to challenge the validity of the client's evidence at this stage. For example, a client could say that a piece of evidence to support his thought that "It's my fault we are homeless" is "We should have used more sandbags to prevent the water from coming into the house," even if it was clear that more sandbags would not have saved the home. The therapist should just encourage the client to write down their evidence on the worksheet. If the evidence is flawed or weak it will only make challenging the thought easier when the time comes.

THERAPIST: In **Step 4**, we begin to **evaluate** the thought. First, ask yourself, "What facts do I have that support my thought?" What are the reasons that supported the thought that you wouldn't be able to evacuate to a safe place? Don't worry about how objective or realistic your reasons are yet. Just brainstorm anything that comes to mind at this point, and we'll evaluate it later.

CLIENT: Well, there was a hurricane watch that was issued.

THERAPIST: Right, so let's write that down. (*Client writes it down*)

CLIENT: And I've heard that this hurricane season is predicted to be worse than last year.

THERAPIST: Okay, add that. (*Client writes it down*) What else?

CLIENT: The last time there was a big hurricane I heard on the news that some people waited so long to evacuate that once they realized they needed to get out it was no longer safe to leave their house. So at that point, there wasn't a safe place to evacuate.

THERAPIST: Okay. So put that one, too. (*Client writes it down*)

Next, the therapist asks the client to consider what evidence there is against their thought. It is important at this stage that the client remain open to considering the evidence against their thought. The goal is for the client to be flexible in their thinking and just consider other possible ways of looking at the situation. The therapist should allow the client to come up with what they can and then ask questions such as "Are there any other ways of looking at this situation?" or "How would someone else look at the situation?"

Another good way to help clients generate evidence against the thought is to ask a question related to any Problematic Thinking Styles they may have identified related to the thought, such as "You said you are catastrophizing. What makes you think that?" Some clients know intellectually that their thought is inaccurate but resist writing down the evidence against it because the thought still "feels" right. In these cases, the therapist should encourage the client to simply write down all the evidence for and against the thought, regardless of how they feel about it. Then, in Step 5, they can make a decision about whether the thought is accurate.

THERAPIST: Now, what facts can you come up with against the thought that there will not be a safe place to evacuate?

CLIENT: Hmm, I'm not sure. Given past storms, this one could be bad too. And there was a watch issued.

THERAPIST: Do you know the difference between a watch and a warning?

CLIENT: Not really.

THERAPIST: Well, a watch means a hurricane might develop, that it is possible in the next few days. A warning means it is expected. So, does that fact that it was a watch make a difference?

CLIENT: Yeah, I would say it's only a watch and that there is time to make a plan.

THERAPIST: Right. So, let's write for evidence against the thought, "It is only a watch, not a warning" and also "I have a few days to make an evacuation plan."

CLIENT: Okay. (*Client writes it down*)

THERAPIST: Now, what other evidence is there? Do you know if most of the time people can't safely evacuate?

CLIENT: Well, I do think there are a lot of people who choose not to evacuate and ride out storms at home.

THERAPIST: Okay, but you did identify Catastrophizing as a Problematic Thinking Style. In what ways do you think you are Catastrophizing? What is the most likely or typical outcome of a hurricane?

CLIENT: Well, you usually don't hear that people die in hurricanes, so I guess most of the time it works out.

THERAPIST: I'd agree. I'm not an expert on hurricanes, but most of the time it seems like if people take precautions they can ride out the storm safely from home.

CLIENT: Should I put down "People don't usually die in hurricanes" or "People can sometimes ride out storms safely at home"?

THERAPIST: How about both? And maybe also, "People can often be rescued." (*Client writes down the evidence*) Anything else you can think of?

CLIENT: Not really.

THERAPIST: Okay, let's look at what we have. Evidence to support the thought that the person won't be able to safely evacuate is that one, there was a hurricane warning; two, the hurricane season is predicted to be worse than last year; and three, if you wait too long, sometimes it is not safe to evacuate.

CLIENT: Yes.

THERAPIST: And what was the evidence against it?

CLIENT: That it was a watch, not a warning, that there is time to come up with an evacuation plan, people don't usually die in hurricanes, that people can sometimes ride out hurricanes safely at home, and that people can get rescued.

Once all of the evidence has been identified, the therapist helps the client review it all and determine whether it mostly supports or does not support the upsetting thought. It is important that this review is not a simple count of the number of things that support versus do not support the thought; instead, it should be a careful consideration of whether the evidence against the thought is stronger than the evidence supporting the thought. The therapist helps the client determine the quality (or weight) of the evidence by asking whether the evidence is based on facts rather than feelings and whether the client could convince another person that the evidence supports the thought. It can help to ask clients if they think they could convince a judge or a jury that their thought is supported by the evidence. If the evidence against the thought is stronger than the evidence that supports it, then in Step 5 the client checks "**NO**, the evidence does *not* support my thought" and comes up with a more balanced and accurate thought based on the evidence.

In an ideal situation, when the evidence does not support the thought the client will be able to identify an alternative thought that is supported. If the client can come up with a new thought, but does not find it very believable, the therapist should help them try to identify a new thought that is more believable than the old thought. Given that the client has already concluded that the evidence does not support their old thought, it is important that the evidence used to challenge the old thought is reflected in the new thought. Encourage the client to talk about the evidence against the thought in order to prompt a more realistic appraisal of the situation.

THERAPIST: The last step of cognitive restructuring, **Step 5**, involves making a **decision**. Once you've weighed the evidence, it's time to decide whether the evidence supports or doesn't support your thought. Consider all the available evidence, and decide if your thought or belief is accurate or not. Ask yourself if you could convince another person that your belief is true. In this situation, after hearing the hurricane watch on the radio, do you think the evidence mostly supports your thought or doesn't support the thought that you won't be able to safely evacuate?

CLIENT: It doesn't support it. Right now it is just a watch, and there is still time to come up with a plan.

THERAPIST: Perfect. Since you have decided that the evidence does not support the thought, you would check the box here (*points to form*) and then come up with a new, more accurate or balanced thought. What would be a more accurate thought in this situation?

CLIENT: A hurricane might be developing, but there is time to come up with a safe evacuation plan.

THERAPIST: Excellent, and which thought is more distressing, that there is a hurricane coming and no safe place to evacuate, or that a hurricane might be developing but there is time to come up with an evacuation plan?

CLIENT: Obviously, the second one.

THERAPIST: Okay, so let's complete the worksheet and write the new thought in Step 5. [See Figure 9.1.]

If instead the client believes their thought is supported by the evidence, they check "**YES**, the evidence *does* support my thought" and develop an Action Plan for dealing with the situation. The therapist should then use basic problem-solving skills to help the client formulate this Action Plan. Using the Action Plan Worksheet (Handout 29 in Appendix B on the APA website at http://pubs.apa.org/books/supp/hamblen), together the client and therapist (1) define the problem, (2) brainstorm possible solutions and select the best ones, (3) plan the necessary steps for implementing the solution(s), and (4) follow the plan. In the example just described, if the client thought the evidence supported their thought that there was no safe evacuation plan, then they would try and identify a plan using problem-solving skills. Possible solutions might be to identify the list of potential shelters in their area, call a friend to see if they could stay with them, get a hotel room, and so on.

FIGURE 9.1. A Sample Completed 5 Steps of Cognitive Restructuring Worksheet

---

1. SITUATION

Ask yourself, "What happened that made me upset?" Write down a brief description of the situation.

Situation: <u>Hearing a hurricane watch on the radio</u>

2. FEELING

Circle your strongest feeling (if more than one, use a separate sheet for each feeling):

(Fear/Anxiety) Sadness/Depression Guilt/Shame Anger

3. THOUGHT

Ask yourself, "What am I thinking that is leading me to feel this way?" Use your Guide to Thoughts and Feelings (Handout 24) to identify the thought that is most strongly related to the feeling circled above. Write down your thought(s) below and circle the thought most strongly related to the feeling.

Thought: <u>(I might not be able to evacuate to a safe place in time.)</u>

<u>Other people might not be able to evacuate to a safe place in time.</u>

If your thought is a Problematic Thinking Style, circle which one(s):

All-or-Nothing Overgeneralizing Must/Should/Never

(Catastrophizing) Emotional Reasoning Overestimation of Risk

Self-Blame

4. EVALUATE YOUR THOUGHT

Things that DO support my thought:

- There is a hurricane watch

- This hurricane season is predicted to be worse than last year

- If you wait too long to evacuate, it can be unsafe to leave your house

Things that DO NOT support my thought:

Ask yourself, "What evidence do I have for this thought?" "Is there an alternative way to look at this situation?" "How would someone else think about the situation?" Use the questions from Handout 27 for help.

(continues)

FIGURE 9.1. A Sample Completed 5 Steps of Cognitive Restructuring Worksheet (*Continued*)

- It is only a watch not a warning

- I have a few days to make an evacuation plan

- People don't usually die in hurricanes

- People can sometimes ride out storms safely at home

- People can often be rescued

5. MAKE A DECISION

Ask yourself, "Do things mostly support my thought or do things mostly

NOT support my thought?"

☒ **NO,** the evidence does *not* support my thought.

If the evidence does NOT support your thought, come up with a new and more

accurate thought that is supported by the evidence. These thoughts are usually

more balanced and helpful, and are associated with less distress. Write your new

thought in the space below. Remember, if you have your old upsetting thought in a

similar situation in the future, replace it with your new and more accurate thought.

New Thought: A hurricane might be developing but there is time to come up with

an evacuation plan

Optional Action Plan: Although your new and more accurate thought should be

less distressing than your old thought, you may nevertheless still find it somewhat

distressing. In this situation, you should then develop an Action Plan. Complete the

Action Plan Worksheet (see Handout 29) to address the problematic situation and

alleviate your distress.

☐ **YES,** the evidence *does* support my thought.

If the evidence DOES support your thought, decide what you need to do next in

order to deal with the situation. Ask yourself, "Do I need to get more information

about what to do?" "Do I need to get some help?" "Do I need to take steps to

make sure I am safe?" Complete the Action Plan Worksheet (see Handout 29) to

address the problematic situation and alleviate your distress.

Then the Action Plan would be writing down the steps necessary to carry out whichever solution is most promising.

In some situations, coming up with a new, balanced thought and an Action Plan are both indicated. For example, in the preceding example, even if the client accepted the new and more accurate thought that they had time to come up with an evacuation plan, it might still be a good idea to actually identify such a plan. In other cases, an Action Plan might involve taking steps to deal with any negative feelings that may remain after a new thought has been identified. For example, some clients may understand that the upsetting event is only a hurricane watch but might still be afraid. Practicing their breathing retraining, arranging to stay overnight with a friend, checking their hurricane preparedness kit, or reviewing an existing evacuation plan might all be possible considerations for the optional Action Plan.

When teaching the 5 Steps of Cognitive Restructuring it is imperative that the therapist manages their time well. At the beginning of these sessions they should try and complete any cognitive restructuring worksheet that was begun during a particular session. One advantage of this is that it maximizes the chance that the client will have a reduction in negative feelings. This decrease in distress is reinforcing and will increase the chances that the client will continue to use the skill on their own. A worksheet should never be stopped after the client has begun to generate the evidence for their upsetting thought without coming up with any evidence against their thought. This could have the effect of strengthening the negative thought. If the therapist needs to stop, however, we recommend that the break happen after Step 3. The client would therefore write down the situation, the feeling, and the thought and would then be ready to challenge the thought on their own, as practice. Therapists might also intentionally choose to start a difficult cognitive restructuring worksheet by helping the client identify the situation, the feeling, and the thought and then have them weigh the evidence for homework. In this way, the therapist can ensure that the client is set up to weigh the evidence on the thought that can most readily be challenged.

COGNITIVE RESTRUCTURING IN SUBSEQUENT SESSIONS AND HOME PRACTICE

Once the 5 Steps of Cognitive Restructuring have been taught, in the remaining sessions clients hone their skills. Clients use Handout 27 as a reference if needed. Each session begins with a review of any cognitive restructuring worksheets the client completed at home, and the therapist makes suggestions and corrections as needed. For example, the therapist might help the client learn how to make an upsetting thought more specific in order to facilitate challenging it, teach the client how to identify disaster-specific cognitions underlying upsetting thoughts, or guide the client in coming up with both more accurate and more believable thoughts about a situation when close examination of a distressing thought indicates it is not supported by the evidence. In addition to determining whether the skill is being used correctly, the therapist will want to determine whether the client is experiencing a reduction in distress when using the skill, a topic we address in Chapter 10. Subsequent sessions are then spent working through either a cognitive restructuring worksheet that the client completed at home but experienced significant problems with, or applying the 5 Steps of cognitive restructuring to a new upsetting situation. Over the next few sessions the therapist should look to ensure that the client is becoming more capable of using the skill on their own (rather than the therapist leading them through the skill) and that the skill is addressing core disaster-related beliefs.

Strategies for Teaching the Specific Steps of Cognitive Restructuring

In this section, we focus on each of the five steps and provide suggestions for how therapists can address some of the more common issues that can arise during the teaching of each step. In Chapter 10, we provide further information on strategies for dealing with additional challenges that can occur when clients are learning to apply the 5 Steps of Cognitive Restructuring.

Step 1: Describe the Situation

Clients are taught that the cue for determining when to use cognitive restructuring is when they feel negative emotion. In the beginning, it is more important that clients learn the skill than that they apply cognitive restructuring to specific disaster-related beliefs. Therefore, any upsetting situation that occurs over the week is acceptable. The client is encouraged to write down a brief description of what they were doing when the upsetting feeling occurred, such as "argument with my partner," "watching a news story about a shooting," or "out jogging when I had a memory of my mother."

Sometimes, however, a client will say that no upsetting situations occurred between the sessions. In this case, the therapist has several options. First, the therapist could bring up a situation that was discussed earlier in therapy, for example, during the psychoeducation sessions (Sessions 1 and 2) or the teaching of the Problematic Thinking Styles. The therapist should check with the client to determine whether that situation is still distressing and, if it is, ask the client if that is a situation on which they would be willing to work.

Another option is to identify a situation identified on the Short Post-Traumatic Stress Disorder Rating Interview, Expanded Version (SPRINT-E; Norris & Davidson, 2007) or another symptom measure. For example, if the client reported on the SPRINT-E that they have been bothered by unwanted memories, then that is a situation that could be used for a cognitive restructuring worksheet. A third strategy, which we discuss in more depth later in this chapter, is to help the client identify a disaster-related cognition on which they would like to work.

Step 2: Identify the Strongest Feeling

Early on in the teaching of the 5 Steps of Cognitive Restructuring the therapist should be looking to help the client address the feelings for which they believe the client can achieve the largest reduction in distress. Therefore, in Step 2 the client is directed to circle on Handout 28 the strongest feeling, because this is typically the one that will have the most impact. If the client has more than one strong feeling, they should pick the one that causes the most distress and work through a worksheet on that emotion. Then, if at the end of the cognitive restructuring the other feelings still remain, they can complete a separate worksheet on those.

Sometimes a client is not sure which feeling is most distressing. Upsetting situations are often complicated by the fact that there are many emotions as well as several associated automatic underlying thoughts. In this case, rather than picking a single emotion and moving forward to Step 3, the client can be encouraged to explore each of the feelings and their associated thoughts before picking the strongest, most upsetting one. Using the Guide to Thoughts and Feelings (Handout 24), the client can identify the specific thoughts related to each of the four feeling states (e.g., fear and anxiety, sadness and depression, guilt and shame, and anger). Once they have considered all of the possible feelings and thoughts, they can then go back and circle the one that is strongest.

The therapist should be aware that anger can be a difficult emotion to challenge because clients often believe their anger is justified and feel energized and empowered by the external focus of blame on someone (or something) else. Clients may see cognitive restructuring as an attempt to invalidate their angry feelings or make them go away by shifting the focus of attention away from others and toward themselves, where an internal focus of attention is more threatening and less comfortable. As a result, clients may be less motivated to examine the evidence against thoughts related to angry feelings as opposed to other negative feelings, such as sadness, anxiety, or guilt. For this reason, when possible it is preferable to focus on other negative feelings first when clients are learning cognitive restructuring and tackle angry feelings later. We provide suggestions for how to use the 5 Steps of Cognitive Restructuring to address angry feelings in Chapter 10.

Step 3: Identify the Most Distressing Thought

Clients frequently have multiple thoughts associated with the negative feeling they have identified. This leads to the question of which thought to address. There is no single "right" or "wrong" thought to focus on in cognitive restructuring; however, in general, cognitive restructuring is most effective when the selected thought is the most upsetting one and when the thought is more specific. As we discussed earlier, if the client is having difficulty identifying their most upsetting thought, they can use the Guide to Thoughts and Feelings worksheet to consider the different types of thoughts associated with different negative feelings to determine which one is most distressing. For example, a client who was in a synagogue shooting could report feeling afraid and may identify "Synagogues are unsafe" as the thought. To help the client narrow down the thought, the therapist could suggest using the Guide to Thoughts and Feelings, which prompts the client to consider what, specifically, they fear. Several possible answers include "I am afraid of another shooting," "I am afraid I could die," "I am afraid that my children or parents could be hurt," and "I am afraid that I won't be able to attend synagogue." Now that there are several possible thoughts available to challenge, the therapist can ask the client which is most distressing.

Once the client has identified the most upsetting thought, the therapist can help the client make the thought as specific as possible. Specific thoughts are easier to challenge than vague ones, and challenging them increases the likelihood that the client will reject their original upsetting thought as inaccurate and replace it with a more accurate, less distressing thought. One strategy for identifying these deeper thoughts is to try and drill down by asking the client, "If this thought were true, what would it mean or say about you?" For example, "What would it mean to you if there was another shooting?" The client might answer, "That I would die," or "That I would no longer be able to attend synagogue." The therapist could dig deeper and ask again, "And what would it mean if you could not attend synagogue?" The client might answer, "That I would lose a part of who I am" or "That I would not be able to raise my children in the Jewish faith." These thoughts are both specific and challengeable, making them good candidates for cognitive restructuring. Other questions that can help drill down to more specific thoughts are "If this happened, what would happen then?" and "What would be so bad about that?" The most important thing is that the client regularly sees that identifying new, more accurate thoughts results in a decrease in distress.

Step 4: Evaluate the Thought

In Step 4, the therapist asks the client to generate all the evidence they can in favor of the thought and then all the evidence against the thought. In generating evidence that supports the thought, the therapist should at this point allow the client to suggest evidence that is weak and may not hold up under closer scrutiny and wait until the next step before helping the client carefully evaluate the quality of the evidence. At this stage, the most important thing is to understand why the client holds a particular belief. After the client comes up with as much evidence for their thought as possible, the therapist prompts them to consider evidence against the thought.

One good place to start when identifying evidence against the thought is with the Problematic Thinking Styles. In Step 3, if the client indicated that the distressing thought might be a Problematic Thinking Style (by circling one or more of the Problematic Thinking Styles on the worksheet), they have already shown that they think their thought might be inaccurate. The therapist can prompt the client to consider the specific reasons why they indicated that their thought was a specific Problematic Thinking Style and use these reasons as evidence against the thought. Other questions can then be asked to elicit further evidence against the thought. Because the ultimate goal is for clients to be able to ask themselves these questions, we created Handout 27, which contains a list of questions clients can ask themselves when they are trying to challenge their thoughts (see Exhibit 9.1).

Step 5: Make a Decision

In the fifth and last step of cognitive restructuring, the client evaluates all of the evidence together and makes a decision about whether the evidence supports their thought. Clients should be helped to be as objective as possible and reminded that they should put the greatest weight on the strongest evidence and be able to convince someone else of their decision. If a client decides

---

EXHIBIT 9.1. Questions to Ask When Challenging Your Thoughts

1. Is there any alternative way of looking at the situation?
2. Is there an alternative explanation?
3. How would someone else think about the situation?
4. Are my judgments based on how I felt rather than what I did?
5. Am I setting for myself an unrealistic and unobtainable standard?
6. Am I overestimating how much control and responsibility I have in this situation?
7. What would be the worst thing that could happen if my fear were true?
8. Am I underestimating what I can do to deal with the problem or situation?
9. Am I confusing a low-probability event with one of high probability?
10. What are the advantages of holding onto this belief?

that the thought is not supported by the evidence, they need to develop a new, more accurate thought. This new thought should be more believable than the old thought and firmly supported by the evidence. For this reason it is best if the client, not the therapist, comes up with the new thought. The new thought is typically based on some of the evidence against the old thought that was most convincing to the client. For example, in the hurricane example presented earlier, a new thought, such as "I will be able to evacuate to a safe place in time" might not be more believable than the original thought that "I might not be able to evacuate to a safe place in time." However, the thought "A hurricane might be developing, but there is time to come up with an evacuation plan," is more believable because it incorporates the evidence against the old thought that there is usually time to make an evacuation plan.

If the thought is not supported by the evidence, an Action Plan is developed (see Handout 29). An Action Plan may also be developed when the client rejects their original thought and comes up with a new, more accurate thought but still feels some distress associated with the new thought. Action Plans involve the exploration of different solutions for dealing with the specific situation and then laying out specific steps for implementing the most effective solution. For example, if a client determined that the thought "I can't pay my bills" is accurate, an Action Plan would be completed to identify concrete steps to address the problem, such as contacting a credit specialist.

One common reason for developing an Action Plan is when the client's distressing feeling is not completely resolved by identifying a more accurate, believable thought. In the hurricane example, even though a new, more accurate thought was created, the client might still feel distress. Therefore, an Action Plan was created that included, among other things, the client reviewing an existing evacuation plan and checking their hurricane preparedness kit.

Another common reason for developing Action Plans is to address genuinely problematic situations that are distressing but are not associated with inaccurate or distorted thinking styles. In fact, as we noted at the beginning of this chapter, one of the major advantages of the 5 Steps of Cognitive Restructuring skill is that it is useful for dealing with any upsetting feelings, including those associated with an accurate appraisal of the situation. Not all of the distress people feel in different situations is due to inaccurate thinking. There are many situations in which any logically thinking person would feel concerned, upset, or distressed, such as if their safety and well-being were threatened. What is needed in those situations is action aimed at addressing the problem at hand, not modifications to one's thinking. Creating an Action Plan provides a standardized problem-solving approach to addressing the practical challenges for dealing with many life difficulties. Disasters create a wide range of life disruptions, such as financial difficulties and housing problems and displacement, that Actions Plans can be used to address.

Finally, Action Plans may be created to focus on improving coping and reducing specific symptoms. For example, trouble sleeping may be distressing even in the absence of inaccurate thinking. Each psychoeducation handout in Appendix B (on the American Psychological Association website, http://pubs.apa.org/books/supp/hamblen) includes strategies for managing the specific symptoms. In addition, a condensed list of symptoms and strategies is included in Exhibit 9.2. Action Plans can incorporate these strategies, and clients can select the strategies they think will be most effective at improving their management of the symptom.

Additional Example of Cognitive Restructuring

In the next chapter, we address specific challenges that can occur when teaching the 5 Steps of Cognitive Restructuring. Here we provide a full transcript of a therapist and a client completing a 5 Steps worksheet during a session, with commentary included to help therapists understand some of the choices and decision points to consider. In this example (which is a composite case that blends the personal experiences of several different clients), the client is Katherine, a 45-year-old married woman with a 17-year-old teenage daughter. Katherine had gone to watch the Boston Marathon at the finish line in 2013 because her best friend was running in it. Katherine's friend had started the race in Wave 3 at 10:40 a.m. and was hoping to complete it in about 4 hours. Katherine was watching at the finish line, ready to cheer. At 2:49 p.m., the first of two bombs exploded. Katherine was thrown off her feet. Her memory was not clear after that, but when she woke up at Massachusetts General Hospital she was informed that her lower left leg had been amputated. Katherine enrolled in CBT-PD almost 2 years after the bombings. The following transcript is from Session 7, when Katherine had begun to use the cognitive restructuring skill to evaluate disaster-related thoughts.

THERAPIST: Katherine, do you have any situations from last week you'd like to work on?

KATHERINE: Yes, my daughter and I had a big fight. She got invited to a concert at [a large stadium arena] and wanted to go. I said it was unsafe and that she couldn't go. She was furious. She started yelling and throwing a fit. She told me to "get over it" and to stop trying to control her life. It went on and on until she stormed out of the house and drove off. I heard her come home late that night, and we haven't really talked since. She just storms around.

EXHIBIT 9.2. Coping Strategies for Common Postdisaster Symptoms

Symptom	Coping strategy
Reexperiencing the disaster (e.g., intrusive thoughts, getting upset at reminders)	Practice breathing retraining Practice acceptance of memories Engage in pleasant, meaningful activities Practice good self-care Download the PTSD Coach app or the Mindfulness Coach from iTunes (https://apps.apple.com/us/app/ptsd-coach/id430646302 and https://apps.apple.com/us/app/mindfulness-coach/id804284729, respectively) or Google Play (https://play.google.com/store/apps/details?id=is.vertical.ptsdcoach&hl=en_US&gl=US and https://play.google.com/store/apps/details?id=gov.va.mobilehealth.ncptsd.mindfulnesscoach&hl=en_US&gl=US, respectively)
Avoidance of disaster-related thoughts and situations	Use breathing retraining or self-talk when in the situation Have someone accompany you at first Set gradual goals
Inability to feel positive emotions	Schedule pleasant activities Connect with others instead of self-isolating
Overarousal	Use breathing retraining Practice mindfulness (download mindfulness apps) Get physical exercise Find your own space where you can be calm Learn to recognize triggers, and prepare for them
Problems with concentration	Remove distractions Use breathing retraining Practice mindfulness Schedule rest breaks when sustained attention is required
Difficulty sleeping	Limit alcohol and caffeine Set a regular sleep schedule Don't nap Do something relaxing before bedtime Free your sleeping area from distractions Don't stay in bed if you are not sleeping Download the Insomnia Coach app from iTunes (https://apps.apple.com/us/app/insomnia-coach/id1341944736) or Google Play (https://play.google.com/store/apps/details?id=gov.va.mobilehealth.ncptsd.insomniacoach&hl=en_US&gl=US)
Nightmares	Get out of bed and interrupt the nightmare Use positive self-talk Use grounding Create a different ending to the nightmare
Anger	Use breathing retraining Practice mindfulness (e.g., download a mindfulness app) Take a time-out

Note. PTSD = posttraumatic stress disorder.

THERAPIST: Okay, did you try and do a cognitive restructuring on your own when this first happened?

COMMENTARY: The ultimate goal is for people to be able to use the 5 Steps of Cognitive Restructuring in the moment; however, when clients are learning the skill they need to complete a worksheet as soon as possible after they experience the negative feeling. By asking if the client had done a cognitive restructuring on her own, the therapist is emphasizing that any time there is an upsetting situation she should initiate a cognitive restructuring.

KATHERINE: I tried, but I just got more and more upset about it. I know I did the right thing. It's my job to keep my daughter safe, not to be her friend.

THERAPIST: I understand. I'm really glad you tried. It can be hard at first to do these worksheets on your own. Let's try it together. Soon you will be able to do then on your own, though. What do you want to write in Step 1 of the 5 Steps of Cognitive Restructuring Worksheet?

COMMENTARY: Here the client acknowledges trying to begin a cognitive restructuring worksheet but did not succeed and is still clearly feeling upset over the situation. Therefore, this is a perfect opportunity to complete a cognitive restructuring with the therapist in session. The therapist also successfully avoids getting involved in a conversation with the client about whether she "did the right thing," instead directing her attention to begin the cognitive restructuring.

KATHERINE: How about "Fight with daughter over going to a concert"?

THERAPIST: Perfect. You just need enough to recall the situation. Go ahead and write that down. Now, in Step 2, you circle the strongest feeling that you were experiencing. What was that?

KATHERINE: I was really angry.

THERAPIST: I am sure you were. Sounds like a pretty terrible argument. Do you think you had any other feelings? Sadness? Guilt? Fear?

COMMENTARY: The therapist could have just gone with anger; however, anger is often a cover for deeper emotions. Therefore, the therapist decides to check on some of the other feelings, knowing that they can always return to anger if it appears to be primary. If a therapist believes the client can get more relief from challenging a thought related to a different emotion, asking about other feelings is one way of steering the cognitive restructuring in that direction.

KATHERINE: Well, I felt guilty when she said I should get over it. Sometimes I think I should be doing better than I am. I'm walking okay, but I agree with her that I don't act the same way. But mostly I guess I was angry because I worried that if she went to the concert something bad could happen.

THERAPIST: So, when you think something bad might happen, what feeling is that usually related to?

COMMENTARY: The client does acknowledge another emotion—in this case, guilt—but quickly returns to anger. However, she goes on to say that the anger was driven by worry that something bad could happen. Therefore, the therapist asks her to consider if anger is the primary feeling related to concerns about harm as a way to again direct the cognitive restructuring away from anger and toward a deeper emotion.

KATHERINE: Fear?

THERAPIST: Right. How about you circle "Fear/Anxiety" in Step 2 on your sheet.

COMMENTARY: The therapist has made a choice to go with fear. She could have asked the client which feeling was stronger: fear or anger. But if the client had said anger, then it would be hard to move the cognitive restructuring in another direction. That would have been an acceptable approach; the therapist could always come back to fear at the end. If, however, the therapist believes that a core belief for Katherine is that the world is a dangerous place, then focusing on fear is the preferred option because it is likely to have a larger impact.

KATHERINE: Okay.

THERAPIST: Now what about Step 3? What is the thought? You actually just said it.

KATHERINE: That something bad will happen?

THERAPIST: Right. And specifically, what kind of bad thing do you worry about happening?

COMMENTARY: Although the client has provided the thought "that something bad will happen," it can be helpful to try and elicit a more specific thought.

KATHERINE: If I let my daughter go to the concert she could be killed.

COMMENTARY: This more specific thought will be easier to challenge when examining the evidence for and against it.

THERAPIST: Okay, write that down in Step 3.

KATHERINE: (*Writes down "If my daughter goes to the concert she could be killed."*)

THERAPIST: What problematic style of thinking might that be? Go ahead and use the Problematic Thinking Styles handout (Handout 25) if you need a reminder of those definitions.

KATHERINE: Catastrophizing? Or maybe All-or-Nothing Thinking?

THERAPIST: Right. In both cases you are expecting the worst. Go ahead and circle both of those Problematic Thinking Styles on your cognitive restructuring sheet. Okay, so now we are at Step 4.

For this step, you're basically gathering evidence both for and against your thought that if your daughter goes to the concert she could be killed. The first thing you want to do is write down whatever you can think of that supports that thought.

KATHERINE: Well, concerts are crowded places full of lots of young people. They are dark and sort of chaotic, with people jumping around and yelling. It would be hard for security to even realize something was happening until it was too late. It's the perfect place to set off a bomb if your goal is to hurt and scare people. It's better to be safe than sorry.

THERAPIST: Okay, so let's try and write some of this down. So, one piece of evidence is that concerts are crowded, another is that they are dark, another is that young people go to concerts, another is that they are chaotic, and then you also said it is hard for security to know what is going on. You also said it's better to be safe than sorry. Anything else?

COMMENTARY: The therapist helps the client identify the separate pieces of evidence, then asks if there is any other evidence before moving on. The therapist is often most effective if they appear neutral. If they seem too eager to prove the client is wrong, the client may become defensive and less open to being flexible in their thinking. By asking if there is any other evidence supporting the thought, the therapist is demonstrating her openness to considering all the possible evidence.

KATHERINE: No. I think that covers what I was worried about. Well, actually, I also think if something happened there could be a riot and it would be hard to get out of the stadium. At least the marathon was outside.

THERAPIST: Okay, so maybe add "If something happened, it would be hard to get help." Any other evidence for your thought that we should write down?

KATHERINE: Not that I can think of.

THERAPIST: Okay, now what about evidence against your thought. Can you think of some things that do not support the thought that if your daughter goes to the concert she could be killed?

COMMENTARY: Early on, clients can have trouble coming up with evidence against their own thoughts; however, the therapist should always give the client the opportunity to generate evidence against the thought on their own. Another tip demonstrated here is that the therapist has reminded the client about the specific thought. Instead of asking, "Can you think of things that don't support the thought?" the therapist focuses the client by asking, "Can you think of things that don't support the thought that if your daughter goes to the concert she could be killed?"

KATHERINE: Well, they do check bags on the way in. But I am sure you could sneak something in.

THERAPIST: Okay, but can we at least put down "The security people check bags"?

COMMENTARY: The therapist does a nice job of avoiding challenging the client on whether people could sneak a weapon into the concert; instead she focuses on what was provided and has the client write down that security provides bag checks.

KATHERINE: Yes.

THERAPIST: What else?

KATHERINE: I am not sure.

COMMENTARY: Although the client was able to come up with one piece of evidence against the thought, she cannot think of another. At this point the therapist can either ask questions or direct the client to the questions included on Handout 27.

THERAPIST: Well, you also said concerts have security. Could you put that down?

KATHERINE: I guess, but I don't think that is enough.

THERAPIST: Okay; do you think security has improved over recent years? That they have learned from past events and have new practices in place?

KATHERINE: I guess so.

THERAPIST: So, what could you write for that?

KATHERINE: There are trained security officers at concerts.

THERAPIST: Good. What else can you think of that does not support your thought? (*Pause*) Has there been a terrorist attack at a concert?

KATHERINE: No, but there could be. No one expected a bomb at the marathon, either, though.

THERAPIST: That's true, but is what I said wrong?

KATHERINE: I guess not; I can add that.

COMMENTARY: The fact that there had not been a terrorist attack at a concert when this cognitive restructuring was taking place was not strong evidence against the thought; in fact, there have now been several mass shootings at concerts. The goal, however, is to help clients consider all the evidence, and at the time it was true that no terrorist attack had occurred at a concert. Today, a better question might focus on the likelihood of an attack at a concert by considering, for example, the number of such attacks at concerts compared with the number of concerts that have occurred without attacks.

THERAPIST: Can you know in advance what is safe and what is not safe?

COMMENTARY: Rather than focusing on whether or not concerts are safe, the therapist brings up a new line of questioning about how people make decisions.

KATHERINE: No, but I can try and make good decisions.

THERAPIST: Are other parents letting their kids go?

COMMENTARY: Asking about what others would do or think in a situation is a good way to get clients to consider alternative perspectives.

KATHERINE: The O'Neils are letting their daughter go. They seem to think it's fine, but they did not have the same kind of close call that we have had. The Smiths are actually going with the girls, so that is different. They don't have to worry.

THERAPIST: Different how?

KATHERINE: Well, they will be there if something happens to their daughter.

THERAPIST: Oh, what can they do?

KATHERINE: I don't know. They can look to see if anything seems out of place. They don't have to worry like I do because I won't be there.

THERAPIST: Hmm, let's see how we can use this information. Do you think the fact that other parents, like the O'Neils, are not worried could be evidence against the thought that something bad will happen?

KATHERINE: I guess so.

THERAPIST: Okay, then write that down. Now what about the fact that the Smiths will be there? Does that change the situation in any way?

KATHERINE: Well, at least there will be an adult there who is looking out for them.

THERAPIST: All right, let's add that. Now, if something were to happen, do you think the Smiths would look after all three girls or just their own?

KATHERINE: I'm sure they would do everything they could.

THERAPIST: Okay, so go ahead and write that down as evidence against your thought. Do you think there could be other people at the concert who would help your daughter if she were hurt or in trouble?

COMMENTARY: It is very useful when the therapist has specific information they can use to help the client challenge a thought. In this case, the therapist remembered that the client had been helped by strangers when she was injured at the marathon bombings and was able to prompt her to consider how strangers might help if an incident occurred at a concert.

KATHERINE: I'm not really sure, but I'd like to think so. And actually, it was complete strangers who carried me to safety after the marathon bombings.

THERAPIST: So, from your own personal experience, you've seen that in a crisis situation strangers can pull together to help others. Do you think we should list this as evidence against your thought?

KATHERINE: I am not convinced that everyone would help her—but I think some people would. So, yes, I think it is worth writing it down.

THERAPIST: Now, this question is a little harder, but even if something were to happen, what do you think is the most likely outcome?

COMMENTARY: The therapist has decided to consider another line of inquiry. The client has already said she is catastrophizing; she is assuming the worst: that there will be an attack and that her daughter will die. Here the therapist is helping the client explore if that is what would be the most likely outcome.

KATHERINE: What do you mean?

THERAPIST: I mean do you think it is highly likely that your daughter would be killed if something happened?

KATHERINE: I don't know, but I wouldn't want to risk it.

THERAPIST: Of course not, but the truth is that even in very serious events, most people are still all right. At the marathon most people were unharmed, right? Three lost their lives, and some people, like yourself, were very seriously injured, but out of the thousands who were there, most were not hurt, right? So maybe we can add that it is unlikely that if something happened that your daughter would be hurt, and if something did happen the Smiths would be there to help.

KATHERINE: I see what you are getting at. Okay.

THERAPIST: Now I want to ask you one other thing: What will happen if you don't let your daughter go?

COMMENTARY: At this point the therapist has helped the client generate enough evidence to challenge the belief that if her daughter goes to the concert she is likely to be killed. Here the therapist shifts tactics to explore the client's assumption of her ability to prevent her daughter from attending the concert.

KATHERINE: She will be pissed at me. Sometimes I worry that if I am too strict, she will just do things behind my back.

THERAPIST: Okay, so then we have two more considerations related to telling your daughter she can't go to the concert. One, that she will be very angry with you. And the other, that she might do it, or something like it, anyway. Why don't we move on to the final cognitive restructuring step.

COMMENTARY: In this case, asking what would happen if the mother said no resulted in strong evidence against the thought. The purpose of Katherine saying no was to protect her daughter, but now it appears that it may not have that effect. The fact that the therapist suggests moving on to Step 5 indicates that she thinks they have enough evidence against the thought to successfully challenge it, and there is no other evidence they want to explore.

THERAPIST: In Step 5, you make a decision about whether the evidence mostly supports the thought or mostly does not support the thought. Let's review. What evidence do you have that supports your thought that if you let your daughter go to the concert that she could get killed?

COMMENTARY: It is always a good idea to review all of the evidence for and against the upsetting thought before making a decision.

KATHERINE: One, concerts are crowded; two, concerts are dark so it's hard to see what's happening; three, young people go to concerts; four, security can't watch everything; five if something happens it could be hard to get out.

THERAPIST: And now, let's look at the evidence against the thought. What do you have listed on the sheet?

KATHERINE: They have trained security officers at concerts, there has not been an attack at a concert, security checks bags, other parents are letting their kids go and must think it's safe, the Smiths will be there, the Smiths will help if something happens, even if an attack happened not everyone would be killed, my daughter will be angry if I say no, and my daughter might go anyway or do something else that is more risky.

THERAPIST: When you read it all over, do you think that the things supporting your thought are stronger or more persuasive as the things against the thought?

COMMENTARY: After a complete review of the evidence, it is important to let the client make the determination of whether the evidence does or does not support the thought. The therapist should not make assumptions about whether the evidence that was generated was strong enough to change the thought. The therapist should remain neutral.

KATHERINE: Well, the things supporting my thoughts are not all that rational. I guess the things that are *not* supporting my thought are more rational. They are better arguments.

THERAPIST: I would agree. Although the things you wrote down that support your thoughts are emotionally powerful, they are not as rational or logical. The evidence for the thought is not strong because it is based on feelings rather than facts. Go ahead and check off on your sheet the box that says the weight of the evidence does *not* support your thought that if you let your daughter go to the concert she could get killed. Now, how could you take all of the evidence you've written down into consideration and come up with a new, more accurate thought about the situation?

KATHERINE: Well, I am still really nervous about her going. I see that it's unlikely that she would be hurt or killed, but I still don't want to take that chance.

THERAPIST: We are not deciding whether she can go right now. All we are doing is examining the evidence and deciding if the thought "If I let my daughter go to the concert she could die" is accurate.

COMMENTARY: The therapist avoids getting distracted by the client's comment that she still does not want her daughter to go. Although the client acknowledges that her thought that her daughter will get killed if she lets her go to the concert is not strongly supported by the evidence, she doesn't have an alternative way of looking at the situation yet, and so her feelings are still driven by that thought. Therefore, it is important to help her come up with a new, more accurate thought if she is going to feel relief. This more accurate and realistic thought will be the primary determinant of what actions the client will ultimately take with her daughter.

KATHERINE: I guess it's not accurate. I am just afraid something might happen, and I want to keep her safe.

THERAPIST: So, what is a more accurate thought, then, for this situation?

KATHERINE: Although I am afraid my daughter could be hurt or killed, there is good security at the concert, and my daughter will be well supervised.

THERAPIST: That's perfect. Telling yourself that she might die is much more anxiety provoking then telling yourself that she will have good supervision. Go ahead and write that in Step 5. Does that new thought result in less distress than your original one?

KATHERINE: Yes, but I am still afraid.

THERAPIST: Okay, so your fear is reduced, but you still have some anxiety over letting her go. Let's consider if you were to let her go. Is there an Action Plan you would want to put into place?

> **COMMENTARY:** This is a situation in which the new thought was not enough to help the client feel better. Therefore, it is appropriate to consider an Action Plan. The therapist may want to use the Action Plan Worksheet (Handout 29), or she can just walk the client through the steps of creating an Action Plan.

KATHERINE: Well, I would want to talk to the Smiths first.

THERAPIST: Okay; what else?

KATHERINE: I would also want my daughter to be alert and on the lookout.

THERAPIST: Do you think if you talked to her about this that she would take the conversation seriously?

KATHERINE: Absolutely. She was pretty frightened by what happened to me. It's taken her a long time to get back to doing things. In fact, I see her looking over her shoulder a lot still.

THERAPIST: So maybe it's a good sign that she is ready to do something like this?

KATHERINE: Yeah. I'm just not sure I'm ready.

THERAPIST: Okay; do you think if you talk to her you will put fears in her head?

KATHERINE: I don't think so. We have talked about this before. I think I would just want to remind her to be aware of her surroundings.

THERAPIST: That sounds good. Anything else you would want to do as part of your Action Plan?

KATHERINE: Well, I would want to stay home in case something happened.

THERAPIST: (*Smiling*) Do you have a cell phone?

KATHERINE: Yes. I get it. If something happened she could reach me on my cell. Well, maybe I would want to go to movies or something to pass the time faster. Otherwise I will just sit around and worry.

THERAPIST: Okay, that makes sense. So, what do you think you will do?

KATHERINE: I think I'll talk to my husband and then probably tell her she can go.

THERAPIST: Originally, when you thought about letting your daughter go to the concert you were scared that she would die. What about now?

KATHERINE: Well, I am still worried, but much less so than before. And I actually think she should go. It will be good for her. And maybe me too.

COMMENTARY: This was a very successful cognitive restructuring. The client was able to come up with a more accurate, less distressing thought, and the therapist helped the client come up with an Action Plan to manage her remaining fear.

CONCLUSION

The 5 Steps of Cognitive Restructuring is a powerful and flexible tool for helping clients deal with negative feelings. It is effective for distress related to a problematic situation, regardless of whether it is disaster related, as well as distress that is part of a posttraumatic reaction. In each case, the 5 Steps allow clients to either change inaccurate thinking, develop a plan for managing the symptoms, or both. Once the 5 Steps of Cognitive Restructuring have been taught, work in most of the remaining sessions of CBT-PD involves helping clients use the steps and to eventually incorporate the skill into their daily lives. The therapist should monitor changes in the client's SPRINT-E scores to watch for signs of improvement. They should also determine how effectively the client is completing the worksheets and if the 5 Step worksheets are challenging core beliefs about the disaster. In Chapter 10, we provide suggestions for how to address common challenges when teaching cognitive restructuring.

Finally, it is important that as attention shifts to cognitive restructuring, the therapist does not neglect the other skills that have been taught. Clients should be asked about how the breathing retraining has been working and reminded to use it both when they are anxious and as a way to focus and relax. For example, clients might try and use the breathing before completing a cognitive restructuring sheet to help them focus their attention, or they could use it during cognitive restructuring if thinking about a particular situation is upsetting. Similarly, clients may need to be reminded to use activity scheduling, to continue to engage in pleasant and rewarding activities. Even if the cognitive restructuring is effective, clients will continue to benefit from this.

10

COGNITIVE RESTRUCTURING 3

Advanced Techniques

The 5 Steps of Cognitive Restructuring (hereinafter in this chapter "the 5 Steps") is a rich skill that can be used to help people cope with a wide range of negative feelings in a variety of different situations, including ones related and not related to the disaster itself. It is not unusual to encounter different obstacles when teaching clients how to use the 5 Steps, and having effective solutions to overcoming those obstacles can make a critical difference in the likelihood of the person learning the skill. In addition, the 5 Steps can be used in creative and unexpected ways to address some of the most important challenges experienced by people recovering from the effects of a disaster, such as making important decisions about how to live one's life going forward. In Chapter 9, we reviewed the basics of the 5 Steps, and in this chapter we address some of the nuances of teaching the skill and provide solutions to common difficulties. We then describe some alternatives to the 5 Steps for clients who have difficulty mastering them.

https://doi.org/10.1037/0000237-010
Treatment for Postdisaster Distress: A Transdiagnostic Approach, by J. L. Hamblen and K. T. Mueser

ADDRESSING DIFFICULT FEELINGS

The 5 Steps are useful for reducing the broad range of negative feelings that can predominate after a disaster, including fear and anxiety, depression, shame and guilt, and anger. However, there are special challenges to addressing some feelings that may occur, including excessive self-blame or guilt, anger, and grief. Specific strategies for using the 5 Steps to address those feelings are described in the next few sections.

Challenging Beliefs Related to Excessive Self-Blame or Guilt

A common emotion experienced by people who have survived a natural disaster or mass violence event is guilt. People may feel guilty about how they responded in the moment when the event was happening, or in the immediate aftermath of the event. For example, a person may feel guilty that they did not do enough to help or save someone, or that they were too preoccupied by their own safety and concerns after the event to attend to others' needs. These feelings emerge naturally in the wake of a disaster as people look back on the incident in a calmer state of reflection and with the knowledge of what happened and what they could have done differently. Despite the well-known adage that "hindsight is always 20/20," meaning that everyone knows how they could have acted more effectively in a situation after it has passed, people often hold themselves responsible and feel guilty about how they responded, especially when significant injury to others or loss of life has occurred.

Guilt can be difficult to challenge because when people hold themselves responsible for a negative event, however implausible the idea that it was really their fault may be, they often maintain some illusion of control over preventing such events from occurring in the future. For example, a client who believes "I should have evacuated from the flood the first time I heard the warning; then no one would have been hurt" may feel a greater sense of security about the future, believing that if another flood were to occur, then as long as they evacuate in time, nothing bad would happen. Although this belief has the advantage that it may make the world feel a little safer to the person, the guilt itself takes its own toll, making it difficult for them to move past the "What if?"

One strategy for helping people challenge strongly held beliefs about their personal responsibility for negative consequences related to the disaster is to ask them whether they would blame someone else for acting the same way in the same situation. When asked, most people admit that they would not blame another person for the events that transpired in the same way they blame themselves. Framing this response as "evidence" against the person's belief that they are responsible for the negative consequences of the disaster, the therapist can again ask the client whether they still think they are to blame for what happened. This often results in a decrease in self-blame and a more realistic appraisal of what happened.

Sometimes, however, clients insist on higher standards of perfectionism for themselves and cling to beliefs about greater personal responsibility while acknowledging that these standards and beliefs are at odds with their expectations for others. In these circumstances it may be helpful to inquire of the client why they think they should be capable of meeting such impossibly high standards. For example, the client can be gently asked "What makes you so special?" to help them consider whether their reasons are good and justified. The exploration of answers to this question can lead to a discussion of the worthiness of pursuing high ideals of personal responsibility and perfectionism while at the same time acknowledging everyone's limitations at achieving those ideals and that "to err is human." This discussion can help clients maintain their striving for perfection while allowing them to give themselves a break when they do not meet their ideals. Such an approach is consistent with the notion of teaching people *self-compassion* (Gilbert, 2005; Gilbert & Choden, 2014), or how to feel and show the same compassion one often feels for others in difficult situations for oneself.

Sometimes, beliefs about excessive responsibility or perfectionism are related to learning experiences from childhood. For example, a client may have been told by a parent that they are responsible for everything that happens, and were even punished when things have happened that were out of their control, and they may have internalized these beliefs. Clients can be helped to identify experiences in their childhoods that may have led to unrealistic expectations of personal responsibility and perfection and encouraged to challenge the basis for those beliefs.

Using Cognitive Restructuring to Address Angry Feelings

Anger is frequent after a traumatic event, and it can persist for a long time. There is plenty to be angry about after a disaster. Survivors often are looking for someone to blame for the situation. It is not unusual to be angry at the perpetrator of the event if there is one (e.g., the terrorist or shooter), as well as at the government for either not protecting people before the event (e.g., through gun control legislation, better mental health services) or for not responding adequately after the fact (e.g., resources are slow to be allocated or are insufficient). Although strong angry feelings are understandable, they can be highly disruptive and interfere with effective functioning, including in interpersonal relationships, work, and parenting, and they can reduce positive feelings, disrupt a sense of well-being, and diminish one's overall enjoyment of life. For some people, persistent angry feelings about a traumatic event can prevent them from moving on with their lives.

The key to working with anger effectively is to recognize how it is different from other negative feelings, such as anxiety, depression, and guilt. Feelings of anger are related to beliefs of having been wronged, by someone or something else, that shift the focus of attention away from oneself and onto "responsible" parties. As a result of this external focus of blame on others, and associated beliefs of righteousness and injustice, strong angry feelings are often energizing and empowering and do not feel unpleasant or distressing like other negative feelings. Although most people would like their angry feelings to go away by "justice being served," such as the consequences of the event somehow being reversed, or the guilty parties forced to accept responsibility, they are usually not motivated to simply make the feelings themselves go away without any action. In contrast, negative feelings such as anxiety, depression, and guilt can be extremely unpleasant and immobilizing, and people are highly motivated to make them go away, making it easier to get clients to closely examine their thoughts related to these feelings than their thoughts related to anger. Nevertheless, there are effective strategies to helping people deal with their angry feelings and move beyond the disaster and on with their lives.

The therapist can target the anger directly through cognitive restructuring or may instead focus on one of the deeper feelings that the anger may be masking. When using cognitive restructuring to address anger directly, the therapist can ask questions to encourage the client to thoroughly consider the evidence supporting and not supporting their belief, but they should avoid getting into a debate with the client, even when exaggeration or minimization of evidence are prominent. One approach is to explore how the angry feelings have been affecting the client and their relationship with others since the disaster occurred. Oftentimes the client can see that their anger is misplaced and an overreaction to the circumstance. For example, a parent might recognize that they have a short fuse with their child. In these cases, the 5 Steps can often be used to modify the thought that triggered the anger. Instead of thinking, "Joey never listens" the new, more balanced thought might be "I need to help Joey listen better, but my anger is really due to my frustration with how slow the legal system has been."

If, instead, the client continues to firmly believe that their thought is supported after a thorough review of the evidence, or still feels angry even after coming up with a new, more accurate thought, the therapist should accept this and move on to helping them create an Action Plan instead of attempting to dissuade them. Continued debate on the accuracy of thoughts or beliefs underlying angry feelings can lead to alienation of the client, who may feel they are being badgered to alter their accurate perceptions of situations. Moving on to developing an Action Plan resolves the immediate problem situation without modifying the underlying thought that led to the angry feeling. To the extent that disaster-related beliefs may have contributed to angry outbursts, there will be other opportunities for bringing those thoughts into focus and examining them closely together later in therapy.

Sometimes, angry feelings related to a disaster persist for months and years after the event has ended. Disaster survivors may hold onto anger at terrorists or shooters responsible for the event, or they may focus their anger on the politicians blocking gun control legislation or not paying attention to climate change legislation that might have prevented a disaster from occurring. When that anger becomes a dominant feature of the client's life and is no longer a productive outlet, the therapist's job is to help the client see that their anger is no longer serving a useful purpose and in fact is controlling and consuming their life—preventing them from enjoying what life still has to offer them.

In these cases, it can be useful to use the Payoff Matrix described later in this chapter to evaluate what the client is getting from holding onto their anger and what they give up by letting it go, as well as what holding onto the anger is costing them and what the costs of letting it go might be. A systematic examination of the benefits and costs of holding onto anger versus letting it go can clarify to the client the price that is being paid for maintaining anger and can identify concerns about the perceived costs of giving the anger up, which can then be carefully examined with the 5 Steps. For example, it is not unusual for people who are angry after a shooting or other incident of mass violence to believe that a disadvantage of letting go of their anger is that they will "let their guard down" and no longer maintain the same level of vigilance aimed at preventing a similar incident from occurring again. With such people, the thought "If I let go of my anger about this incident and reduce my vigilance, there is a good chance that a similar incident could happen" can then be the focus of close examination with the 5 Steps. The therapist can examine with the client the evidence about just how likely it is that a similar incident might occur again and whether the client's maintenance of a high level of anger and vigilance could prevent it. A primary advantage to such an examination is that it focuses on the fear underlying the client's angry feeling and is easier to challenge because it reflects one of the common Problematic Thinking Styles (Overestimation of Risk; see Chapter 8). A close examination of the thoughts and beliefs related to letting go of anger often leads to the identification of exaggerated concerns about risk that, when successfully challenged, can enable the client to loosen their angry fixation on the disaster without putting themselves at increased risk.

Addressing Grief

Many disasters unfortunately result in the loss of lives, and for each person lost there are loved ones left behind to grieve. Grief can result in strong feelings of sadness, loneliness, fear, anxiety, resentment, anger, and even guilt. In the Cognitive Behavior Therapy for Postdisaster Distress (CBT-PD) program grief may therefore come up as part of the psychoeducation around each of the four feeling states (i.e., fear and anxiety, sadness and depression, guilt and shame, and anger; see Chapter 8). There may be sadness and depression related to thoughts such as "I will never be happy again"; anxiety related to thoughts such as "I won't be able to support myself"; anger related to thoughts such as "How could he leave me when I needed him most?"; and guilt related to thoughts such as "If I had been there, maybe this wouldn't have happened."

Therapists may be concerned that examining the client's grief-related thoughts could be interpreted as invalidating the basis for these feelings. It is critical that the therapist demonstrate deep and genuine empathy for the client's loss and convey the understanding that anyone who experienced such a loss would feel devastated. A mutual bond of understanding and empathy is needed in order for the therapist to work closely with the client to gently examine and challenge inaccurate thoughts related to their loss that can increase their distress and interfere with the normal grieving process.

Through the use of the 5 Steps, the therapist can help the client see when their upsetting thoughts are not completely accurate and how new, more balanced thoughts can reduce the associated distress. In many cases involving grief, significant distress persists even after new, more accurate thoughts have been identified. In fact, while correcting inaccuracies in the old thought, the new thought might acknowledge that it will take time before the person feels better. For example, a more balanced thought for "I will never be happy again" might be "It is normal to feel sad after a death, but over time I will start to feel better." Although this new thought is more accurate, an Action Plan is still needed to help the client cope with their grief as effectively as possible (see Exhibit 10.1 for suggestions).

EXHIBIT 10.1. Suggested Action Plans for Dealing With Grief

1. Schedule positive and meaningful activities to bring joy and a sense of purpose to your life.
2. Connect with friends and family, especially those who knew the deceased well.
3. Write a letter to the deceased to say goodbye, to update them or your life, to say you are sorry, and so on.
4. Engage in a ritual to remember the deceased, such as planting a tree as a memorial; getting together with loved ones; doing something the deceased used to do, such as going for a hike, and so on. Consider making it an annual event.
5. Honor the loss. Look for ways to make meaning of the deceased person's life, and pay tribute to their accomplishments, such as making a donation in their name to a cause they cared about.
6. Remember the deceased's accomplishments. Share those memories with others.
7. Write about your feelings about the death and how you are currently feeling.
8. Engage in healthy coping: Eat well, exercise, limit drinking, get good sleep.

Guilt and shame are often part of the grieving process. It is not unusual for people who have lost a loved one to wonder whether there is something they could have done (or done differently) that would have led to a different outcome, for example, thinking "I wish I had insisted we evacuate," or "I should have never let my daughter go to . . .," or "If only I had stayed, then. . . ." Each of these thoughts implies that the bereaved person had some responsibility for, or control over, the event. One useful technique for addressing feelings of guilt and shame is to ask the client what the deceased person would say to them. If the client thinks "I wish I was there when the shooting happened so that I could help" the deceased might respond "I'm glad you weren't there. We might both have been killed, and the kids need you."

If the client is still experiencing considerable grief toward the end of CBT-PD, the therapist might consider referring them for treatment that specifically focuses on addressing their grief, such as complicated grief therapy, a cognitive behavioral approach that focuses on seven core themes: (a) understanding grief, (b) managing painful emotions, (c) thinking about the future, (d) strengthening relationships, (e) telling the story of the death, (f) learning to live with reminders, and (g) remembering the person who died. The treatment was used after the September 11, 2001, terrorist attacks (Donahue et al., 2006) and in several randomized controlled trials that compared complicated grief therapy with standard interpersonal psychotherapy (Shear et al., 2005, 2013, 2014). For information on the assessment of complicated grief, see the website of the Center for Complicated Grief (https://complicatedgrief.columbia.edu/professionals/complicated-grief-professionals/overview/).

STRATEGIES FOR ADDRESSING SPECIFIC CHALLENGES
TEACHING THE 5 STEPS OF COGNITIVE RESTRUCTURING

The 5 Steps is a complex but rich skill that has broad-scale potential to directly target and change thoughts and beliefs that underlie posttraumatic stress disorder and other postdisaster symptoms, to alleviate negative feelings by correcting inaccurate thinking and reasoning processes, and to prompt action to address genuinely problematic situations in people's lives. As with teaching any rich skill, however, clinicians may encounter a variety of challenges when teaching it. In the following sections we describe strategies for addressing some of the most common challenges encountered when teaching clients the 5 Steps.

Client Does Not Use the 5 Steps of Cognitive Restructuring to Examine Disaster-Related Thoughts

In the CBT-PD program, the 5 Steps is taught as a skill that can be used to deal with any upsetting situation. To have the greatest impact on a client's symptoms of postdisaster distress, however, it is important that the client challenges some of their disaster-related thoughts and beliefs. The therapist should not be concerned if the client does not begin to address trauma-related thoughts during the early sessions, when the basics of cognitive restructuring are being taught, including recognizing and challenging Problematic Thinking Styles and the 5 Steps; however, if some trauma-related thoughts or beliefs have not been the focus of cognitive restructuring by the sixth or seventh session the therapist should look for ways of bringing such cognitions into focus and helping the client examine them closely.

During the psychoeducation portion of CBT-PD, and again when teaching clients how to recognize and change Problematic Thinking Styles, the therapist should be listening for distorted cognitions to challenge later on in the program. For example, the therapist might recall that, when reviewing the Problematic Thinking Styles, the client gave the example "Police can't be trusted" when learning about All-or-Nothing Thinking.

THERAPIST: So, now that you have learned the 5 Steps of Cognitive Restructuring, would you be willing to begin using it on some of the disaster-related thoughts you had shared with me previously?

CLIENT: Sure; like what?

THERAPIST: Well, how about the thought that "Police can't be trusted"?

CLIENT: Okay, but that is how I feel. I mean, if they had been doing their job on the day of the school shooting maybe no one would have died.

THERAPIST: Well, that's how you feel before challenging the thought (*smiles*), but are you up for going through the 5 Steps and challenging the thought "The police can't be trusted"?

CLIENT: Yes.

A second way for the therapist to discover disaster-specific cognitions is through the routine monitoring of outcomes. For example, if the client says they are bothered by unwanted memories of the event, the therapist can explore the situation to identify what they were thinking at the time. This line of exploration can directly lead to disaster-related cognitions, which can then be examined with the 5 Steps. In the following vignette, the client completed the Short Post-Traumatic Stress Disorder Rating Interview, Expanded Version (SPRINT-E; Norris & Davidson, 2007) at the beginning of the seventh CBT-PD session. The therapist begins by reviewing the completed assessment:

THERAPIST: Let's take a look at your SPRINT-E together to see how things have been going for you over the past week.

CLIENT: Okay.

THERAPIST: I see that you indicated being bothered "a moderate degree" over the past week by unwanted memories of the disaster. Can you tell me more about that?

CLIENT: Well, hurricane season is starting up, and there was a story on the news about how this hurricane season is predicted to be worse than past years. I got really upset.

THERAPIST: I see. And when did that happen, and how long did it last?

CLIENT: It was over the weekend.

THERAPIST: And what were you thinking when you got upset?

CLIENT: That I will just fall apart. I just can't do it again.

THERAPIST: That sounds pretty upsetting. How long were you having those thoughts and feelings?

CLIENT: Most of the weekend. I felt liked a basket case.

THERAPIST: I understand. That must have been hard. How about if we use the 5 Steps of Cognitive Restructuring to examine your thought "If another hurricane hits, I will fall apart"?

CLIENT: Okay, I can try.

A third way of bringing disaster-related cognitions into the focus of cognitive restructuring is to use two optional worksheets we developed to help clients identify their thoughts and beliefs about the disaster. Handout 31, My Disaster-Related Thoughts and Feelings Worksheet (available in Appendix B on the American Psychological Association [APA] website at http://pubs. apa.org/books/supp/hamblen) prompts the client to identify specific disaster-related thoughts tied to each of the four negative feeling states (fear and anxiety, sadness and depression, guilt and shame, and anger). Asking about disaster-related thoughts within the context of these four broad feeling states can sometimes help the client identify thoughts that they may not be able to recognize on their own. If the client is still not able to identify distressing thoughts or beliefs related to the disaster, they can use Handout 32, Common Thoughts About the Disaster Worksheet (available in Appendix B on the APA website at http://pubs.apa.org/books/supp/hamblen), which provides a list of common disaster-specific cognitions that may be relevant. The client simply checks the cognitions that are true for them and then completes a 5 Steps worksheet on the thoughts that were identified.

Challenging a Thought Leads to Only Small Reductions in Distress

Sometimes a client who has learned cognitive restructuring experiences only small reductions in distress, despite having successfully challenged an upsetting thought and identifying a more accurate thought. There are several strategies for dealing with such apparently small effects. First, it is important to determine whether the client experienced *any* reduction in distress after the successful challenge and modification of an inaccurate or unsupported thought. If it is unclear whether reductions in distress have occurred, the therapist can ask the client to first rate the distress associated with their original thought on a subjective units of distress scale, for example, one that ranges from 0 (*No Distress*) to 100 (*Extreme Distress*; see Figure 10.1). The

FIGURE 10.1. Subjective Units of Distress Scale (0–100)

0	25	50	75	100
No Distress	*Mild Distress*	*Moderate Distress*	*Severe Distress*	*Extreme Distress*

client then can be asked to rate the distress associated with their new, more accurate thought. If the client believes that the evidence does not support the initial thought and comes up with a new and more accurate thought, some reduction in overall distress should be expected. The therapist should reinforce even small reductions in distress ratings that occur after cognitive restructuring and point out that upset feelings often gradually improve after inaccurate or distorted thoughts are replaced with more accurate and balanced ones. This gradual improvement is due to the fact that it takes time for the person to get used to the new thought, and they may need to keep reminding themselves of the new thought before the old one is successfully replaced. As long as there is some reduction in distress related to the new thought compared with the old one, additional steps may not need to be taken.

If the client indicates that the new thought is not associated with a reduction in distress, the therapist should determine whether the client finds the new thought more believable than the old one. Again, using a scale that ranges from 0 (*Not at All Believable*) to 100 (*Completely Believable*; see Figure 10.2), the therapist can ask the client to first rate how believable their original thought is (now that they have weighed the evidence for and against that thought and concluded it is inaccurate) and then how believable their new thought is (which should take into account the evidence against the old thought).

The less believable the old thought is, and the more believable the new thought is, the greater the reduction in distress should be. If the new thought is only somewhat more believable than the old thought, and the reduction in distress is small, the therapist can then help the client increase the believability of the new thought. One way to do this is to help the client develop a new thought that incorporates some of the evidence against the thought into the new thought. If the client still reports little change in distress, even after coming up with a more believable thought that incorporates evidence against the thought, the therapist can explore whether there might be another thought that is driving the distress. As we discussed in both Chapters 8 and 9, many upsetting situations are associated with multiple feelings

FIGURE 10.2. Believability Scale (0–100)

and thoughts. It may be that another thought related to the situation might be more effective. A second cognitive restructuring can be completed on the same situation but with a different thought and feeling.

Finally, if a new and more accurate thought is still associated with significant distress, albeit somewhat less distress than the old thought, then an Action Plan should be considered to help the client deal with the upsetting situation. For example, recall the vignette in Chapter 9 in which the client, Katherine, felt anxious even though she had come up with the new thought "There is security at the concert, and my daughter will be well supervised." Katherine, with her therapist, then created an Action Plan that included talking to her daughter about being alert, talking to the parents who would be chaperoning, and keeping busy so that she does not worry. Action Plans should also be used when there is only a modest reduction in distress after an old thought has been replaced with a new one. In this case, the Action Plan can be created to address the specific distressing symptom. For example, as we discussed in Chapter 9, it is not unusual for people to have symptoms even after they have successfully challenged beliefs, and this may be why they still feel distressed. In these cases the Action Plan can be used not only to come up with solutions to remaining problems but also to develop coping skills for managing the specific symptoms.

Difficulty Using Cognitive Restructuring to Address Nightmares

Nightmares are a common symptom after a disaster. They sometimes involve a repetition of part of the disaster, but more often they are bad dreams that may be thematically linked to the disaster without actually replaying memories of the event itself. Regardless of the nature of the nightmares, they are often a major source of distress to clients, and they frequently interfere with sleep, both by causing the client to awake unexpectedly and by contributing to anxiety about going to sleep.

There are two general approaches to treating nightmares with cognitive restructuring. First, it can be used to challenge negative thoughts related to the content of the nightmares themselves. It is helpful for clients to maintain a journal of the nightmares they have. This journal can be kept by the bedside, and when the client is awakened by a nightmare, or when they awaken the next morning, they can write down a description of the nightmare. During the therapy session the therapist should review recent nightmares the client has described in the journal and collaborate with the client in either identifying a common theme across several of the nightmares that appear to be related to the disaster, or focus on one specific nightmare for cognitive restructuring. After a specific event or theme has been identified, the therapist can go through the steps of cognitive restructuring with the client, first identifying the negative feeling related to the event or theme, then the underlying thoughts or beliefs related to that emotion, and so on. The primary purpose of cognitive restructuring is to address core thoughts or beliefs related to the traumatic experience(s) that underlie the nightmare. By addressing these beliefs, distress associated with nightmares, as well as the frequency of the nightmares, can be reduced.

Second, cognitive restructuring can be used to help clients deal with the anxiety or other negative feelings they have about nightmares when they are trying to go to sleep or trying to get back to sleep after being awakened by a nightmare. Under these circumstances, Cognitive restructuring can be used to help clients address Problematic Thinking Styles that may interfere with coping with the nightmares, such as Catastrophizing (e.g., "I can't stand it if I have another nightmare tonight; I won't be able to go through the day tomorrow if I don't get at least 6 hours of sleep"), All-or-Nothing Thinking (e.g., "I'm a basket case because I keep having nightmares"), or Overgeneralization (e.g., "I'm always going to have nightmares"), and develop more adaptive self-statements for coping with these experiences. In addition, Action Plans can be developed that involve taking steps to improve poor sleep habits (sleep hygiene), such as avoiding naps, avoiding caffeine-containing beverages in the evening, engaging in regular exercise, going to bed at a regular time every evening, and doing something relaxing before going to bed (see Chapter 9, Exhibit 9.2, for a detailed list of coping strategies for clients who have difficulty sleeping). Although improved sleep hygiene may not have a direct impact on nightmares, it may improve the quality of sleep when the person is able to sleep and decrease some of the disruptive effects of the nightmares on sleep.

Addressing Negative Feelings Related to Injuries

Just as with grief and loss, clients who experience a serious injury may have intense emotional feelings that therapists may at first be nervous about challenging. Depending on the injury, a client may have significant challenges ahead with respect to mobility, employment, and relationships. Therapists should not shy away from challenging thoughts such as "I may never walk again," "I can't do the things I used to do," and "I will never be the same," even if they might at first sound accurate. Instead, the therapist should explore the deeper meaning behind these thoughts to identify more specific thoughts to examine. For example, asking a client "What might it mean if you can't walk again?" may prompt them to reveal concerns that they will not be able to take care of their children, find a meaningful job, or be able to enjoy running. In each case, the therapist can help the client challenge these more specific thoughts and replace them with more accurate and less distressing ones. In addition, the process of examining the thought can lead to the discovery of specific problems that can be addressed with an Action Plan.

Recall again the vignette of Katherine. Katherine lost her leg in the Boston Marathon bombing. In the vignette, she and her therapist challenged the thought "If I let my daughter go to the concert, she could be killed." Over the course of the CBT-PD program the therapist also helped Katherine challenge beliefs about herself and her place in the world. Although Katherine's life did change substantially as a result of her injury, she was still a competent and loving mother; a productive member of society; and an attractive, sensual woman. If the therapist had been hesitant to take on realistic concerns, such as that Katherine's life would change, that some of the changes would be difficult, and in some cases there might be things Katherine could no longer do, the therapy would have been a lot less effective. Instead, the therapist helped Katherine replace her inaccurate beliefs, such as "I'll never be close to my daughter again," with the more accurate belief "I miss not being as close to my daughter as I used to be." They also created Action Plans to help Katherine overcome practical obstacles to her goals, such as finding new activities she can do with her daughter, like playing board games and scrapbooking while her mobility was restricted.

Sticking to Beliefs That Are Not Supported by the Evidence

Sometimes people have difficulty letting go of a belief even after a review of the evidence indicates that it is not supported. They may say things like "Even though I know it isn't true, it still *feels* true"; or "I know it isn't true, but I can't help coming back to the thought again and again"; or "I know the evidence doesn't support the thought, but I still think it's true." There are several strategies the therapist can use to help clients address upsetting thoughts and beliefs that persist despite the evidence against them. First, the therapist can point out to the client that they may have held the belief for a significant period of time, that it has been reinforced many times over the weeks and months since the disaster, and that it takes time and practice to unlearn and change these strongly held beliefs. The therapist can assure the client that repeatedly challenging thoughts and beliefs that they know are incorrect, and replacing them with more accurate ones, will gradually feel more natural and become routine.

Sometimes the use of a metaphor can help clients understand the process of changing one's thinking. For example, the therapist can explain to the client how thinking is like a stream of water that gradually erodes the earth to create deeper and deeper pathways (or riverbeds) as it flows downward. It takes time and effort to change the direction of a stream that has been flowing down one pathway for some period and to get the water to flow down another pathway, but if the stream is successfully diverted for a long enough time, eventually the water flows down the new pathway just as naturally and effortlessly as the old pathway. Thoughts and beliefs are like water flowing down a stream—they take time and persistence to change. Although the change may occur gradually, and may at first seem tenuous, over time the new thoughts and beliefs will become just as real and as firmly entrenched as the old ones were.

A second approach to this problem is to help the client distinguish between what *feels* right or correct and what *is* right or correct; in other words, just because a belief feels right does not mean that it is supported by the evidence. The therapist can help the client recognize this thinking pattern as one of the Problematic Thinking Styles: Emotional Reasoning. It makes sense that people who have thought a particular way for a long time will continue to believe that their original thoughts are correct because those thoughts feel so familiar and natural, despite the evidence against them. Acknowledging that long-held beliefs often continue to feel right even after they have been shown to be inaccurate normalizes the experience for the client. The client can be told that as they practice replacing inaccurate and unhelpful thoughts and beliefs with more accurate, adaptive ones these new beliefs will eventually come to feel normal.

A third approach involves constructing a Payoff Matrix (see Handout 33 in Appendix B on the APA website at http://pubs.apa.org/books/supp/hamblen). Instead of the client trying to determine the accuracy of their thinking, the Payoff Matrix shifts the focus onto the consequences of holding or changing the thought. It is, in essence, a two × two table that is set up to weigh the advantages and disadvantage of keeping or changing a thought. Clients can be reluctant to change their thought because they are fearful of the consequences. They often believe that changing the thought will put them, or their families, at risk and that by holding onto the thought they are keeping their families safe. However, this has to be compared with the disadvantage of keeping the thought, which often involves some limitation on their freedom. Having identified the advantages and disadvantages of clinging to an old thought versus changing to a more accurate thought, the therapist and client can then explore and challenge some of these perceived reasons; specifically, therapists may help clients challenge the perceived benefits of holding onto a belief or the perceived costs of giving up that belief. Clients may also benefit from seeing the high cost they pay for holding onto certain beliefs rather than giving them up.

In the following vignette, which took place approximately a year after the September 11th attacks, the therapist works with the client, a Staten Island ferry boat captain who continued to be afraid that his ferry might be a terrorist target. After September 11th, the New York City Department of Transportation received daily briefings about possible threats in and around New York, and this captain believed it was not safe to be transporting passengers on the ferries. Although it is always best if clients can successfully challenge their thoughts and come up with more accurate, less distressing ones, in some cases examining the consequences of holding onto thoughts can help clients shift to endorse the new belief. As always, it is best for the therapist to assume a collaborative stance when reviewing the benefits of holding onto beliefs that are not well supported and the costs of giving up those beliefs.

THERAPIST: It seems like you are having a hard time coming up with evidence against the thought that "The ferry could be a terrorist target."

CLIENT: Yeah. When I tried to come up with evidence against the thought, I just keep coming back to the briefings where we are being told it could happen. I mean, [the terrorists] had inside information.

THERAPIST: Okay; sometimes people are reluctant to challenge their thinking because they are concerned about the consequences of changing their thought. In this case, you are telling me you don't want to change the thought because you feel like it might put you and your passengers at risk.

CLIENT: That's right. Even if I know it's not that likely to happen, it feels risky.

THERAPIST: I wonder whether it might be helpful for us to complete a Payoff Matrix together so you can examine the advantages and disadvantages of keeping your thought compared to changing it. What do you think?

CLIENT: Sure.

THERAPIST: Here is how it works. First, let's look at the pros and cons of keeping your thought. Your thought is that "The ferry could be a terrorist target." Starting with the first column of the Payoff Matrix, what are the advantages of holding that thought?

CLIENT: Well, knowing that it is target means that I can try and be more aware of anyone who looks suspicious.

THERAPIST: Okay. And how would that help?

CLIENT: Well, I might be able to call for help before thousands of passengers die.

THERAPIST: Okay, write that down in this box. And what are the disadvantages of holding the thought?

CLIENT: I guess mostly that I am afraid. I am afraid for the passengers and for myself. I don't sleep well, either. I'm worried all the time, and I can't relax. And to be honest, I think I am distracted when I drive the boat, which also puts the passengers at risk. I spend too much time scanning the passengers and looking at bags when I really need to be focused on driving the boat.

THERAPIST: Okay, so add those here. (*Client fills in worksheet.*) Now let's work on the second column, the advantages and disadvantages of changing the thought. What are the advantages?

CLIENT: Well, sort of the opposite, right? If I wasn't worried about the ferry being a target, I wouldn't be afraid. I could be relaxed and enjoy life again.

THERAPIST: Okay, fill that in. Now what are the disadvantages?

CLIENT: Well, that thousands of people would die.

THERAPIST: Okay, put that down in the last box. (*Client fills in worksheet; see Table 10.1.*) So now you can see the advantages and disadvantages. Holding onto your thought may keep you alert to danger and might help prevent a disaster, but there are consequences as well. You are anxious all the time and can't relax. How often have you been worried about an attack?

CLIENT: Every day since 9/11.

THERAPIST: So for just over a year, then?

CLIENT: Yes.

THERAPIST: And how often has there been an attack?

CLIENT: Never.

THERAPIST: So, every day you worry about it, but it never happens. That sounds like it could be one of the Problematic Thinking Styles.

CLIENT: Yeah, Overestimation of Risk.

TABLE 10.1. Payoff Matrix Worksheet for the Thought "The Ferry Could Be a Terrorist Target"

Keeping the thought	Changing the thought
Advantages	
In what ways does *holding onto* your thought make your life seem more manageable, safer, or easier to handle? Does the thought provide you with a sense of control, security, or predictability?	How could *changing* your thought improve your life? Consider whether changing your thought or belief would reduce negative feelings and free you from concerns about past events.
• If I know the ferry is a target I can look for suspicious passengers and possibly get help before thousands of passengers die.	• I would be relaxed. • I could enjoy life again.
Disadvantages	
In what ways does *holding onto* your thought make your life more difficult? Consider the effects of the thought or belief on negative feelings that prevent you from doing things you would like to do.	What are the possible disadvantages or costs of *changing* your thought? Would changing the thought lead to your feeling less control, security, or predictability?
• I am afraid for my passengers and myself. • I don't sleep well and can't relax. • I am distracted when driving the boat.	• Thousands of people could die if there is an attack.

THERAPIST: And how much do you believe you could stop an attack even if you did spot one?

CLIENT: I don't know. There have been a few times I have seen someone with a backpack where I thought something looked a little off, but then I decided everything was okay, and obviously nothing happened. It's hard to know if I would really be able to tell the difference.

THERAPIST: So, the question is whether it is worth it to hold onto the fear when the chance of an attack happening is relatively low and you may not be able to do anything about it anyway.

CLIENT: I see what you're saying. Since there isn't a lot I can do about the situation, what's the point of worrying?

THERAPIST: Right. It's not really about whether your thought is accurate or not. It is just whether the pros of holding that thought outweigh the cons. It sounds like there are definite costs, and there may not be any real advantages.

CLIENT: Well, when you put it like that, it seems like I am spending a lot of time worrying about something that I can't really control.

THERAPIST: I agree. So let's see if we can come up with an Action Plan. So rather than telling yourself, "The ferry is a terrorist target" when you start to think that way what do you think you could do instead?

CLIENT: Maybe I could try and focus on something else.

THERAPIST: Okay, how would that work? What would you focus on?

CLIENT: Well, if it happens when I am underway, I could focus on the boat instead. I could check my speed, the boat's location, maybe ask the first mate for a report. The things I need to know to do my job.

THERAPIST: Okay. And what about when you are not on the ship? Is there something that you could do that might help you relax or get more engaged in other activities?

CLIENT: Hmm, I think I could try and see if my wife wanted to do something, like go for a walk or see a movie. Usually when I get anxious I isolate and start browsing the internet to see what news I can find. So it would be better if I could get away from that.

THERAPIST: That sounds like a good idea to me. How does that sound to you?

CLIENT: Better than being anxious all the time.

One of the most common disadvantages of giving up unrealistic thoughts or beliefs is having to accept a view of the world as sometimes unpredictable and dangerous. The therapist can explore and evaluate evidence with the client to determine whether the client's perceptions of risk are exaggerated or realistic. Many clients experience relief when they are able to develop more realistic perceptions of risk and danger; however, they may still need an Action Plan to help them manage their distress.

Some clients, on the other hand, experience very high levels of anxiety when they perceive *any* risk, and this anxiety may prevent them from developing more realistic perceptions of their responsibility for and control over events. In these circumstances, instead of continuing to attempt to modify the client's perceptions of risk it is preferable to shift the focus and ask whether the client is able to accept the level of risk in the world rather than trying to change it. In other words, a certain amount of risk in life is inescapable, and in order to get on with their life the client needs to decide whether to accept the risks they face on a day-to-day basis and will likely face in the future. Clients who accept this risk can then be helped to modify their beliefs about excessive control over, or responsibility for, events both past and future. For clients who cannot accept the degree of risk inherent in living their lives, the therapist can focus the discussion on exploring possible lifestyle changes that might reduce their perceptions of risk even further. For example, in the vignette just provided, the client might have concluded that being a captain for a New York ferry is just too great a risk and that he could not accept the responsibility for the safety of his passengers. In that case, the Action Plan would have looked very different; for example, he might have had to consider looking for another job and what that would entail.

Difficulty Using Cognitive Restructuring "In the Moment"

For the 5 Steps to be as effective as possible, clients must be able to use cognitive restructuring in the moment that they experience the negative feelings instead of hours or days later, after the feelings have subsided. For many people, it takes a long time to learn how to do cognitive restructuring in the moment, and this experience should be normalized as a skill that clients will learn through extensive practice. It may be that anxiety in the moment is interfering with the client's ability to use the 5 Steps. In this case, breathing retraining can be offered as a solution. Clients can be encouraged to do some breathing first, to relax and focus, and then begin work on the cognitive restructuring worksheet. Another problem may be that the client does not recognize that they need to do a 5 Step worksheet until the moment has passed. In this case, the therapist can ask the client to consider if they were able to recognize a Problematic Thinking Style in the moment. If they can, this can be the cue that they should do a worksheet instead of relying on identifying that they feel upset.

Finally, the worksheets themselves can be a barrier to using the skill in the moment. Although early on in the CBT-PD program it is important for clients to write everything down, to ensure that they are using the skill correctly, the therapist ultimately hopes the client comes to later sessions reporting that they used the 5 Steps spontaneously. For example, a client might report in Session 9 that they did not complete a worksheet but that when they were reminded of fire by a story on the news, instead of feeling afraid they just told themselves "I am safe, and I have a plan for what to do if the fires start coming close again." If, however, this spontaneous transition does not occur, in later sessions the therapist should begin to encourage the client to try and use cognitive restructuring in the moment. If recalling the steps is part of the problem, the therapist can give the client a pocket card that lists a brief version of the 5 Steps, for example: (1) Situation, (2) Feeling, (3) Thought, (4) Challenging the Thought, and (5) Make a Decision.

ALTERNATIVE COGNITIVE RESTRUCTURING SKILLS

Most clients are able to learn the 5 Steps to deal with their negative feelings and address inaccurate thoughts and beliefs related to the disaster; however, some continue to struggle with the skill even after multiple sessions of CBT-PD. In these situations the therapist can shift to teaching a cognitive restructuring skill that is simpler than the 5 Steps; we discuss some of these in the sections that follow. Although these alternative skills may lack some of the richness and flexibility of the 5 Steps, they may also be easier for clients to learn and to use on their own, which is the ultimate goal of the CBT-PD program.

For cognitive restructuring to be successful, clients need to have some flexibility in their thinking in order to move away from their initial thoughts and develop new, more adaptive thoughts. Although cognitive restructuring is most effective if that flexible thinking leads to an alternative thought that is less distressing, even just recognizing that there is more than one possible thought or perspective in a situation can result in a decrease in distress (Suarez et al., 1987). Another difference between the 5 Steps and these alternative strategies is that the latter do not rely on the client's ability to generate evidence against the thought.

Returning to Problematic Thinking Styles

Problematic Thinking Styles is the first cognitive restructuring skill that clients learn in the CBT-PD program. Although it is taught as a precursor to the 5 Steps, some clients may do better returning to the Problematic Thinking Styles and using that alone as a cognitive restructuring skill. One way to do this is by using the Problematic Thinking Styles Log Worksheet (Handout 26 in Appendix B on the APA website at http://pubs.apa.org/books/supp/hamblen). Clients can use this more basic worksheet because it still results in the identification of a more helpful thought. The client starts with their original thought, identifies the associated Problematic Thinking Style, and then comes up with a more helpful thought. In essence, the client is simply taking a step back to the way they were using cognitive restructuring before they were taught the 5 Steps.

If, however, the client is having difficulty even identifying their initial thought, the Problematic Thinking Styles can still be used alone. Some clients strongly identify with a particular Problematic Thinking Style. If they can identify their characteristic thinking style in an upsetting situation, they can recognize their thinking error and correct it. For example, clients who know they tend toward Catastrophizing can catch themselves and then try and come up with a more realistic thought, or clients who use Self-Blame can correct themselves by considering what else might be contributing to the problem.

Brainstorming Multiple Alternative Thoughts

Another technique that can be useful is to have clients generate multiple alternative thoughts. Here the goal is not to try and prove whether the original thought is accurate or not, or even to come up with a new thought, but instead to help clients become more flexible in their thinking by generating as many alternative thoughts as they can. The client does not have to believe the new thoughts; in fact, they likely will not believe them. However, the process of even considering alternatives forces clients to recognize that other alternatives exists and therefore to become less rigid in their thinking.

THERAPIST: I notice that you are often having a hard time coming up with evidence against the thought. Let's try something new that doesn't require Step 4.

CLIENT: Okay. I am trying, but yeah, it's really hard for me.

THERAPIST: Instead of trying to dispute the thought, let's see if you can just come up with other thoughts, even if you don't believe them. Looking at this 5 Steps worksheet from last week, you tried to challenge the thought "Concerts are a target for terrorists," but you had difficulty coming up with evidence against your thought.

CLIENT: Yeah. When I tried to think of any I just kept coming back to the Harvest Festival shooting [in 2017] and the Ariana Grande concert shooting at the Manchester Arena [in 2017; "Manchester Arena Bombing," 2020]. I just don't see how you can say concerts or really any big gathering at a stadium are safe.

THERAPIST: So, rather than trying to dispute the thought, let's try and come up with other ways to think about it. You don't have to believe these thoughts. I'm just asking what might other people think. A lot of people go to concerts, sporting events, festivals, and so on, where there are large groups of people. Why would they do this?

CLIENT: Obviously some people must think it's safe. But they don't know how fragile life is and how quickly things can turn around!

THERAPIST: I understand what you are saying, but right now all we are doing is thinking about what others might think in the same situation. So, one alternative thought is "People still go to concerts and think they are safe." What is another thought some people might hold?

CLIENT: Well, I think some people think the chances of something happening are extremely low. I've heard other people say they think there have been improvements in security.

THERAPIST: So that is two more alternative thoughts. The first thought is, "The chances of a shooting at a concert I'm attending are very low." The second thought is, "Security is improved." Can you think of any other alternative thoughts? Lots of people still go to concerts, so they must be telling themselves something.

CLIENT: Maybe they think that even if something happened they would probably be okay.

THERAPIST: So that's another alternative thought: "Even if a shooting happened, I would probably be okay." Now we have five different ways to think about the situation. Your original thought was that "Concerts are a target for terrorists," and then there were four more thoughts, including "People still go to concerts and think they are safe," "The chance of a shooting at a concert I'm attending are very low," "Concert security is improved," and "Even if a shooting happened, I would probably be okay."

CLIENT: I guess so . . .

THERAPIST: So, even if you can't convince yourself that one of these four alternatives are true, allowing yourself to even consider that there are alternatives should help your thinking become more flexible over time and can also sometimes lead to a decrease in how strongly someone holds onto the original thought. Has that happened for you?

CLIENT: A little, I guess. I mean, I still believe that concerts are a target for terrorists. I mean they have been, right? But I can also see how other people could think something different, and that does help a little.

While this method does not require that the client accept the alternative, it should be clear that generating alternative thoughts actually does involve considering evidence against the thought. It is that alternative evidence that leads the client to the alternative explanations. Therefore, this strategy can be useful when clients are struggling with the 5 Steps and, in some cases, once clients are willing to consider alternatives the therapist can move back to using the 5 Steps.

CONCLUSION

In this chapter, we have provided therapists with solutions to common problems clients may experience while learning cognitive restructuring, which is the skill that has the greatest potential impact for reducing posttraumatic symptoms after a disaster. Building on the explanation we provided in Chapter 9 for how to teach the 5 Steps, we discussed in this chapter solutions for how to help clients use cognitive restructuring to challenge inaccurate disaster-related thoughts and beliefs, to make the cognitive restructuring more effective at reducing distress, to use cognitive restructuring to address angry feelings, to help clients when they are having trouble letting go of beliefs despite evidence against them, and to increase clients' ability to use cognitive restructuring in the moment.

In this chapter we also have discussed alternative cognitive restructuring strategies that can be taught to clients who have difficulty learning or using the 5 Steps on their own. There are a number of ways that clients can learn to be more flexible and to move their thoughts from rigid, extreme, and distressing ones to more general, flexible, and less distressing ones. Many clients are very successful in changing their thinking by identifying and changing Problematic Thinking Styles, as taught in Chapter 8, and they can return to this skill if they have difficulty mastering the 5 Steps. Others may struggle coming up with a specific alternative thought but can still learn to be more flexible in their thinking by brainstorming alternative thoughts.

11 TERMINATION

Cognitive Behavior Therapy for Postdisaster Distress (CBT-PD) is intended to be a time-limited program. This is communicated to the client at the outset and readdressed throughout the course of the therapy. The therapist continually evaluates and discusses with the client how they are progressing in terms of mastery of the skills, whether disaster-related beliefs are being routinely challenged, and, most important, whether there are clinically meaningful reductions in distress. Around Session 8, the therapist should begin to more directly discuss progress through treatment and whether the client is feeling like they are meeting their therapy goals. Together they should set a termination goal. The therapist typically should be working toward having the client complete the program in approximately 10 to 12 sessions. Some clients with more complex presentations may need a few more, but ideally the program should end by 16 sessions for almost all clients. If CBT-PD is being offered as part of a formal disaster mental health program, it may have a set number of sessions.

There are several steps the therapist can take to help clients prepare for termination. In addition to being flexible about the length of the treatment program, the last few sessions can be scheduled every other week. This can

https://doi.org/10.1037/0000237-011
Treatment for Postdisaster Distress: A Transdiagnostic Approach, by J. L. Hamblen and K. T. Mueser

help build the client's confidence in their ability to use the cognitive restructuring skills on their own. For clients who are concerned about termination, a 5 Steps of Cognitive Restructuring Worksheet (Handout 28 in Appendix B on the American Psychological Association [APA] website at http://pubs.apa.org/books/supp/hamblen) can be completed in an earlier session to challenge the belief that the client needs to continue in therapy. The 5 Steps of Cognitive Restructuring (hereinafter "5 Steps") can also be used to challenge any other fears the client has about upcoming difficulties or situations. Then, in the last session, the therapist reviews the skills that were taught in the program, helps the client identify any specific unmet needs, and develops a plan for handling them.

DETERMINING WHEN TO END THE THERAPY

Cognitive behavioral interventions such as the CBT-PD program are aimed at teaching people critical information and skills to help them manage or reduce problematic symptoms and get on with their lives. Because of the emphasis on teaching skills, all cognitive behavioral approaches, including the CBT-PD program, are provided for a set period of time believed to be required for most clients to learn the requisite skills. Cognitive behavioral interventions have been developed and successfully applied to a broad range of psychiatric disorders and to facilitate the management of numerous acute and chronic medical conditions, and hundreds of studies have documented the long-term effectiveness of these time-limited programs for months and years after they have ended (e.g., Butler et al., 2006; van Dis et al., 2020). There is little evidence that providing cognitive behavioral treatment longer than the recommended period of time leads to better outcomes. In fact, not terminating treatment could be counterproductive because it could foster client dependence on the therapist and hinder the acquisition of the skills necessary to improve symptoms and functioning. Although there is no absolute right number of CBT-PD sessions, there are some things that the therapist can use to guide their decision about when to terminate.

Mastery of Cognitive Restructuring

Determining whether a client has sufficient mastery of cognitive restructuring requires consideration of several different areas. First, does the client understand each of the 5 Steps, and can they correctly identify thoughts and feelings, challenge their thoughts, and come up with more balanced thoughts or Action Plans for the situation? If not, can they use one of the alternative cognitive restructuring techniques to deal with distressing thoughts and beliefs? Although clients do not need to have completely mastered the 5 Steps skill to benefit fully from the CBT-PD program, over the course of the program they should acquire some ability to think more flexibly when experiencing upsetting thoughts and to develop more accurate and balanced thoughts to replace them with.

At the beginning of each session, the therapist should review the 5 Steps worksheets to determine whether the client is using the skill appropriately. The therapist should look for any consistent difficulties the client is having learning the skill, such as not identifying thoughts that are specific enough to challenge, having difficulty coming up with evidence against an upsetting thought, or not being able to determine whether the evidence supports a thought. In Chapters 9 and 10 we provided some suggestions for how to handle common problems such as these.

The general approach to teaching the 5 Steps as outlined in Chapter 9 is that during a session the therapist can help the client rework any 5 Steps worksheets that have not been completed correctly, or they can suggest starting a new worksheet in the session. Early on, after the 5 Steps have been introduced, the therapist may need to provide a lot of support to the client in using the skill. Through Socratic questioning the therapist can lead the client to the answers. As clients begin to master the skill, fewer questions are required, and they become able to work through the thought on their own. Thus, one sign of mastery is 5 Steps worksheets that are completed independently and accurately by the client.

Another indication of mastery is that clients are able to use cognitive restructuring in the moment, when they are feeling distressed. Early in the learning of the 5 Steps clients need to rely heavily on the worksheets in order to challenge their negative thoughts. At first, clients may not even be able to recognize the negative thoughts that underlie their upset feelings because the thoughts are so automatic, and identifying evidence against them may seem impossible without the therapist's help. Over time, though, as clients gain more and more practice using the cognitive restructuring worksheets, they should be completed with increasing accuracy. Ultimately, the goal is for the client to be able to use cognitive restructuring in the moment (instead of well after the event) and in their head (instead of using the worksheet). As the skill becomes more automatic, clients often spontaneously report noticing negative thoughts and replacing them with more accurate ones.

As we discussed in Chapter 10, if the client is not using cognitive restructuring in the moment to deal with negative feelings, there are several strategies the therapist can use to help. For example, when reviewing 5 Steps worksheets the therapist can prompt the client to remember what the next step is rather than just encouraging them to go to the next step on the worksheet. The therapist can also prompt the client during sessions to recall the

5 Steps at a moment when they are feeling distressed and then prompt them to try to deal with the feeling without using the worksheet.

Disaster-Related Cognitions

In the CBT-PD program the therapist helps the client move from learning to use cognitive restructuring as a skill for dealing with any negative feeling to using it to address beliefs related to the disaster that underlie posttraumatic and other symptoms they experience. Throughout the program the therapist should be on the lookout for dysfunctional beliefs the client has and seek to understand how they are associated with disaster-related beliefs. Some clients readily identify disaster-related beliefs and begin to start challenging them as soon as cognitive restructuring is introduced. Others learn how to use cognitive restructuring to deal with upsetting situations that are less clearly related to the disaster or that are not related at all. For these clients, learning the basics of cognitive restructuring by using it to cope with more rudimentary, everyday upset feelings before addressing potentially stronger and more distressing feelings related to the disaster can be helpful. For the CBT-PD program to be most effective, however, cognitive restructuring needs to target core disaster-related cognitions.

When deciding when to end treatment, the therapist should consider whether the client has successfully challenged their disaster-related beliefs. As we discussed in Chapter 10, therapists can use several strategies to help clients identify and challenge disaster-related thoughts. For example, the therapist may suggest a disaster-related belief to be challenged that the client mentioned previously; they can have the client challenge a thought that was identified on one of the two optional worksheets (Handouts 30 and 31 in Appendix B on the APA website at http://pubs.apa.org/books/supp/hamblen); or they can look to the Short Post-Traumatic Stress Disorder Rating Interview, Expanded Version (SPRINT-E; Norris & Davidson, 2007) to identify thoughts related to a specific symptom the client is currently reporting.

Symptom Improvement

Symptom monitoring should be part of any treatment. In the CBT-PD program we recommend using the SPRINT-E, but other outcome measures could be used. As we discussed earlier, throughout the course of the program the therapist and client should be reviewing the changes in symptoms. There are three main trajectories to consider: (a) improving, (b) worsening, and (c) maintaining.

Most clients follow the *improving* trajectory and show at least some improvement in their symptoms, if not a great deal of improvement or even total remission. Clients on this trajectory usually have few to no symptoms by Session 8 or 9, so the decision to end around Session 10 is fairly straightforward. At this point, clients should be exhibiting low levels of distress, and the main consideration is to ensure that they are prepared to use the skills on their own. There may be some anticipatory anxiety about termination, but that can typically be addressed within the 10 sessions.

The therapist may want to add on a few more sessions for clients who have improved but still have significant symptoms Although clients generally will continue to improve even after therapy has ended, additional sessions can still be helpful in solidifying their ability to use cognitive restructuring on their own. The therapist should consider whether there are specific thoughts that have yet to be challenged, whether trying alternative cognitive restructuring skills might be indicated, or whether there are specific symptoms that should be targeted. SPRINT-E item scores that remain high can guide the therapist in determining what symptoms to target.

Unfortunately, in some cases clients improve only a little or not at all (the *maintaining/worsening* trajectory). It is important to try and determine what is preventing the skills they have been taught from being successful. For example, has the client stopped using their breathing retraining and activity scheduling as the focus shifted to cognitive restructuring? Alternatively, is the client using the cognitive restructuring skill correctly but not seeing a decrease in distress, or are they struggling to use the skill at all? Strategies for addressing problems in teaching cognitive restructuring are addressed in Chapter 10. It is rare that clients are able to internalize the skill but do not show improvement. The therapist should encourage struggling clients to continue to practice the skill and explain to them that cognitive restructuring becomes easier with practice. Clients who receive cognitive behavioral treatments often continue to improve after therapy has ended as they become more adept at using the skills they have learned.

Client Goals Are Met

A final indication that it may be time to end treatment is if the client's personal goals have been achieved. Clients describe their goals for treatment in Session 1 and identify important life areas as part of activity scheduling in Session 2. Throughout the treatment, therapists should continue to monitor whether clients are making progress on attaining their goals and use both activity scheduling and the 5 Steps to help address upsetting situations that may occur when pursuing goals. For some clients, the ability to return to work, maintain a close intimate relationship, or pursue an education may be more important than a decrease in symptoms. Any discussion of termination should also include a check-in about whether the client's personal goals have been met.

LAST-SESSION REVIEW

In the second-to-last session, the client is reminded that the next session will be the last one. The therapist should prepare the client for that session by letting them know that the session will focus on a review of the client's progress and the skills that were taught, identifying upcoming challenges that the client foresees, and then coming up with a plan for addressing those challenges. This gives the client a chance to think about any concerns they may want to bring up with the therapist in the final session.

At the start of the final session, the therapist should remind the client of the plan for the session, as illustrated below.

THERAPIST: We have spent the last few months working together to help you better understand and cope with difficult emotions related to disaster. We've now reached our last session of working together. Today, we will begin by looking at how your symptoms have changed throughout the program. Next, we will review the information and skills that we have covered in this program. Then, we'll develop a plan for how to deal with upsetting situations or triggers that may arise in the future, and talk about other ways you can find support now that our work together will be ending. We can also talk about any other concerns you may have about ending therapy and how you have coped with your traumatic experiences. I'd also like to take a few minutes to tell you how much I enjoyed working with you.

Client Progress

As we mentioned earlier, the therapist can use the client's scores on the SPRINT-E in consideration of when to end treatment. A final review of the client's improvement in symptoms is a good way to begin the session:

THERAPIST: When you and I first began working together, your total score on the questionnaire you completed was XX. Today, when you completed the same questionnaire, your score was XX. What do you think of these changes in your symptoms?

If there are very large changes, the therapist should explore with the client which skills they think helped, such as the breathing retraining, activity scheduling, cognitive restructuring, or some combination of these. The client should be encouraged to continue to use the skills in dealing with disaster-related thoughts and beliefs. If more modest decreases are evident, or if the client continues to experience distress despite significant reductions, the therapist should normalize this by informing them that further reductions in symptoms and distress often occur after the CBT-PD has ended, as the person continues to use their skills. If there is less change in symptomatology, the therapist should still emphasize that it may just take some time before the client begins to see a decrease in their symptoms. The client should be encouraged to continue to practice the skills on their own. If in a few weeks the client is still not seeing improvement, a booster session or two can be scheduled.

Showing clients their scores is a concrete way for them to see their progress; however, it is also important to understand how the client feels about their progress:

THERAPIST: How are you feeling now compared with when you began the program? Let's discuss the ways in which you feel you have improved, and also any areas in which you would like to see further improvement. We will take some time at the end of today's session to problem solve about how to address any thoughts, feelings, and situations that continue to feel challenging or problematic.

CLIENT: I do feel better, but there are some things I am still worried about.

THERAPIST: That's understandable. We will spend time today talking about how you can handle upcoming situations.

Overview of Education and Skills

Next, the therapist should review each of the primary components of the treatment (psychoeducation, breathing retraining, activity scheduling, and cognitive restructuring) and discuss with the client what aspects of the treatment they found most helpful. For example, clients who are no longer anxious may not recall how effective breathing retraining was. Reminding them to use their breathing retraining if they start to feel anxious, or experience other posttraumatic overarousal symptoms, increases the chances that they will use this skill in the future.

THERAPIST: Let's review some of the information and skills you've been learning in this program. First, we spent some time talking about the common effects of disaster, such as symptoms of posttraumatic stress disorder, depression, and anxiety. As we have discussed, your reactions to the disaster are similar to the reactions of other people who have had traumatic experiences. It is often helpful to learn about these common reactions in order to put your symptoms into some perspective. Did you find it helpful to learn about common postdisaster reactions?

CLIENT: Yes. I was really surprised to learn that other people were struggling with the same things I was. I don't know why, but it helped me to feel less ashamed.

THERAPIST: Knowing about common symptoms could help you in the future, too. If some symptoms do come back, you will know what they are, and it will be an indication that you should try using some of the skills you learned in this program. So let's review those skills now. In the program, you learned a helpful skill for reducing your physiological arousal and coping with anxiety and tension—breathing retraining. Over the course of the program, I've been pleased to hear about how you practiced this skill and about your ability to use it in a variety of situations where you felt anxious or overstimulated. How has the breathing retraining been helpful? In what situations did you find it helpful?

CLIENT: Well, at first I found it hard to use the breathing. It seemed forced. But what I found was that after only a week or two I could really use it to help me focus. I could catch myself catastrophizing and use the breathing to calm my thinking down. I was even able to use the breathing to focus in the moment so that I could use the 5 Steps of Cognitive Restructuring.

THERAPIST: Perfect. So that is a good thing to remember if you feel too anxious to use the 5 Steps in the moment. Rather than getting stressed and worried that you can't do it, you relax first by breathing and then use the cognitive restructuring skill. Another skill you learned was activity scheduling. Remember that doing more positive and meaningful activities can help improve your mood and can help you target avoidance. Over the course of the treatment you have scheduled more activities into your life. Which activities were most helpful and in what ways?

CLIENT: As you know, I started taking fitness classes again. It was something I used to enjoy, but after we were forced from our home I wasn't close to my gym, and I just didn't feel like going. I had so many other things that seemed more important. But after I found a new gym and started taking classes again I found I really started to look forward to them. And I actually met some new people. I mean, I am not great friends with them, but sometimes we go for coffee after a class.

THERAPIST: So you learned that when you get overwhelmed you have a tendency to stop doing things that make you happy. Now that you know this you can look out for it. If you see yourself starting to pull back from activities, you can make a decision to find ways to keep more active.

CLIENT: That makes sense. If I continue to do things that are fun it will be harder to feel depressed. But once I get depressed it is so much harder to snap out of it.

THERAPIST: Yes. That's how it is for most people. Finally, you learned a skill called cognitive restructuring. This was a primary focus of the program, and we spent a good deal of time on it. This skill has helped you see that unpleasant feelings are often related to inaccurate thoughts. By identifying, challenging, and changing those thoughts you learned you can improve your mood. As we've worked together, I've been impressed by the progress you've made in cognitive restructuring, including your ability to identify and challenge problematic thinking patterns. What stands out for you as having been the most helpful part of cognitive restructuring?

CLIENT: At the beginning, I thought you were telling me that my thinking was wrong. And, I guess in some ways it was. But what I really learned is that I can choose to think about upsetting situations in other ways that make me less upset. Even if a part of me believes my automatic negative thoughts, thinking about it from another perspective makes me feel better.

THERAPIST: Were any of the Problematic Thinking Styles helpful in learning to look at situations from another perspective?

CLIENT: Absolutely! I learned that I overgeneralize. And I mean, a lot of really bad things did happen as a result of the flood, but now I know that doesn't mean that bad things will always happen.

Now I try to catch myself when I overgeneralize, and then I can come up with a less negative thought.

THERAPIST: You have made a lot of progress catching your thinking and replacing negative thoughts with more accurate, less distressing ones. However, as you know, not every 5 Step worksheet results in feeling completely better. Are there specific Action Plans that you developed that you feel were particularly helpful?

CLIENT: Um, like I said, I really like the breathing. I just feel like if I stop and take a moment to focus I can think better. So that is a part of almost all my Action Plans. But I guess I also like the problem-solving. In the past, I would just get overwhelmed by things. But I like that there are specific steps I can take to try and think through a problem. Now when I get anxious about whether there will be another flood, I use my breathing to help me focus and then I review the Action Plan I came up with for the situation, which involved making sure my valuables and important documents are stored on the top floor, that my radio and other electronics are charged, and that my first-aid kit is complete.

THERAPIST: Well, I think you have done a great job learning these skills in this program. Like any skill, such as drawing, sports, or playing a musical instrument, you get better and it comes more naturally with repeated practice over time. We have found that many clients actually continue to improve after therapy is over. For this reason, it's important for you to keep practicing the skills that you've learned in therapy, so that they will become more natural and automatic.

CLIENT: That makes sense.

Aftercare Plan

Building on the review of the skills, in the last part of the therapy the therapist works with the client to identify any areas they may still be concerned about and helps them identify skills for handling them. Together, the client and therapist complete the Aftercare Plan Worksheet (Handout 30) in session.

First, the client lists the things in their life that have improved with the program. This is different from the review of symptoms but could certainly include improved mood. Typical responses might be feeling happier, improved functioning at work or school, a better relationship with a significant other or children, or engaging in more activities.

Next, the client identifies areas on which they want to continue to work, or any upcoming specific challenges they expect. For example, some clients may want to continue to work on getting out more, decreasing their anger, or improving relationships. Upcoming challenges might include attending a large gathering, needing to talk to a boss about a mistake, or going on a date.

In the next section of the Aftercare Plan Worksheet the therapist helps the client identify specific skills that can address the concerns, for example, using activity scheduling to get out more, or cognitive restructuring to challenge thoughts related to anger or feelings of worthlessness. For upcoming situations, clients can anticipate what thoughts they may have in those situations and can do a 5 Step worksheet in advance. For example, the client could challenge the thought "My boss will fire me when I tell him I made a mistake" before going to speak to the boss.

The last section of Handout 30 provides space for the therapist to help the client identify strategies they can use to help them manage distress after the treatment ends. For all clients, reviewing past handouts and worksheets should be added to this list as a strategy for managing distress. These materials are essentially a mini–treatment manual that has been customized for the client. Not only can they review the information on each skill, but also, by reviewing their worksheets, the client can see how they have handled other upsetting situations.

Another possibility is to help the client to identify a friend they could ask for support. This can be especially helpful if the client has already involved a loved one in the program who is familiar with the worksheets, the information, and the skills taught. Some clients even choose to teach a support person the skills because they have found them so helpful that they want their support person to get the same benefit. In some cases, a support person could even attend part of a therapy session with the client to get an overview of the skills and a better understanding of the treatment. This support person can then remind the client of the specific skills that they have used in the past and can encourage the client to use them again if they begin to have symptoms. For some clients, sharing the number for the National Suicide Prevention Lifeline (1-800-273-8255) might be appropriate.

Finally, it is important to end the therapy by providing positive feedback and encouragement. If appropriate, the therapist should emphasize that many clients do not experience the full benefits of the treatment right away. They should explain to clients that they may continue to improve in the months to come as they practice the skills they learned in the program. Some of the following statements may be helpful:

- "I have enjoyed working with you and wish you much luck in the future."

- "It's evident that you are feeling much better and that your hard work has paid off."

- "You had some difficult weeks there, but you persisted with courage and patience, and I can see that your efforts paid off for you."

- "You mentioned that you were disappointed that you had not made more progress in the program. I'd like to tell you that it is not unusual for clients to express the same feelings and then discover that they feel better gradually as time goes on."

- "It takes time to sort out what happened in the treatment. You may continue to feel better as time goes on, especially if you continue to use the skills and techniques you have learned."

- "I think that you're a very strong person to stick with this program and that you've made some definite gains."

- "You have put a lot of hard work into this program, and you have made a lot of (or some) definite gains."

- "I know this program was difficult for you to complete. In fact, there were a few days (weeks) when you wanted to discontinue the program. But you stuck with it and made some real progress."

If the therapist believes the client is in need of continued or more intensive treatment, a referral can also be considered; however, it is best to have the client try and work through the distress for at least a few weeks on their own. In many cases, they will be successful and will be empowered by using their skills and their own supports. Ultimately, though, if the client does need more therapy, we recommend that the therapist who has treated them in the CBT-PD program should not continue working with that client in another type of therapy, even if they are skilled in that additional therapy. This transition from one type of treatment to the next by the same therapist could inadvertently send the message to the client that they can continue on in therapy indefinitely as long as they continue to experience distress. If another clinician is truly unavailable, the therapist should consider formally ending treatment. Then, if several months later the client would like to resume therapy, the therapist can begin a new course of treatment.

CONCLUSION

From the beginning of CBT-PD, the therapist sets the expectation that the program is time limited. Throughout the course of the treatment, the therapist works to build the client's confidence in their ability to manage symptoms effectively on their own. By reminding the client about what has been effective over the course of the treatment, the therapist helps the client recognize their progress, identify any potential upcoming challenges, and problem solve potential solutions. Although many clients will show substantial improvement, some may continue to experience symptoms. Clients should be reminded that continued improvement can be expected with practice.

PART **III** OTHER ISSUES

12 SPECIAL CONSIDERATIONS FOR THERAPISTS

Disaster mental health presents some unique challenges. After a disaster, many people may have a sudden and immediate need for treatment, which can easily overwhelm the capacity of local mental health professionals with experience treating posttrauma reactions related to disasters or other events. Therefore, therapists who have less experience treating these or related problems are often called on to help. Such therapists may themselves be learning new treatment approaches, such as the Cognitive Behavior Therapy for Postdisaster Distress (CBT-PD) program, while they are working with new clients who are in acute distress.

In addition to the challenge of learning new treatment methods, therapists are often survivors and clinicians at the same time, because disasters affect both people individually and the community as a whole. Therefore, therapists are often struggling with some of the same difficulties and stressors as their clients, such as property destruction and repairs, temporary housing, financial hardships, illness or injury, and disruption of work and everyday life. Therapists themselves may also be coping with residual posttraumatic reactions, such as difficulty sleeping, upsetting memories of the disaster, fear and

https://doi.org/10.1037/0000237-012
Treatment for Postdisaster Distress: A Transdiagnostic Approach, by J. L. Hamblen and K. T. Mueser

anxiety, or some combination of these. The unique stresses associated with treating disaster survivors can compound the often emotionally taxing nature of psychotherapy as usually provided, which involves an intense and intimate relationship between a client in distress and a clinician. In this chapter, we address these common issues for therapists who are responding to the needs of disaster survivors. Our aims in this chapter are to increase therapists' ability to help people who are in acute distress process their traumatic experiences and rebuild their lives after a disaster while at the same time enhancing their own personal resiliency and reducing their experience of stress.

LIMITED EXPERIENCE TREATING DISASTER SURVIVORS

Disasters occur with little or no warning. Although some geographic regions are more prone to certain types of events, such as hurricanes or floods, other events, such as mass violence and accidents, can occur anywhere, at any time. The unexpected nature of disasters means that clinicians who lack special expertise in disaster mental health are often called on to use their clinical skills in new and different ways to help the influx of people whose lives have just been turned upside down. Clinicians may feel unprepared to treat disaster survivors and at the same time find it difficult or impossible to obtain outside training or support for their clinical work, yet their experience, skills, and compassion are sorely needed to reduce the high distress and impaired functioning of survivors who are often living in the same community as the clinician.

Clinicians should rest assured that they are capable of rising to the occasion, learning new approaches to treating the posttraumatic effects of disasters, and effectively treating disaster survivors in need of their services. This book is designed to provide therapists with the guidance needed to competently deliver the CBT-PD program and alleviate the postdisaster distress in their clients' lives. In the early chapters of this book, we provided the background and theoretical framework for conceptualizing postdisaster reactions, to help therapists better understand their clients' reactions and how to help them. We then gave specific guidance for each component of the CBT-PD program, including sample dialogues and case vignettes to illustrate the techniques, which are supplemented with educational handouts and worksheets to facilitate the teaching of each of the skills in the program. Finally, we devoted a specific chapter to challenges that may arise when using cognitive restructuring and another chapter that alerts therapists to special considerations when treating survivors of specific types of disasters.

We recognize that some therapists may feel a little uncomfortable when first using the CBT-PD program with their clients because they must quickly become familiar with the information and skills taught in the program. Some background in cognitive behavior therapy or trauma work will be helpful to clinicians who have not worked with disaster survivors before, but it is not a prerequisite to learning the program and developing expertise in it. Clinicians should get thoroughly acquainted with the educational material presented in the handouts and worksheets for clients by reading them carefully. (These materials are available on the American Psychological Association [APA] website at http://pubs.apa.org/books/supp/hamblen, where they can be downloaded and printed out for clinical use.) In addition, we recommend that all clinicians who are learning the CBT-PD program develop some personal expertise with the three core skills taught in the program—breathing retraining, activity scheduling, and cognitive restructuring—through practicing and learning these skills by routinely incorporating them into their lives for a period of at least several weeks and up to several months. Seeing and experiencing how these skills work in their own lives will provide a better understanding of them and how to teach them to their clients than any training could deliver.

Therapists are also encouraged to seek and engage in peer supervision and/or case consultation, especially when there are other therapists in the area who are providing the CBT-PD program as well. As we discuss in Chapter 13, the nature of some disasters have common themes of impact on people's lives and their outlook on the world, and consulting with others who are using the same program can help identify strategies that are effective in addressing some of these themes. Therapists who are looking for training opportunities to bolster their skills will find trainings in the CBT-PD program, as well as more broadly focused cognitive behavioral interventions for posttraumatic stress disorder, anxiety disorders, or depression, can be useful.

DUAL ROLE OF SURVIVOR AND THERAPIST

It is not uncommon for clinicians who are responding to the mental health needs of people recently exposed to a disaster to also have been affected by the disaster, placing them in the dual role of therapist and survivor. Like their clients, therapists often have to deal with the same or similar practical, real-life consequences of the disaster. They may also be experiencing some of the same posttraumatic reactions as their clients, such as recurrent distressing memories of the event or sleep difficulties. Experiencing these and other symptoms may help the therapist empathize with the client's situation, but unless the therapist successfully copes with or deals with the effects of the disaster on their own life these problems can interfere with their ability to be maximally effective in treating their clients. This is especially important in terms of the therapist's own thoughts and beliefs about the disaster, how they responded to it, and the meanings they attach to it. If the therapist holds the same or similar inaccurate disaster-related thoughts or beliefs as the client, they will be less able to help them identify evidence against their inaccurate thoughts and replace them with more accurate ones.

In the next section, we address how therapists can become aware of their own reactions to a disaster and how to address them so those reactions do not interfere with their clinical work. We then discuss how to use the shared experience of a disaster with the client as a therapeutic tool to enhance their effectiveness as a clinician.

The Importance of Addressing Therapists' Postdisaster Reactions

For illustrative purposes, we begin with a vignette of a therapist, Rita, who recently experienced a hurricane that has had a significant impact on her and her family's life.[1]

Rita is a 35-year-old married social worker with two elementary school–age children. Her house flooded after a major storm in Houston, Texas, dropped more than 17 inches of rain in a single day, leading to widespread flooding. No one was hurt in Rita's family, but their house is currently uninhabitable. Luckily, her in-laws live about 30 minutes away. The in-laws have one spare room, which the whole family is currently sharing it. Because they are staying outside of their school district, there is no school bus, and therefore either Rita or her husband must leave early each morning to drop their children off at school on their way to work. Throughout the day, calls must be made to contractors, to their insurance company, and to the Federal Emergency Management Agency (FEMA) to follow up on their flood insurance claim. The soonest a contractor has been able to commit to coming is 4 months away, and the price they have been given is significantly higher than they expected. Rita and her husband have scheduled the repair but are continuing to make calls to see if they can find anyone who can come sooner or who charges less. Meanwhile, any free time Rita or her husband has is spent at the house trying to do as much cleaning up as they can on their own. They have managed to remove the damaged carpet and the kitchen cabinets, but the house is still far from livable. The kids are unhappy. They miss their toys, their rooms, and their friends. They cannot just go outside and see their friends, and they are upset that their parents don't seem to have time to take them on play dates. They are acting up at home, and there is a lot of shouting and misbehavior. Although Rita's in-laws have not complained, she feels guilty because she knows the situation is hard on them.

---

[1]The personal details in the vignette have been disguised to protect the clinician's confidentiality.

In the next two scenarios, we illustrate the impact of difficulty versus success in Rita's management of her postdisaster reactions on her ability to help her client critically examine and challenge her own thoughts and beliefs about the event. In the first scenario, Rita has negative feelings about her postdisaster circumstances that are related to inaccurate beliefs she has about how she is handling the events following the hurricane.

> *Although Rita's in-laws invited her family to stay, she worries they are wearing out their welcome. Rita thinks she is failing as a mother because she has a short temper and is constantly yelling at the kids. She knows the kids are having a hard time and believes she should be more patient with them, but her irritability is interfering with her parenting. Worse, when she does yell, she can see the look in her mother-in-law's eye passing judgment, and she believes her mother-in-law thinks she is letting her family down. Finally, Rita is frustrated that all of her free time is spent trying to fix the house, and she blames FEMA for not providing more support to families sooner.*

Rita is working with a client who has also been displaced from her home and is struggling to balance the challenges this presents. In one session the client brings up the thought "I am letting my family down because I am so distracted by all the work to be done around the home repairs."

CLIENT: I feel like I am letting my family down all the time.

RITA: Okay, let's do a 5 Step worksheet on that. Can you tell me the last time you had this thought? What happened?

CLIENT: The kids wanted to go to their friend's house. We were all invited over to play at their pool. But I said I couldn't go because my husband and I had to meet a repairman at the house. My in-laws couldn't take them, either. They said it wasn't fair, and then I just lost it and yelled at them.

RITA: So what is the specific thought you would challenge?

CLIENT: I guess that I am letting my family down because I am so distracted by the home repairs.

RITA: Okay, now what evidence do you have against the thought that you are letting your family down?

CLIENT: I don't know. I just feel like I'm so busy with other things. I don't have time for my kids, my husband, or myself. And I am moody and yell a lot.

RITA: How might others look at the situation?

CLIENT: I think they would agree that I haven't been spending as much time with them as I used to.

RITA: I see. Can you think of any examples of when you are not letting your family down—where you are actually doing a good job?

CLIENT: Not really.

The problem with this scenario is that when the client tries to come up with evidence against the thought, Rita, who herself feels similarly, has trouble guiding the client toward evidence against the thought. Rita cannot see another way to think about the situation, and therefore her questions do not elicit evidence against the thought. She is stuck, and so she inadvertently reinforces the client's belief that she is letting her family down.

In the second scenario, Rita has coped with and overcome some mild post-disaster reactions and is not experiencing any symptoms. She has a balanced outlook on life despite the stress she is under, and she does not harbor any strong inaccurate postdisaster beliefs about herself or other people.

> *Rita is currently dealing with a lot of stressors related to the disaster, but she feels she is fortunate that no one in her family was hurt or injured. Rita counts herself lucky because she and her husband kept their jobs and their kids can still attend their regular school. Although things are a little tense with her in-laws, they are working on it together. Rita feels good that her family has a safe place to live, and she is confident that they will eventually be able to move back into their home.*

In this second scenario, Rita is able to more quickly recognize that her client's thoughts about neglecting her family are not completely accurate, enabling her to effectively guide the client in identifying evidence against those thoughts. Picking up the prior vignette from the point at which the client identified the thought "I am letting my family down because I am so distracted by all the work to be done around the home repairs," we illustrate how a change in the therapist's response can lead to a different outcome:

RITA: So what is the specific thought you would challenge?

CLIENT: I guess that I am letting my family down because I am so distracted by the home repairs.

RITA: Okay, now what evidence do you have against the thought that you are letting your family down? Why are you spending so much time away from your family?

CLIENT: Well, there's just so much to do. If I put it off it will just delay the amount of time it takes to get moved back in.

RITA: So you are not doing this because you prefer to be away?

CLIENT: Of course not.

RITA: Or because you are lazy and don't have the energy?

CLIENT: I am tired, but no. I really feel like I have to focus on these things in order to make things better for my family.

RITA: That sounds like evidence against the thought that you are letting your family down.

CLIENT: Yeah. I'll write that down.

Other questions that might lead to evidence against the thought are "Have you done anything with the kids lately?" "What does your husband say about whether you are letting family down?" and "What do the kids say?" These questions may have elicited responses such as "We went to the playground yesterday after school" and "The kids have been great. Most of the time they say they understand that I need to spend time at the house. But this time, when my in-laws couldn't take them to their friend's they got upset." When Rita was better able to help the client examine her thought, she was more effectively able to help reduce the client's distress instead of reinforcing the inaccurate thought.

Self-Assessment of the Impact of the Disaster

Therapists can determine the impact the disaster has had on them through self-assessment. Just as they can use the Short Post-Traumatic Stress Disorder Rating Interview, Expanded Version (SPRINT-E; Norris & Davidson, 2007) to identify clients who have significant distress related to the disaster and to track improvements in disaster-related distress over the course of the CBT-PD program, therapists who have had significant exposure to the disaster can complete the SPRINT-E themselves to evaluate their own reactions to the event. If the therapist is experiencing significant distress related to the disaster, they can use the SPRINT-E repeatedly over time to monitor reductions in their distress, similar to how the instrument is used with clients. Self-awareness of one's own reactions to the disaster, as well as self-management when appropriate, is critical for the therapist to ensure that they can be as effective as possible in working with their clients.

A score of 3 or higher on the SPRINT-E indicates that the therapist is having some postdisaster reactions and that they could benefit from using the skills taught in the CBT-PD program. Scores of 7 and above indicate more severe postdisaster symptoms, which are important to address before providing the CBT-PD program to others. Therapists who have SPRINT-E scores above 3, including those with higher scores (e.g., above 7) and more severe symptoms, are encouraged to use the skills taught in the CBT-PD program to manage their own distressing symptoms and to monitor the effects of their self-management by repeated administration of the instrument.

Breathing retraining and activity scheduling are highly effective strategies for managing stress that therapists can readily incorporate into their lives. Furthermore, practice and mastery of the cognitive restructuring skills taught in the CBT-PD program (including routine use of the Problematic Thinking Styles Log Worksheet [Handout 26 in Appendix B on the APA website at http://pubs.apa.org/books/supp/hamblen] and the 5 Steps of Cognitive Restructuring Worksheet [Handout 28 in Appendix B at http://pubs.apa.org/books/supp/hamblen]) can enable the therapist to identify and change their own negative, inaccurate beliefs about the disaster. Completing the Action Plan Worksheet (Handout 29 in Appendix B at http://pubs.apa.org/books/supp/hamblen) can help them come up with practical solutions to many of the real-life problems associated with a disaster.

Regular practice and use of these skills will be effective at reducing most of the postdisaster symptoms therapists may be experiencing over a 3- to 6-week period. However, if SPRINT-E scores do not decline during this time period, or they decline only a little (e.g., remain over 7), the therapist should consider seeking treatment for themselves. Therapists who are experiencing significant symptoms of suicidality or substance use disorder should seek outside treatment immediately and refrain from treating clients.

The Benefit of Shared Experience and the Role of Self-Disclosure

The fact that the therapist may share the experience of the disaster with the client can be of therapeutic benefit to the client. In usual practice, therapists share very little personal information about themselves with their clients; for example, if a client talks about having been sexually abused as a child, the therapist usually does not reveal whether they also were abused. However, after a widespread disaster in which almost everyone has been affected in some way, it may sometimes be useful for the therapist to draw on their own experience when working with a client. As with any therapeutic self-disclosure, the purpose should be to help the client.

For example, "I know, I can't believe how hard it is to find a contractor" or "I miss having down time. Sometimes I wish I could just go to movies instead of always working on the house" are modestly revealing comments that may make the client feel the therapist has a deeper understanding of what they are experiencing because they are currently dealing with the same issues. Of course, therapists should not reveal deep personal struggles (e.g., "I'm worried if my claim does not get processed that I might not be able to pay my bills," "The stress I am under is taking a toll on my relationship with my husband"), because these types of comments could shift the attention away from the client to the therapist's own issues.

Limited, selective self-disclosure can also be useful in helping clients challenge or modify unhelpful beliefs. For example, after the September 11th, 2001, terrorist attacks, one therapist used her own experience to help a client who had trouble letting go of a belief even after generating sufficient evidence against the thought. After September 11th, many people in New York were afraid to fly, enter tall buildings, or even take the subway. Each of these activities were seen as potential terrorist targets. Clients being seen as part of New York's Project Liberty enhanced services program (the disaster response program initiated after the September 11th attacks; Donahue et al., 2006) frequently identified thoughts such as "It is unsafe to fly" or "New York City is a terrorist target" as ones to challenge. In the following example, though, after a client was unsuccessful in changing a thought despite abundant evidence against it, a therapist uses her own experiences to encourage the client to conduct a cost–benefit analysis using the Payoff Matrix we described in Chapter 10.

THERAPIST: Even though you came up with some evidence against the thought "New York is a terrorist target," it sounds like you still think the evidence is stronger to support that New York is a target. I get that. It's hard to know if the thought is accurate or not. My husband was in the Twin Towers signing papers earlier that morning on 9/11, and I know sometimes I wonder if it is safe to live in New York City. For me, the pros of living here outweigh the cons. Could we try and complete a Payoff Matrix and see how that might influence your thoughts?

COMMENTARY: The therapist uses some self-disclosure to acknowledge the shared experience; however, the self-disclosure is brief, and the therapy is quickly redirected toward the client.

CLIENT: I guess so. What do I have to lose?

THERAPIST: That's a good question. Let's start by looking at the pros and cons of keeping the thought "New York is a terrorist target." What are the pros? What are the advantages to holding that thought?

CLIENT: Well, if I continue to believe that New York is a terrorist target I can be on the lookout for danger.

THERAPIST: And what does that look like?

CLIENT: Well, I can try and avoid crowds, like a parade, sporting event, or concert. And I can be on the lookout for people who don't look right.

THERAPIST: And would that keep your family safe?

CLIENT: Well, maybe. Yeah, I think we would be safer if we avoided those things.

THERAPIST: If you had been on the lookout on 9/11, would you have avoided going into the World Trade Center that day?

CLIENT: I mean, I probably wouldn't have seen plane coming, so I guess not.

THERAPIST: Okay, so an advantage of holding onto that thought is that you would try and avoid being in places where you could be a target, such as crowds. Right?

CLIENT: Right.

THERAPIST: Okay. But it sounds like you also recognize that you can't foresee every possible danger. Something could still happen, even if you had your guard up.

CLIENT: I guess so.

THERAPIST: Okay, now let's talk about possible disadvantages of keeping the thought. Can you think of any disadvantages to thinking New York is a probable terrorist target?

CLIENT: Well, obviously we couldn't go to those places—any place there might be a crowd.

THERAPIST: So you wouldn't go to the Macy's Day Parade or go to a concert?

CLIENT: Right.

THERAPIST: What about walking around Central Park, going shopping, or skating at Rockefeller Center? Or taking tourists from out of town to the Statue of Liberty?

CLIENT: Probably not.

THERAPIST: Last week I had out of town guests. I took them to a show on Broadway. Would you do that, or would that be another place you'd avoid as well?

CLIENT: I think I would have to avoid Broadway shows, too, if I believed that New York was a target.

COMMENTARY: Here, the therapist used self-disclose to make the consequences of holding the belief more real.

THERAPIST: Okay, now let's consider some of the advantages of changing the thought to something like, "New York *is* a safe place to live." Can you think of any advantages to thinking that New York is safe?

CLIENT: Well, we could go anywhere and do anything we wanted. There are lots of great attractions in New York. That's one of the reasons we moved here in the first place.

THERAPIST: Have you been to any crowded places recently that were fun?

CLIENT: Actually, yes. We went to a Yankees game. We are huge baseball fans. It was actually really fun.

THERAPIST: So if you changed the thought you'd be freer to do more fun things?

CLIENT: Yes.

THERAPIST: What about other advantages to changing the thought? I found when I stopped focusing on all the bad stuff that could happen, I was actually a lot more relaxed. If you were able to change the thought, do you think you would be less on guard?

CLIENT: Definitely. That would be an advantage.

COMMENTARY: Here, the therapist used her own experience of feeling more relaxed to help the client explore whether he would have a similar reaction. This was an important consideration because clients sometimes discount the toll that negative feelings can take on them.

THERAPIST: Okay, and what are the disadvantages of changing the thought? Are there any possible negative consequences to thinking that New York is safe?

CLIENT: Well, like I said, we might go places where something bad would happen.

THERAPIST: So you'd be putting yourself in harm's way?

CLIENT: Yes.

THERAPIST: All right, so now that we have considered the pros and cons, you can see that the advantage to keeping the thought is it might keep you safe, and the disadvantage is that it prevents you from doing things you want to do and makes you feel on guard. So the question is, is it worth it?

CLIENT: You mean, is it worth it to give up those things to be safe? I don't know.

THERAPIST: Okay, well how much safer are you?

CLIENT: What do you mean?

THERAPIST: Well, you said there was no way to know the World Trade Center would be hit by a plane on 9/11, right? So if you had had an appointment to sign some papers that morning, like my husband did, you would have gone?

CLIENT: I guess so.

THERAPIST: So even though you would avoid some places, you might not avoid the right places at the right time.

CLIENT: Mm-hmm.

THERAPIST: And what about what you would be giving up? Seems like you had a great time at the ball game.

CLIENT: I did.

THERAPIST: So, is it worth it? From what you are saying, there is no way to know what situations to avoid, and instead you would just be missing out on things that are enjoyable.

CLIENT: I see what you are saying, but . . .

THERAPIST: For me, it is a question of how I want to live my life.

CLIENT: What do you mean?

THERAPIST: Well, some of my clients have examined the thought that "New York is unsafe" and decided that it's not accurate, that New York really is a safe place to live, or as safe as anywhere else, so they feel safe living here. Other people who have examined the same thought have been less convinced that it's inaccurate, and that another terrorist attack won't happen again. For me, I decided that I think New York is safe enough for me to live in. When I weigh the pros and cons, I can see that I am happier when I am out with my family and friends enjoying New York. I don't want to stay shut in, even if it might keep me a little safer. I'm not willing, partly because I am not sure staying shut in would keep me safer and partly because it's just not how I want to live my life. It seems like you too feel like you would be missing out if you tried to avoid going to crowded events. So, you will have to decide if that is how you want to live your life.

COMMENTARY: Again, the therapist is selectively choosing to share information that she believes could be helpful to the client.

CLIENT: I see what you're saying now. I did really have fun at the ball game. And I am not sure anyone really knows how to stay completely safe. It's really too bad that the world is like this.

THERAPIST: It is. But the question is whether you are going to be controlled by those fears or not. I've decided I love New York and I want to live here. So that's what I am going to do. You have to decide for yourself whether it is worth it to you.

It is important for the therapist to carefully attend to the impact of their self-disclosure on the client. In some cases, such disclosure can help clients feel more understood; however, there is also the risk that if the therapist's feelings are different enough from those of the client, the client may feel invalidated and may be less forthcoming about their thoughts and feelings in the future. Being attentive to how the client responds to the therapist's self-disclosure, and whether it seems helpful or not, can inform them about the potential use of self-disclosure in the future.

MANAGING STRESS

An issue that all therapists face, and that is often compounded when a disaster has recently occurred, is coping with stress. This additional stress may be due to a multitude of factors, including the direct and often-widespread consequences of the disasters, the acute distress experienced by many survivors and the desire of therapists to help them, and the internal and external pressures therapists may feel to work long hours and do as much as possible to help during or after the crisis. The result is that therapists may neglect their own needs while attending to those of others. Managing stress effectively is essential in order for therapists to do their best with clients and to have the stamina to function well for as long as the postdisaster period lasts.

Therapists may be familiar with a variety of self-care strategies from their usual work with their clients; however, knowing about self-care and using it are not the same thing. Good sleep, exercise, healthy eating, connecting with others, and scheduling some down time for oneself serve as the foundation for self-care. Therapists can take these and other steps to improve their ability to manage stress. In the sections that follow, we suggest several strategies, many of which are included in the CBT-PD program.

Increase Social Connection

Social support from friends and family is a means of reducing stress (Hensel et al., 2015; Stevanovic & Rupert, 2004). Just as social support serves as a buffer against developing postdisaster distress, so too does it protect one from becoming stressed and exhausted. Long hours, combined with trying to address what may feel like the endless and desperate needs of clients, can result in therapists taking important time away from friends and family and "recharging" their energy as needed.

Social support can come from different sources. Spending time with friends, colleagues, significant others, and children can be rejuvenating. In some cases, neglecting these relationships, such as not spending time with one's children or partner because of long work hours, can lead to added stress and guilt. Therapists should plan ahead to spend time with colleagues, friends, and family, and scheduling such events should be given the same priority as any work-related appointments. Planning ahead for specific times to spend with friends and family can help the therapist feel more relaxed by knowing that there will be time to connect with people they care about. In Exhibit 12.1, we provide suggestions of ways to increase social connectedness at work and home.

EXHIBIT 12.1 Activities to Increase Social Connectedness

Home activities	Work activities
Have family dinners	Pick a day where colleagues all eat lunch together
Go for a bike ride with friends	
Schedule a weekly family game night	Go for a walk or jog with a coworker before or after work
Go on a date	
Call a friend	Start the day with a group mindful meditation
Attend an exercise class with a friend	Schedule an office potluck once a month
Go out to lunch	Plan an office outing after work, such as going for drinks or trying something new, such as painting pottery or going to an "escape room"
Join a book club	

Reduce Stress

There are a wide variety of stress reduction techniques therapists can use. Therapists will already be familiar with the breathing retraining taught in the CBT-PD program. Breathing retraining is an excellent and easy-to-learn technique to manage stress and focus attention. Yoga is another popular and effective stress-reduction technique. There are many different types of yoga, and it is increasingly available in many communities. For those without access to a studio, many classes are streamed online and available on demand, which makes them very convenient.

In recent years, increasing numbers of people have been turning to mindfulness and meditation as ways to cope with stress. *Mindfulness* involves paying attention to the present moment, in a nonjudgmental and nonreactive way (Kabat-Zinn, 2013). There are numerous ways to learn how to be more mindful and practice mindfulness. In many cases, the exercises do not take very long and can be used in the moment to refocus. For example, paying attention to the taste and texture of chocolate on one's tongue; focusing on one's breathing; and mindful watching, whereby the person consciously attends to a specific object with the goal of focusing their attention, are all quick and easy mindfulness exercises. Meditation is a component of mindfulness, and there are many different types of meditation from which to choose. Therapists are encouraged to try several different strategies to see which ones work best for them. There are now several mindfulness apps that offer a variety of tools and strategies that therapists (and clients) can try, including Mindfulness Coach and Calm, both of which are available for download in iTunes (https://apps.apple.com/us/app/mindfulness-coach/id804284729 and https://apps.apple.com/us/app/

calm/id571800810, respectively) and Google Play (https://play.google.com/
store/apps/details?id=gov.va.mobilehealth.ncptsd.mindfulnesscoach&hl=
en_US&gl=US and https://play.google.com/store/apps/details?id=com.calm.
android&hl=en_US&gl=US, respectively).

Set Limits on Work and Schedule Rewarding and Meaningful Activities

We strongly encourage therapists to set limits on the number of hours they
work. Seven years after the bombing of the Alfred P. Murrah Federal Building
in Oklahoma City, Norris et al. (2005) interviewed providers about their
experiences in providing disaster mental health services to the community.
Providers frequently spoke of "self-imposed pressure" or an "internal need to
hurry, hurry, hurry" that resulted in them putting in long hours for an extended
period of time. Some said they found it hard to keep a professional distance
from the pain of the people they were treating. In sum, no matter how
distressed their clients may be, or how rewarding the clinical work is, therapists need time to engage in other activities in order to rejuvenate their energy
and spirits.

Even therapists who do not work extended hours may need to pay attention to their need to engage in rewarding and meaningful activities outside
of work. People who are under stress can easily become overwhelmed and
reduce or stop doing some of the things they enjoy most and care the most
about in life and, just like for everyone else, engaging in fewer rewarding and
meaningful activities takes a toll on the enjoyment of life, dampens the spirits,
and increases the risk of depression.

The activity scheduling component of the CBT-PD program is an excellent
way to shift attention away from work and toward alternate rewarding and
meaningful activities. Therapists are encouraged to start with Handout 22,
Personally Meaningful Life Areas (in Appendix B on the APA website at http://
pubs.apa.org/books/supp/hamblen), and identify at least one life area they
want to focus on other than work. Next, they should identify specific activities
to engage in that can help fulfill that goal. For example, if the therapist picks
"intimate relationships with a partner" as their identified life area, then activities should include concrete things they can do to improve that life area, such
as spending time together, asking about their partner's day, or showing affec-
tion. The therapist may also want to identify additional activities unrelated
to personal life goals that are simply enjoyable (e.g., reading a good book).
Just as therapists help clients schedule and follow through on these activities,
they themselves need to commit to a time in the week when they will do the
activity and follow through on it as planned, no matter how busy they are or
whether they feel like it at the moment.

Engage in Values Clarification

It is sometimes difficult for people who are under high levels of stress to remember what is most important and meaningful to them in their lives, such as their family life, work, volunteer activities, or spirituality. Recognizing and reconnecting to values can help therapists identify concrete choices that create a more fulfilling work and home experience. Many exercises are available to do this. Here is one example:

1. Imagine that it is many years in the future and someone has decided to throw you a party. Consider what the party would be like. Where it would be? Who would be there?

2. Think of three people who would speak at your party and what you would want them to say about the kind of person you are, what you accomplished, what you cared about, and your effect on other people.

3. Reflect on the three most important qualities that you want to be said about you by each speaker. For example, would you want to be described as caring, giving, selfless, fun, a risk-taker, smart, hardworking, intelligent, a great parent, a great son or daughter, a good friend, conscientious, understanding? There is no right or wrong answer.

4. Knowing what qualities you value can help you identify personal goals. Identify one goal to work on.

5. Identify steps to meet that goal.

When therapists are aware of their values and goals, they can achieve a better balance between their work and the rest of their lives. For example, after completing the exercise we just provided, some people realize that, looking back, they wished they had spent more time with family, whereas others may feel that they want to do more to help other people, outside of their families. By taking the time to reflect on what is most important, therapists can decide how they can best spend their time. Even if the exercise does not result in a change in behavior, remembering what it is about the work that is fulfilling can be a buffer against stress.

CONCLUSION

Responding to a disaster raises some unique issues for providers. Being aware of these issues can help therapists be better prepared to respond effectively to their clients' needs. First, those new to disaster mental health response may find they are learning as they go. Few therapists have prior experience dealing with disasters, and even in communities where certain types of disasters are more prevalent (e.g., hurricanes) therapists may have more experience but not be familiar with the CBT-PD program. We recommend that therapists interested in the treatment of postdisaster distress read this book and the educational handouts with care and practice the skills in their own lives in preparation for an event.

A second unique issue that can arise in disaster mental health work is the dual role of being both a therapist and a survivor. Whereas some events, such as a shooting or a tornado, are more contained, others, such as a hurricane, have effects that are more widespread, increasing the chances that therapists are also affected by it. If therapists are going to be optimally effective in helping clients challenge inaccurate thoughts, they must be able to recognize which thoughts are not supported by the evidence. Therefore, we recommend that all therapists who have been directly affected by the disaster take a self-assessment (e.g., the SPRINT-E) before initiating work with clients, to determine their level of postdisaster distress. Even low levels of symptoms should be attended to, either by working through the skills taught in CBT-PD or by seeking one's own treatment.

A last consideration we addressed is that disaster mental health work can be extremely stressful. Therapists often feel an internal pressure to help others manage their postdisaster reactions, sometimes at the expense of their own needs. In this chapter, we have reminded therapists about the importance of attending to their own needs, and we have provided some basic strategies to manage stress.

Despite the challenges, therapists often find disaster work to be incredibly meaningful and fulfilling. Although all therapy is directed at improving the quality of a client's life, being part of a disaster mental health response goes beyond the individual client. When disasters are intentional, such as terrorism or mass violence, therapists help restore a sense of safety and trust in their communities. Even when disasters are naturally caused, therapists bring communities together by helping people reengage with friends and families. After a disaster, when many people feel at their most powerless, therapists make contributions toward recovery by offering hope and assistance that has an impact throughout the community.

13

APPLYING CBT-PD TO DIFFERENT TYPES OF DISASTERS

To the survivor, each person's experience of a disaster is unique. Even when other people have been through the same, or similar, events, such as a hurricane, shooting, or fire, their hurricane, shooting, or fire occurred in a specific context that can be fully understood only by them alone. And so, every event is different. But as our colleague Dr. Fran Norris used to say, "Every event is different and every event is the same."

Regardless of the nature and specifics of the disaster, including whether the disaster is natural (e.g., flood, hurricane), technological (e.g., industrial accident), or intentional (e.g., mass shooting, terrorist attack), many people's reactions are similar, as we have noted throughout the chapters. They experience fear and anxiety, whether the fear is about a future attack, another storm, or a health crisis. They feel sad about the losses they have experienced, whether the losses are of costly or sentimentally valued possessions after a natural disaster, a loved one, or the sense of safety and security they once had. They are often angry that the world can be so unfair and believe that they are owed something in return for their suffering. Some events generate national and media attention, such as the September 11, 2001,

https://doi.org/10.1037/0000237-013
Treatment for Postdisaster Distress: A Transdiagnostic Approach, by J. L. Hamblen and K. T. Mueser

terrorist attacks ("September 11 Attacks," 2020); the 2004 Indian Ocean tsunami ("2004 Indian Ocean Earthquake and Tsunami," 2020); and Hurricane Katrina in 2005 ("Hurricane Katrina," 2020). In each of these cases, donations poured in from around the world, and funds were established to help victims. Even aid can lead to difficult feelings, however, whether it is anxiety over when promised assistance will arrive, anger over some survivors getting more than others, or something else. In other disasters, where little or no assistance is available, survivors often feel that their experiences and hardships did not receive the attention and support they deserved. Finally, survivors often experience guilt and shame. Many question their own actions at the time of the event and look back in anguish, wishing they had made different decisions. They may also feel ashamed that, even long after the event, they are continuing to struggle and have difficulty "getting on" with their lives.

Despite these common reactions, and the unique facets of each person's experience, different types of disasters can lead to specific posttraumatic challenges. In this chapter, we discuss some important ways in which disasters differ, and the particular challenges associated with them, as well as how the Cognitive Behavior Therapy for Postdisaster Distress (CBT-PD) program can be used to help survivors overcome them. Although space limitations preclude a discussion of every type of disaster, we describe some of the unique aspects of different types of disasters and provide suggestions for how to address them. Factors such as intentionality, ongoing threat, property damage, displacement, and disruption of community services are some of the important variables that must be recognized in order for the program to be optimally effective.

TERRORISM AND MASS VIOLENCE

We address terrorism and random acts of mass violence (e.g., school shootings) together because each case involves one or more people whose goal is typically to kill as many people as possible. The intentionality of these events, as well as the high rates of death and injury that usually occur in a limited range of people, distinguishes this type of disaster from others. Motive, above and beyond intentionality, can also be an important factor to consider in how people respond to a disaster. Terrorism is politically motivated, and the general population of a country is the target. For example, incidences of Islamic extremism have occurred in recent years, such as the September 11th attacks, the 2005 London bombings ("7 July 2005 London Bombings," 2020), and the Paris bombing in 2015 ("November 2015 Paris Attacks," 2020).

Mass violence and shootings can be motivated by a variety of factors, including personal grievances, ideology, race, or religion, such as the Tree of Life synagogue shooting in Pittsburgh, Pennsylvania in 2018 ("Pittsburgh Synagogue Shooting," 2020). The 2011 Norway terrorist attacks are an example of mixed motives ("2011 Norway Attacks," 2020). The shooter endorsed extreme Islamophobia as well as far-right ideology and set off a bomb in a government complex, then targeted youth at a Labour Party summer camp. Sometimes the motives of perpetrators of acts of mass violence are unknown, which can present its own challenges, such as in the Route 91 Harvest Festival shooting in Las Vegas. In that incident, a man killed 58 people and wounded 867 more by shooting from a hotel window down into the crowd. To this day, there is no known motive for his actions ("2017 Las Vegas Shooting," 2020).

Intentionality

Intentionality is one of the most defining features of these types of events. Unlike natural disasters and accidents, terrorism and acts of mass violence, and shootings, are often carefully planned and executed. In some cases the motivation of the perpetrator is clear. As we noted, the offender may be making a political statement, as in cases of terrorism; a social statement about racism, religion, or gender identity; or they may be spurred on by a revenge motive, such as in the case of a school shooting by a student who felt picked on or bullied. Even if the act itself is intentional, however, the targets of these events are often random, selected only because they happen to be at a specific location at a specified time, or because they represent something to the perpetrator. Even in more personal cases, where there is an intended target, the perpetrators are often indiscriminate in their killing.

Regardless of the motive, for the victims the event seems to come from out of the blue, with no warning. Therefore, survivors of these events often have trouble feeling safe and trusting others. They are fearful of future attacks and may avoid crowds, believing that crowds are likely targets. They also need help challenging thoughts such as "An attack could happen at any time," "No one can be trusted," and "Social situations are unsafe." Catastrophizing, All-or-Nothing Thinking, and Overestimation of Risk are common Problematic Thinking Styles that often come into play.

In almost all situations in which a seemingly random act of violence by an individual or group of individuals occurs, a critical job for the therapist is to help the client understand that what happened was an event of extremely low probability and that the chances of something like it happening again to the person are also extremely low. Although it is true that one can never know when one of these types of events will occur, the frequently overlooked fact is that they are in fact rare, more rare than most people, especially anyone who has recently been exposed to such an event, think. One factor contributing to these common misperceptions is the fact that mass shootings and terrorist attacks are often featured in headlines or lurid stories in the mass media even when relatively few people are affected (Morse, 2018), leading to the impression that they occur more often than they do. Thoughts that bring a new perspective on the situation and are more balanced because they take into account information that is ignored in the original negative thought, such as "Terrorist attacks are rare," "Security has been improved at large venues," and "Most people are good," can lessen a client's distress. When clients are unable to modify their thoughts, the Payoff Matrix (see Chapter 10) can help them weigh the risks they perceive against the benefits of freely engaging in activities.

Along with fear, anger is also common after intentional events. As we teach in Handout 24, the Guide to Thoughts and Feelings (available in Appendix B on the American Psychological Association [APA] website at http://pubs.apa.org/books/supp/hamblen), anger is the result of feeling that something is unfair. Given that in most cases the client did nothing to elicit the attack, it is understandable that they would perceive the situation as unjust. In Chapter 10, we outlined a number of strategies for addressing anger and challenging beliefs that underlie angry feelings.

Death and Injury

Terrorism and mass violence often, although not always, result in death and injury. Clients who may have almost lost their life, or who had a friend or loved one seriously injured or killed, have difficulty believing that these extreme outcomes are rare. Combined with the idea that these events can happen at any time, their life-threatening nature further reinforces clients' fears that the world is an unsafe place. The therapist works to help the client understand that even if the worst thing *can* happen, that does not mean it is *the most likely* outcome. Even small shifts in thinking can have large changes in distress. We offered suggestions for helping clients manage grief related to the loss of a loved one and for challenging cognitions related to disaster-related injuries in Chapter 10.

Damage and Destruction Are Localized

One characteristic of terrorism and mass violence that distinguishes these events from other disasters is that the resulting damage tends to be localized.

There usually is no widespread destruction of property or disruption of community services. This means that people can usually return to their homes after the event (or after they are released from the hospital). Being at home, rather than displaced, means that survivors have access to their support networks. Likewise, secondary stressors, such as job loss due to businesses closing, extensive home repairs, or limited resources, are less likely to be experienced. There are often jobs and homes to return to, and community services are intact. This factor can often be worked into the cognitive restructuring component of CBT-PD; for example, when a client catastrophizes (e.g., "Nothing will ever be the same"), the therapist can help them see the parts of their life that are still intact and going well.

Localized damage also increases the chances that clients will continue to have access to their support networks and that they can engage in both pleasant and meaningful activities. Unlike events with widespread destruction, clients who experience terrorism or a mass shooting usually have friends and family who were not present at the event. These nonaffected people are therefore available to provide important support because they are not dealing with their own reactions to the event. Therapists can work with clients to help them reach out to these people for emotional support and to maintain their connection. As we discussed in Chapter 4, supportive others can sometimes play a valuable role in helping the client understand their postdisaster reactions and practice and use the skills taught in the CBT-PD program. This approach is most effective when a plan is developed with the client to systematically review the information and skills covered in the program with a supportive person over the course of treatment. This is done by either encouraging the client to routinely share the handout materials and skills taught in the program with the support person or by reviewing the information and skills in brief portions of sessions that include the support person with the client.

NATURAL DISASTERS

Natural disasters are the result of physical processes of the earth; floods, earthquakes, hurricanes, fires, tornados, tsunamis, drought, and winter storms are all examples. These typically are brief events that last for up to a few hours, as in the case with a hurricane or tsunami, but they can also persist for days, weeks, or longer, such as with a wildfire, flood, or aftershocks that follow a major earthquake. In all disasters, the immediate aftermath of the event can be chaotic and last longer than the event itself, and it can be as traumatic, or more so, than the disaster itself.

Although forecasting is improving for some types of natural disaster, most occur with little to no warning. Even when there is warning about an impending disaster, it may occur only a few minutes before the event (e.g., a tsunami, tornados). When more advanced warnings of a disaster are possible, the specific regions expected to be affected, and the severity of the event, often change up to the last minute before impact. Natural disasters often cause widespread damage and destruction. This is especially true in developing countries, where housing provides less protection because of the lack of building codes to regulate construction, and where the social safety networks are weaker, resulting in minimal emergency assistance. As a result of the damage, many people are forced to leave their homes and may have to move to find housing or jobs.

Damage and Disruption of Community Services

The defining feature of natural disasters is the amount of damage and disruption they cause. Damage to property is often widespread. Homes, businesses, and roads may be destroyed, and there can be considerable disruptions of community services. Electricity can be knocked out, transportation may be blocked by hazardous debris, and emergency services may be limited. In addition, the extent of the damage can mean that the situation on the ground is prolonged. In some cases, employees cannot physically get to their workplaces. People may be stranded in hard-to-reach locations, such as when a bridge has been washed away or a road flooded. There may not be a sufficient number of emergency personnel or construction workers, supplies may be scarce or unavailable, and financial support from the government may be delayed. For example, 1 month after Hurricane Maria hit Puerto Rico on September 20, 2017, 88% of the islanders remained without power, 29% did not have tap water, and 40% had no cell service ("Effects of Hurricane Maria," 2020).

Although people do not typically participate in CBT-PD immediately after a disaster, the prolonged nature of the recovery means that clients may still be dealing with the consequences many months later. These secondary stressors can be worse for some people than the event itself. Clients may experience severe anxiety due to the uncertainty of their situation; for example, they may not know when they will be able to go back to work or where they will be living.

Cognitive restructuring can help clients develop more accurate and less catastrophic beliefs about their situations. Nevertheless, many of their concerns may be accurate, and multiple Action Plans may be needed to help them formulate practical solutions to their many new problems, implement those solutions, and troubleshoot them as needed. The anxiety accompanying clients' multiple concerns can be so overwhelming that it interferes with their ability to use cognitive restructuring and problem solve effectively. These people can benefit from increased attention to learning and practicing breathing retraining to reduce their anxiety, which can provide a level of calm necessary to engage in cognitive restructuring to examine their most distressing concerns.

The widespread physical damage associated with natural disasters is often accompanied by a profound sense of loss over possessions. When people lose their homes, most of their possessions are destroyed as well. Some things, like family heirlooms and older family photographs, cannot be replaced. The meaning ascribed to these one-of-a-kind items can result in grief and sadness. Relatedly, people whose possessions and homes are destroyed may experience a loss of their sense of identity. A person's home is more than the sum of their possessions: It is a safe place that has provided stability and security. Without the anchor of a home, people can feel lost and vulnerable.

For clients to process and deal with these types of loss, it is important that therapists help them separate the tangible loss of a home or their possessions from the meaning they ascribe to it. For example, just because an heirloom is destroyed does not mean that the person (or people) who passed down the heirloom will be forgotten. People can experience the loss and associated sadness while at the same time recognizing that it is just an object and that their memories are still intact. These thoughts can be addressed through cognitive restructuring. An Action Plan about the lost item, such as how it could be remembered or whether it could be replaced with something else that would be meaningful in its own right, also can help. Similarly, therapists can also help clients recognize that although one's home provided a sense of identity and security, a new home can do this as well. Thoughts such as "Without a home I will never be safe again" or "I will never find a place where I belong again" can be challenged and replaced with more accurate thoughts, such as "I have a safe place for me and my family to live right now, even though it is not my home" and "It took me awhile to get connected to my community, but I did it once, and I can do it again in a new place."

In addition to sadness over the loss of possessions and damage, many survivors of natural disasters experience anger. Although there is no one to blame for a natural event itself, many survivors feel angry over how the disaster response was handled, especially if the situation was clearly mishandled, as in the case of Hurricane Katrina (Brinkley, 2007). Resources are often limited and may not be distributed equally across all groups, which can result in resentment and further anger. Unlike major terrorist attacks and events of mass violence, few natural disasters receive media attention or large donations. It is not uncommon to hear survivors say that they feel they were either initially forgotten or were forgotten as soon as the next event hit the news cycle and replaced their story. Cognitive restructuring is often effective at addressing these lingering feelings of anger, which may emerge many months or more after the event occurred. In Chapter 10, we provided further suggestions for helping clients deal with persistent anger after a disaster.

Displacement

Displacement from one's home is closely related to damage and destruction. As we just discussed, natural disasters may damage homes, making them uninhabitable. For some people this displacement is temporary while they wait for their homes to be repaired. The lucky ones are able to stay locally with friends and family and then return to their homes. Others may not have this option and must move away from their communities to find work or housing. This displacement can be very stressful. Daily activities that were relatively easy at home can become overwhelming in a new place. Childcare and carpools have to be worked out, support networks may be disrupted, transportation may be challenging, and a lack of familiarity with the areas and what is available may complicate all of this. Home repairs, if required, are difficult to negotiate from afar. Clients are often frustrated with these tasks. They may experience hopelessness and believe things will never improve. They may have realistic fears about where they will live in the long term.

As a consequence of these stresses, people who are displaced from their homes by a disaster and must temporarily live elsewhere have a greater chance of developing posttraumatic stress disorder and other negative outcomes than similar people who are able to obtain temporary housing in the same community (Cofini et al., 2015). Therapists may need to help clients challenge their inaccurate beliefs about their ability to eventually resume their lives as before. Action Plans may need to be developed to help them address many of the practical problems they may be facing in their new living situation.

Financial Problems

Because the damage and destruction associated with natural disasters are often widespread, many survivors experience financial problems. Job loss may result because the survivor cannot get to their place of work, has other responsibilities that make it impossible for them to work, or because they have been laid off from a business that has temporarily shut down for repairs or permanently closed. Survivors who are injured may have health expenses.

There may also be added costs related to childcare or eldercare. Home repairs are costly and frequently not fully covered by insurance or disaster relief funding.

It can be easy for the therapist to be distracted by the pressing problems of the client. Damage, destruction, displacement, and financial loss are all practical difficulties that therapists may feel compelled to assist with; however, therapists are cautioned against spending too much time providing case management. Although they may indeed be able to address some of the client's most immediate needs, in many cases there are others who can fulfill that role.

In contrast, the therapist likely is the only one who can help clients develop skills to decrease their disaster-related distress. Working within the framework of cognitive restructuring, the therapist can help the client cope with the upsetting situations. For example, a client may come to a session upset that they will be losing their Federal Emergency Management Agency–supplied trailer next week. A 5 Steps of Cognitive Restructuring Worksheet can be done on the thought "I am going to lose my trailer and be homeless." A more balanced thought might be "I have several people I can call to find out about housing options." Then, as part of an Action Plan, the therapist could link the client to some resources or help them determine what other options are available if they cannot find a new place to live; for example, perhaps they can stay with friends or family.

ACCIDENTS AND ENVIRONMENTAL DISASTERS

By their very nature, accidents are a class of disasters that are unintentional. They include a wide range of events, such as transportation accidents (plane, train, maritime, road, and space events), explosions, nuclear and industrial accidents, stampedes, structural collapses, and fires. Some of these, however, can also be caused intentionally and would then be in a different category, such as a plane being deliberately shot down by a propelled rocket. When these accidents have environmental consequences, they are called *environmental disasters*. Some examples of major environmental disasters include the India Bhopal gas leak tragedy in 1984, which exposed more than 500,000 people to a toxic gas and killed thousands ("Bhopal Disaster," 2020); the 1986 Chernobyl and 2011 Fukushima nuclear disasters ("Chernobyl Disaster," 2020; "Fukushima Daiichi Nuclear Disaster," 2020); the U.S. *Deepwater Horizon* explosion and oil spill in 2016 ("*Deepwater Horizon* Explosion," 2020); and the Boeing 737 MAX airplane crashes in 2018 and 2019 ("Lion Air Flight 610," 2020; "Ethiopian Airlines Flight 302," 2020).

These types of disasters usually involve complex systems that incorporate numerous safety checks at multiple levels, mechanisms for warning facility operators, and options for automatically responding to problems. Although these systems are designed to prevent accidents, some have argued that conventional engineering approaches to safety add further complexity to the systems and may in and of themselves contribute to accidents, leading to such accidents being inevitable or "normal" (Perrow, 1999, 2007). Nevertheless, the fact that these accidents involve man-made technologies means that whenever they happen there is an immediate rush to identify the parties at fault and try to hold them accountable. For example, after the Bhopal disaster one side believed that the gas leak was the result of poor maintenance, whereas the other said it was the result of sabotage. The Chernobyl accident is thought to be caused by a reactor design flaw that malfunctioned during a safety test when unprepared staff were on duty. The Fukushima accident was later determined to be caused by both poor oversight and insufficient standards as well as an inadequate crisis management plan after the event, and the *Deepwater Horizon* explosion shared blame among BP, the rig owner, and the cementer.

Although it may be difficult or impossible to know who is truly responsible for a technological disaster, the victims of these types of incidents often harbor deep anger at those whom they see as guilty for the event. Helping clients examine the personal costs of holding onto their anger using a Payoff Matrix is one strategy. Sadness and depression also are common. These disaster survivors are confronted with an event that was preventable, and therefore the losses they suffer (e.g., the loss of innocence, the loss of loved ones) seem unnecessary, which can add to the pain they are feeling. Cognitive restructuring is often focused on helping the client recognize the difference between an intentional act and an accident and to understand that, even if there is someone to blame, that person likely did not intend the outcome.

RIOTS

Riots typically occur as a reaction to an event, often related to race, religion, or governmental oppression, that people feel is unjust. Some riots occur as a protest of the status quo and may be aimed at least partly at inciting change, although not everyone involved may have the same intention, and some may see it simply as an opportunity to get something for nothing (e.g., by looting). Other riots may occur during moments of mass jubilation, such as after the victory of a sports team, and may be more generally focused on creating mayhem. Riots are complicated because they may start out as a peaceful protest or celebration but then unexpectedly morph into violence and destruction of property, affecting a wide range of people.

A client who presents with distress related to a riot may be someone who was engaged in a peaceful protest that turned unruly or violent. The survivor can also be someone who became caught up in the moment and engaged in some of the destruction or violence, which they may or may not later regret. A person may have joined the group for one purpose and then found themselves in a very different and unexpected situation. This can be complicated further when the person is caught in a crowd and physically unable to separate from it.

Police and other law enforcement officials may also seek treatment for disaster-related distress. They may find themselves obligated to take action against people who are breaking the law even if they agree in principle with what is motivating the outrage. This inner conflict between doing one's job and living by one's values may require careful unpacking by the therapist. In addition, given the volatile nature of riots, law enforcement officials may find it more difficult than usual to be calm and controlled and may themselves be carried away in the moment, acting more aggressively than is necessary and prompting potential backlash from protesters.

Other people affected by riots are business owners whose shops are damaged or looted, bystanders who witness the violence, or community members who live in the area. These people may be scared of future riots or of being retaliated against. The underlying issue often is not quickly resolved, and so riots can pop up again with little warning. In addition, there is often a lot of anger both at the protestors and law enforcement as well as at the system that is seen to have caused the riot in the first place.

Therapists should be careful not to assume they understand the source of the client's distress. It is important to ask open-ended questions about the event and the client's reactions to it. It is not for the therapist to challenge whether the riot or the client's actions were justified, or whether the grievances that underlie the riot are valid. The therapist should focus on helping the client examine their thoughts with the goal of reducing their distress.

DISEASE OUTBREAKS

A disease outbreak occurs when there is a sudden increase in the number of cases of a virus or other sickness. An outbreak becomes an *epidemic* when there is a rapid spread of the disease within a particular region and a *pandemic* when the spread has global reach. One of the most deadly pandemics in recent history was the Spanish flu, which lasted just over 2 years, from 1918 to 1920, infecting more than 500 million people and killing tens of millions ("Spanish Flu," 2020). More recent epidemics include AIDS, which peaked worldwide in the 1980s ("HIV/AIDS," 2020); severe acute respiratory syndrome (SARS), which peaked in 2003 ("Severe Acute Respiratory Syndrome," 2020); the avian flu (H1N1 virus), which peaked in 2009 ("Pandemic H1N1/2009 Virus," 2020); Ebola, which peaked in West Africa from 2014 to 2019 ("Ebola," 2020); the 2015–2016 Zika virus ("Zika Virus," 2020); and coronavirus disease 2019 (COVID-19), which began in 2019 ("Timeline of the COVID-19 Pandemic," 2021).

As with other types of disasters, the severity of exposure to a disease outbreak is one of the most important determinants of its mental health impact. Aside from people who have lost a loved one to an outbreak of a disease, by virtue of their profession, health care workers experience some of the highest levels of exposure. Health care workers not only are often exposed to the disease and its lethal consequences for prolonged periods of time but also are at increased risk of contracting viral diseases themselves, such as with COVID-19. The inherent stress of working in these situations can then be compounded when there is uncertainty as to how the virus is transmitted, leading to a fear of passing the virus to their loved ones, and feelings of powerlessness about the insufficiency of available treatments. Although research indicates that the majority of health care workers who respond to a disease outbreak do not suffer from significant postdisaster mental problems such as posttraumatic stress disorder or depression (e.g., Lancee et al., 2008), they are nevertheless at increased risk for symptoms of postdisaster distress (Lai et al., 2020; Preti et al., 2020). The CBT-PD program may be particularly useful for this group.

As one example, activity scheduling can help health care workers obtain a better work–life balance by identifying their values and prioritizing activities that help them reconnect with friends and family instead of maintaining a singular focus on their patients. Breathing retraining can be used to help health care workers reduce arousal and focus their attention. Using the 5 Steps of Cognitive Restructuring, the therapist can help health care worker clients challenge beliefs related to fears that they might contract the virus or pass the virus to loved one (or develop practical Action Plans to minimize risk to family members), address guilt associated with feeling that they are not doing enough for their patients, and assuage anger at various systems (e.g., hospital administrators or city, state, or federal government) that may not be providing them with enough personal protective equipment or that is perceived to be mismanaging the outbreak. As we suggested in Chapter 10, the Payoff Matrix may be especially useful for helping clients gain insight into their reluctance to let go of their guilt or anger and accept that the world can sometimes be an uncertain place.

The public at large can also be affected by disease outbreaks, especially vulnerable populations, such as people with a preexisting psychiatric disorder (Van Rheenen et al., 2020; Wang et al., 2021). Disease outbreaks can be very frightening because a disease has no boundaries and, in some cases, no cure. To prevent the spread of infection people may have to socially isolate, which has myriad negative effects on them (Miller, 2020; Pietrabissa & Simpson, 2020). Furthermore, disease outbreaks can result in major economic hardships related to the loss of jobs. Although there is no panacea for these problems, the CBT-PD program can reduce the acute psychological distress some people experience during a disease outbreak and help them rebuild their lives after its conclusion.

Ongoing Threat

One aspect of a disease outbreak that differs from most other types of disasters is that the threat is often ongoing, and it may last or occur intermittently for years, until a vaccine is found or sufficient numbers of people have been infected that herd immunity occurs. Furthermore, when a new virus appears, often little is known about it, such as how it is transmitted, whether people need to be symptomatic to spread it, and whether having been infected gives the person immunity from reinfection. This lack of knowledge can further increase people's fears of infection, which may be experienced for an extended period of time.

Therapists may be concerned that it is not possible to challenge thoughts that, on the surface, seem like true statements. For example, thoughts related to COVID-19 such as "It is unsafe to go out in public"; "If I go back to work, I could get infected"; or "My parents cannot have visitors because they are elderly and at increased risk" may seem difficult to challenge. This is partly because the specific evidence needed to evaluate many thoughts may depend on the person's specific situation, including where they live, the current phase of the pandemic, the nature of their work, and personal risk factors for a worse course of illness (e.g., older age, preexisting health conditions, compromised immunity). However, these are the same reasons it is important to gather the evidence necessary to comprehensively weigh the evidence for and against a distressing thought and to correct it to make it more accurate and less distressing when appropriate. For example, the alternative thought "If I follow physical distancing guidelines and wear a mask, my risk of catching the virus in public is much lower" is a more accurate and less distressing thought than

"It is unsafe to go out in public." Similarly, the alternative thoughts "My workplace has taken precautions to lower the risk of transmission" and "The risk of my parents catching the virus is lower if they only see a few visitors and the visit takes place outside" are more accurate and less distressing.

Unknown Outcomes

In addition to the question of how long a disease outbreak will last, anxiety and uncertainty are further exacerbated by other many unknowns. How contagious is the disease? How is the virus transmitted? What are the risk factors for severe illness and death? Can you develop immunity? What treatments are effective? Will a cure be found? We know that fear and anxiety are caused by the expectation that something bad will happen. In disease outbreaks, there is a tendency to jump to the worst possible outcome because of a lack of knowledge. The media may contribute to these fears by broadcasting stories about unusual cases, making it appear as if these outcomes are more likely than they may in fact be. At the same time, accurate, transparent risk communication on the part of the media can decrease fears.

Cognitive restructuring is based on identifying the facts. In challenging cognitions related to outbreaks, it is important for therapists to rely on scientific information. For example, in the early days of AIDS, people believed one could get infected by being near someone who had the disease. It was only later that scientists showed that people can contract AIDS only by coming in direct contact with certain body fluids from an infected person. Therapists may find it necessary to provide some clients with sources of accurate information to help them challenge disease-related cognitions. Therapists also should help clients understand what the most likely outcomes are, as opposed to the worst outcomes.

There may also be situations with which a client identifies that involve considerable risk or in which a close friend or loved one becomes sick. Here again, the flexibility of the 5 Steps of Cognitive Restructuring can be used to help them cope with their upset feelings. Therapists help clients evaluate their thoughts and ideally help them develop a more accurate and less distressing thought. For example, the thought "My father has the virus and is going to die" is more distressing than the thought "My father has the virus and is getting the best care available" or "My father has the virus, and the doctors are learning new ways to treat it every day." Action Plans should also be used to help clients continue to solve difficult problems related to managing their situation. For example, the client may develop a new thought about his father but still feel upset that they cannot be with him. An Action Plan could therefore include steps the client can take to reduce this distress, such as setting up daily video calls when his father is feeling up to it, having the grandchildren send artwork to him that he can put up on the walls, or making a short family video to send that his father can watch.

In the event that a client does lose a close friend or loved one, the therapist can help them manage their grief or guilt associated with the loss. Just as with other upsetting situations, the therapist helps the client identify the most upsetting thought, such as "No one will ever understand me the way my father did" or "I should have been there with him when he died" and then challenge them to come up with more accurate thoughts, such as "There are others, like my wife, who understand me" and "My father knows I loved him and that I did everything I could to be with him through the virus." Action Plans in these situations are more about coping with specific symptoms than problem-solving. An Action Plan in this example might involve the client scheduling pleasant activities, keeping to a routine, and journaling about some of the memories of his father.

Isolation

Isolation is a part of many disasters. The displacement that is commonplace with natural disasters can result in a person being isolated from friends and family. The financial problems that occur after some disasters can result in a lack of resources to be able to go places, see friends, and participate in recreational activities, which also can be isolating, and the fear of future terrorist attacks or mass violence can result in avoidance that is socially isolating. Activity scheduling is used in the CBT-PD program as a form of behavioral activation to help clients reengage in meaningful and rewarding activities. Disease outbreaks, however, have a stricter type of isolation associated with them. At varying points during the COVID-19 pandemic, more than 90% of the United States, and more than one third of the world population, was on lockdown ("National Responses to the COVID-19 Pandemic," 2020). These mobility restrictions varied by state and country but generally involved a shutdown of schools, universities, and nonessential businesses, as well as travel restrictions. People were told to stay home except to exercise, go to the grocery store, or see a doctor. This led to significant levels of loneliness, especially in single people living alone. Domestic violence also increased, likely because of the combined effects of the heightened stress on everyone and increased levels of contact between intimate partners.

These issues may be especially pertinent when restrictions require the provision of therapy by video or telephone, although many may linger long afterward. For example, one issue to consider during periods of restricted mobility is how to help clients engage in interesting activities when they can no longer take part in their usual pursuits. Some activities to consider include learning a new skill, taking an online class, taking a walking tour, taking up a new hobby, exercise, journaling, cooking or baking, and online calls with friends. Cognitive restructuring can help clients challenge thoughts related to hopelessness such as "Things will never be normal again," fears such as "It will never be safe to leave the house," and anger such as "The government has no right keeping me inside."

Economic and Societal Impact

With the COVID-19 pandemic came a worldwide economic impact. The stay-at-home orders and shutdowns of nonessential businesses led to high rates of unemployment and financial hardships that contributed to other ongoing stressors. These practical problems often require more than examination and correction of negative, inaccurate thinking. Although thoughts may be modified to be more accurate and less distressing, Action Plans may be frequently needed to help clients develop and work through practical solutions to their numerous real problems. Finding new employment, connecting with programs that offer financial assistance, and developing new ways of connecting with friends and family are just some of the issues therapists can help clients problem solve.

Therapists should also closely monitor the level of depression and suicidal intent in their clients. Suicidality is closely related to hopelessness and the combination of health concerns, lack of social support, and suffering from significant financial hardships. The last item on the Short Post-Traumatic Stress Disorder Rating Interview, Expanded Version (Norris & Davidson, 2007; see Appendix A on the APA website at http://pubs.apa.org/books/supp/hamblen) is a screen for suicide. Although it is not included in the total score with the other items, it is a way for therapists to monitor suicidal ideation in clients. Respondents simply reply "Yes" or "No" to the question "Is there any possibility that you might hurt or kill yourself?" A positive response requires immediate follow-up.

CONCLUSION

In this book, we have presented a transdiagnostic treatment program that is both flexible and specific. It can be used with clients who have experienced all types of disasters. Although each disaster is unique, the ways people respond to these events are quite similar. In this chapter, we have reviewed some of the common presentations therapists will face for each type of disaster. In each case, the same core skills that are taught throughout the CBT-PD program can be applied.

Psychoeducation provides the foundation for the treatment. Regardless of the client's specific symptom profile (e.g., more anxious vs. more depressed), psychoeducation helps the client recognize their symptoms and offers strategies for coping with them through the treatment. The therapist explains and teaches the four feeling states (i.e., fear and anxiety, sadness and depression, guilt and shame, and anger) and returns to them as the basis for cognitive restructuring. Residual symptoms can be addressed through specific Action Plans.

Breathing retraining is also broadly applicable to a range of clinical presentations. For anxious clients, the breathing helps calm them. For angry clients, the breathing acts like a time-out, allowing them to slow down and regroup before acting. Others use the breathing as a way to focus. The breathing can be used alone or as part of an Action Plan.

Activity scheduling is most often considered an intervention for depression. By engaging in pleasant and meaningful activities, clients feel better, which reinforces continued engagement and involvement in those activities. In the CBT-PD program, activity scheduling is also used to target the avoidance and isolation that can develop after a disaster. Activity scheduling can help clients connect with a new community; meet their personal goals, such as improved relationships; and improve their overall mood.

Finally, the cognitive restructuring taught in the CBT-PD program is particularly flexible. To recap, cognitive restructuring is first taught as a skill that can be applied to any negative thought, not just disaster-related cognitions. Therefore, clients can use cognitive restructuring on any upsetting thought, making it very generalizable. Second, there are several different approaches provided to help clients learn to recognize and change their thinking. Although the 5 Steps of Cognitive Restructuring is the main focus, Problematic Thinking Styles, the Payoff Matrix, and other strategies are also taught. Third, problem-solving is integrated into the cognitive restructuring such that clients learn to develop practical approaches to dealing with upsetting situations. This is important because the very nature of disasters means that clients will be faced with real problems over and above distress that may be related to inaccurate thinking.

Together, these four skills give therapists the tools they need to address the heterogeneous clinical presentations of clients who are coping with post-disaster distress, whether they are fearful clients who have been through a terrorist attack, sad clients who have lost all their possessions in a flood, or angry clients who feel their disaster was preventable. Although the skills are applied in a systematic way across clients, the delivery of the skills is specific to each client. The CBT-PD program is therefore tailored to each client, focusing on the thoughts and feelings that are most distressing to that client and examining the client's specific reasons for holding certain thoughts. Finally, the focus on each client's specific treatment goals further individualizes the treatment in that the client's goals serve as the road map that helps guide how upsetting situations are addressed.

References

Addis, M. E., & Jacobson, N. S. (2000). A closer look at the treatment rationale and homework compliance in cognitive-behavioral therapy for depression. *Cognitive Therapy and Research, 24*(3), 313–326. https://doi.org/10.1023/A:1005563304265

American Psychiatric Association. (1980). *Diagnostic and statistical manual of mental disorders* (3rd ed.).

American Psychiatric Association. (2013). *Diagnostic and statistical manual of mental disorders* (5th ed.). https://doi.org/10.1176/appi.books.9780890425596

American Psychiatric Association. (2020). *View and comment on recently proposed changes to* DSM-5. https://www.psychiatry.org/psychiatrists/practice/dsm/proposed-changes

Arnberg, F. K., Gudmundsdóttir, R., Butwicka, A., Fang, F., Lichtenstein, P., Hultman, C. M., & Valdimarsdóttir, U. A. (2015). Psychiatric disorders and suicide attempts in Swedish survivors of the 2004 southeast Asia tsunami: A 5 year matched cohort study. *The Lancet Psychiatry, 2*(9), 817–824. https://doi.org/10.1016/S2215-0366(15)00124-8

Arnberg, F. K., Johannesson, K. B., & Michel, P. (2013). Prevalence and duration of PTSD in survivors 6 years after a natural disaster. *Journal of Anxiety Disorders, 27*(3), 347–352. https://doi.org/10.1016/j.janxdis.2013.03.011

Barlow, D. H., & Craske, M. G. (2000). *Mastery of your anxiety and panic: Client workbook for anxiety and panic MAP–3* (3rd ed.). Psychological Corporation.

Barlow, D. H., Raffa, S. D., & Cohen, E. M. (2002). Psychosocial treatments for panic disorders, phobias, and generalized anxiety disorder. In P. E. Nathan & J. M. Gorman (Eds.), *A guide to treatments that work* (pp. 301–335). Oxford University Press.

Barton, A. H. (1969). *Communities in disaster: A sociological analysis of collective stress situations*. Doubleday Anchor.

Başoğlu, M., & Salcioglu, E. (2011). *A mental healthcare model for mass trauma survivors: Control-focused behavioral treatment of earthquake, war, and torture trauma.* Cambridge University Press. https://doi.org/10.1017/CBO9780511975936

Başoğlu, M., Salcioglu, E., & Livanou, M. (2007). A randomized controlled study of single-session behavioral treatment of earthquake-related post-traumatic stress disorder using an earthquake simulator. *Psychological Medicine, 37*(2), 203–213. https://doi.org/10.1017/S0033291706009123

Başoğlu, M., Salcioglu, E., Livanou, M., & Acar, G. (2005). Single-session behavioral treatment of earthquake-related post-traumatic stress disorder: A randomized waiting list controlled trial. *Journal of Traumatic Stress, 18*, 1–11. https://doi.org/10.1002/jts.20011

Beck, A. T. (1952). Successful outpatient psychotherapy of a chronic schizophrenic with a delusion based on borrowed guilt. *Psychiatry, 15*(3), 305–312. https://doi.org/10.1080/00332747.1952.11022883

Beck, J. S. (1995). *Cognitive therapy: Basics and beyond.* Guilford Press.

Berkowitz, S., Bryant, R., Brymer, M., Hamblen, J., Jacobs, A., Layne, C., & Watson, P. (2010). *Skills for psychological recovery: Field operations guide.* National Center for PTSD and National Child Traumatic Stress Network.

Bhopal disaster. (2020, November 2). In *Wikipedia.* https://en.wikipedia.org/wiki/Bhopal_disaster

Bisson, J. I., Roberts, N. P., Andrew, M., Cooper, R., & Lewis, C. (2013). Psychological treatment of post-traumatic stress disorder (PTSD). *Cochrane Database of Systematic Reviews.* https://doi.org/10.1002/14651858.CD003388.pub3

Bolton, E. E., & Mueser, K. T. (2009). Borderline personality disorder. In K. T. Mueser, S. D. Rosenberg, & H. J. Rosenberg (Eds.), *Treatment of post-traumatic stress disorder in special populations: A cognitive restructuring program* (pp. 225–238). American Psychological Association. https://doi.org/10.1037/11889-011

Bondjers, K., Willebrand, M., & Arnberg, F. K. (2018). Similarity in symptom patterns of posttraumatic stress among disaster-survivors: A three-step latent profile analysis. *European Journal of Psychotraumatology, 9*(1), 1546083. https://doi.org/10.1080/20008198.2018.1546083

Boscarino, J. A., Kirchner, H. L., Hoffman, S. N., Sartorius, J., Adams, R. E., & Figley, C. R. (2011). A brief screening tool for assessing psychological trauma in clinical practice: Development and validation of the New York PTSD Risk Score. *General Hospital Psychiatry, 33*(5), 489–500. https://doi.org/10.1016/j.genhosppsych.2011.06.001

Boston Marathon bombing survivor to speak on the power of perseverance. (2019, October 2). Connect2Commerce Springfield Regional Chamber. https://springfieldregionalchamber.com/boston-marathon-bombing-survivor-to-speak-on-the-power-of-perseverance/

Bovin, M. J., Marx, B. P., Weathers, F. W., Gallagher, M. W., Rodriguez, P., Schnurr, P. P., & Keane, T. M. (2015). Psychometric properties of the PTSD Checklist for

Diagnostic and Statistical Manual of Mental Disorders–Fifth edition (PCL–5) in veterans. *Psychological Assessment, 28*(11), 1379–1391. https://doi.org/10.1037/pas0000254

Bram, J., Haughwout, A., & Orr, J. (2002). Has September 11 affected New York City's growth potential? *Economic Policy Review, 8*(2), 81–96.

Brewin, C. R., Fuchkan, N., Huntley, Z., Robertson, M., Thompson, M., Scragg, P., d'Ardenne, P., & Ehlers, A. (2010). Outreach and screening following the 2005 London bombings: Usage and outcomes. *Psychological Medicine, 40*(12), 2049–2057. https://doi.org/10.1017/S0033291710000206

Brewin, C. R., Rose, S., Andrews, B., Green, J., Tata, P., McEvedy, C., Turner, S., & Foa, E. B. (2002). Brief screening instrument for post-traumatic stress disorder. *The British Journal of Psychiatry, 181*(2), 158–162. https://doi.org/10.1192/bjp.181.2.158

Brewin, C. R., Scragg, P., Robertson, M., Thompson, M., d'Ardenne, P., & Ehlers, A. (2008). Promoting mental health following the London bombings: A screen and treat approach. *Journal of Traumatic Stress, 21*(1), 3–8. https://doi.org/10.1002/jts.20310

Brinkley, D. (2007). *The great deluge: Hurricane Katrina, New Orleans, and the Mississippi Gulf Coast*. HarperCollins.

Brown, L., Syvertsen, J., Schinka, J., Mando, A., & Schonfeld, L. (2007). *Project Recovery: Final program evaluation*. Louis de la Parte Florida Mental Health Institute, University of South Florida

Bryant, R. A., Ekasawin, S., Chakrabhand, M. L. S., Suwanmitri, S., Duangchun, O., & Chantaluckwong, T. (2011). A randomized controlled effectiveness trial of cognitive behavior therapy for post-traumatic stress disorder in terrorist-affected people in Thailand. *World Psychiatry, 10*(3), 205–209. https://doi.org/10.1002/j.2051-5545.2011.tb00058.x

Brymer, M. J., Layne, C. M., Jacobs, A. K., Pynoos, R. S., Ruzek, J. I., Steinberg, A. M., & Watson, P. J. (2006). *Psychological first aid: Field operations guide* (2nd ed.). The National Child Traumatic Stress Network and National Center for PTSD.

Bustamante, V., Mellman, T. A., David, D., & Fins, A. I. (2001). Cognitive functioning and the early development of PTSD. *Journal of Traumatic Stress, 14*(4), 791–797. https://doi.org/10.1023/A:1013050423901

Butler, A. C., Chapman, J. E., Forman, E. M., & Beck, A. T. (2006). The empirical status of cognitive-behavioral therapy: A review of meta-analyses. *Clinical Psychology Review, 26*(1), 17–31. https://doi.org/10.1016/j.cpr.2005.07.003

Carmassi, C., Bertelloni, C. A., Massimetti, G., Miniati, M., Stratta, P., Rossi, A., & Dell'Osso, L. (2015). Impact of *DSM-5* PTSD and gender on impaired eating behaviors in 512 Italian earthquake survivors. *Psychiatry Research, 225*(1–2), 64–69. https://doi.org/10.1016/j.psychres.2014.10.008

Carmassi, C., Dell'Oste, V., Barberi, F. M., Pedrinelli, V., Cordone, A., Cappelli, A., Cremone, I. M., Rossi, R., Bertelloni, C. A., & Dell'Osso, L. (2020). Do somatic symptoms relate to PTSD and gender after earthquake exposure?

A cross-sectional study on young adult survivors in Italy. *CNS Spectrums*, 1–7. https://doi.org/10.1017/S1092852920000097

Chernobyl disaster. (2020, October 28). In *Wikipedia*. https://en.wikipedia.org/wiki/Chernobyl_disaster

Clement, S., Schauman, O., Graham, T., Maggioni, F., Evans-Lacko, S., Bezborodovs, N., Morgan, C., Rüsch, N., Brown, J. S. L., & Thornicroft, G. (2015). What is the impact of mental health-related stigma on help-seeking? A systematic review of quantitative and qualitative studies. *Psychological Medicine*, *45*(1), 11–27. https://doi.org/10.1017/S0033291714000129

Cofini, V., Carbonelli, A., Cecilia, M. R., Binkin, N., & di Orio, F. (2015). Post traumatic stress disorder and coping in a sample of adult survivors of the Italian earthquake. *Psychiatry Research*, *229*(1–2), 353–358. https://doi.org/10.1016/j.psychres.2015.06.041

Corrigan, P. W. (2004). How stigma interferes with mental health care. *American Psychologist*, *59*(7), 614–625. https://doi.org/10.1037/0003-066X.59.7.614

Courtois, C. A., Sonis, J., Brown, L. S., Cook, J., Fairbank, J. A., Friedman, M. J., & Schultz, P. (2017). *Clinical practice guideline for the treatment of post-traumatic stress disorder (PTSD) in adults*. American Psychological Association. https://www.apa.org/ptsd-guideline

Creamer, M., Burgess, P., & McFarlane, A. C. (2001). Post-traumatic stress disorder: Findings from the Australian National Survey of Mental Health and Well-being. *Psychological Medicine*, *31*(7), 1237–1247. https://doi.org/10.1017/S0033291701004287

Cyniak-Cieciura, M., Popiel, A., & Zawadzki, B. (2015). General self-efficacy level and changes in negative posttraumatic cognitions and posttraumatic stress disorder (PTSD) symptoms among motor vehicle accident survivors after PTSD therapy. *Studia Psychologiczne*, *53*(1), 18–29.

Davis, L. L., Kyriakides, T. C., Suris, A. M., Ottomanelli, L., Mueller, L., Parker, P. E., Resnick, S. G., Toscano, R., Scrymgeour, A. A., & Drake, R. E. (2018). Effects of evidence-based supported employment vs. transitional work on achieving steady work among veterans with posttraumatic stress disorder: A randomized clinical trial. *JAMA Psychiatry*, *75*(4), 316–324. https://doi.org/10.1001/jamapsychiatry.2017.4472

Dawson, K. S., Bryant, R. A., Harper, M., Tau, A. K., Rahman, A., Schafer, A., & van Ommeren, M. (2015). Problem Management Plus (PM+): A WHO trans-diagnostic psychological intervention for common mental health problems. *World Psychiatry*, *14*(3), 354–357. https://doi.org/10.1002/wps.20255

Deepwater Horizon explosion. (2020, November 2). In *Wikipedia*. https://en.wikipedia.org/wiki/Deepwater_Horizon_explosion

Dell'Osso, B., Glick, I. D., Baldwin, D. S., & Altamura, A. C. (2013). Can long-term outcomes be improved by shortening the duration of untreated illness in psychiatric disorders? A conceptual framework. *Psychopathology*, *46*(1), 14–21. https://doi.org/10.1159/000338608

Dell'Osso, L., Stratta, P., Conversano, C., Massimetti, G., Akiskal, K. K., Akiskal, H. S., Rossi, A., & Carmassi, C. (2014). Lifetime mania is related to post-traumatic stress symptoms in high school students exposed to the 2009 L'Aquila earthquake. *Comprehensive Psychiatry, 55*(2), 357–362. https://doi.org/10.1016/j.comppsych.2013.08.017

Descilo, T., Vedamurtachar, A., Gerbarg, P. L., Nagaraja, D., Gangadhar, B. N., Damodaran, B., Adelson, B., Braslow, L. H., Marcus, S., & Brown, R. P. (2010). Effects of a yoga breath intervention alone and in combination with an exposure therapy for post-traumatic stress disorder and depression in survivors of the 2004 South-East Asia tsunami. *Acta Psychiatrica Scandinavica, 121*(4), 289–300. https://doi.org/10.1111/j.1600-0447.2009.01466.x

Difede, J., Cukor, J., Jyasinghe, N., Patt, I., Jedel, S., Spielman, L., Giosan, C., & Hoffman, H. G. (2007). Virtual reality exposure therapy for the treatment of posttraumatic stress disorder following September 11, 2001. *The Journal of Clinical Psychiatry, 68*(11), 1682–1689. https://doi.org/10.4088/JCP.v68n1102

Dimidjian, S., Barrera, M. J., Jr., Martell, C., Muñoz, R. F., & Lewinsohn, P. M. (2011). The origins and current status of behavioral activation treatments for depression. *Annual Review of Clinical Psychology, 7*(1), 1–38. https://doi.org/10.1146/annurev-clinpsy-032210-104535

Donahue, S., Jackson, C., Shear, M. K., Felton, C., & Essock, S. M. (2006). Outcomes of enhanced counseling services provided to adults through Project Liberty. *Psychiatric Services, 57*(9), 1298–1303. https://doi.org/10.1176/ps.2006.57.9.1298

Duffy, M., Gillespie, K., & Clark, D. M. (2007). Post-traumatic stress disorder in the context of terrorism and other civil conflict in Northern Ireland: Randomised controlled trial. *British Medical Journal, 334*(7604), 1147–1150. https://doi.org/10.1136/bmj.39021.846852.BE

Ebola. (2020, November 29). In *Wikipedia.* https://en.wikipedia.org/wiki/Ebola

Effects of Hurricane Katrina in New Orleans. (2020, November 20). In *Wikipedia.* https://en.wikipedia.org/wiki/Effects_of_Hurricane_Katrina_in_New_Orleans

Effects of Hurricane Maria in Puerto Rico. (2020, November 9). In *Wikipedia.* https://en.wikipedia.org/wiki/Effects_of_Hurricane_Maria_in_Puerto_Rico

Ehlers, A., Ehring, T., & Kleim, B. (2012). Information processing in post-traumatic stress disorder. In J. G. Beck & D. M. Sloan (Eds.), *The Oxford handbook of traumatic stress disorders* (pp. 191–218). Guilford Press.

Ehring, T., Ehlers, A., Cleare, A. J., & Glucksman, E. (2008). Do acute psychological and psychobiological responses to trauma predict subsequent symptom severities of PTSD and depression? *Psychiatry Research, 161*(1), 67–75. https://doi.org/10.1016/j.psychres.2007.08.014

Ethiopian Airlines Flight 302. (2020, December 2). In *Wikipedia.* https://en.wikipedia.org/wiki/Ethiopian_Airlines_Flight_302

Federal Emergency Management Agency. (2020a). *Declared disasters.* https://www.fema.gov/disasters/year

Federal Emergency Management Agency. (2020b). *Summary of disaster declarations and grants*. https://www.fema.gov/data-visualization-summary-disaster-declarations-and-grants

Feeny, N. C., Zoellner, L. A., & Kahana, S. Y. (2009). Providing a treatment rationale for PTSD: Does what we say matter? *Behaviour Research and Therapy*, *47*(9), 752–760. https://doi.org/10.1016/j.brat.2009.06.007

Flory, J. D., & Yehuda, R. (2015). Comorbidity between post-traumatic stress disorder and major depressive disorder: Alternative explanations and treatment considerations. *Dialogues in Clinical Neuroscience*, *17*(2), 141–150. https://doi.org/10.31887/DCNS.2015.17.2/jflory

Foa, E. B., Hembree, E. A., Cahill, S. P., Rauch, S. A. M., Riggs, D. S., Feeny, N. C., & Yadin, E. (2005). Randomized trial of prolonged exposure for post-traumatic stress disorder with and without cognitive restructuring: Outcome at academic and community clinics. *Journal of Consulting and Clinical Psychology*, *73*(5), 953–964. https://doi.org/10.1037/0022-006X.73.5.953

Foa, E. B., Hembree, E. A., Rothbaum, B. O., & Rauch, S. A. A. (2019). *Prolonged exposure therapy for PTSD: Emotional processing of traumatic experiences—Therapist guide* (2nd ed.). Oxford University Press.

Foa, E. B., & Kozak, M. J. (1986). Emotional processing of fear: Exposure to corrective information. *Psychological Bulletin*, *99*(1), 20–35. https://doi.org/10.1037/0033-2909.99.1.20

Foa, E. B., McLean, C. P., Zang, Y., Zhong, J., Powers, M. B., Kauffman, B. Y., Rauch, S., Porter, K., & Knowles, K. (2016). Psychometric properties of the Posttraumatic Diagnostic Scale for *DSM-5* (PDS–5). *Psychological Assessment*, *28*(10), 1166–1171. https://doi.org/10.1037/pas0000258

Fortney, J. C., Unützer, J., Wrenn, G., Pyne, J. M., Smith, G. R., Schoenbaum, M., & Harbin, H. T. (2017). A tipping point for measurement-based care. *Psychiatric Services*, *68*(2), 179–188. https://doi.org/10.1176/appi.ps.201500439

Fukushima Daiichi nuclear disaster. (2020, November 7). In *Wikipedia*. https://en.wikipedia.org/wiki/Fukushima_Daiichi_nuclear_disaster

Fusar-Poli, L., Solmi, M., Brondino, N., Davies, C., Chae, C., Politi, P., Borgwardt, S., Lawrie, S. M., Parnas, J., & McGuire, P. (2019). Transdiagnostic psychiatry: A systematic review. *World Psychiatry*, *18*(2), 192–207. https://doi.org/10.1002/wps.20631

Galea, S., Ahern, J., Resnick, H. S., Kilpatrick, D. G., Bucuvalas, M. J., Gold, J., & Vlahov, D. (2002). Psychological sequelae of the September 11 terrorist attacks in New York City. *The New England Journal of Medicine*, *346*(13), 982–987. https://doi.org/10.1056/NEJMsa013404

Galea, S., Vlahov, D., Resnick, H. S., Ahern, J., Susser, E. S., Gold, J., Bucuvalas, M., & Kilpatrick, D. G. (2003). Trends of probable post-traumatic stress disorder in New York City after the September 11 terrorist attacks. *American Journal of Epidemiology*, *158*(6), 514–524. https://doi.org/10.1093/aje/kwg187

Garcia, J., Lasiter, P. S., Bermudez-Rattoni, F., & Deems, D. A. (1985). A general theory of aversion learning. *Annals of the New York Academy of Sciences*, *443*, 8–21. https://doi.org/10.1111/j.1749-6632.1985.tb27060.x

Ghafoori, B., Neria, Y., Gameroff, M. J., Olfson, M., Lantigua, R., Shea, S., & Weissman, M. M. (2009). Screening for generalized anxiety disorder symptoms in the wake of terrorist attacks: A study in primary care. *Journal of Traumatic Stress, 22*(3), 218–226. https://doi.org/10.1002/jts.20419

Gilbert, P. (2005). Compassion and cruelty: A biopsychosocial approach. In P. Gilbert (Ed.), *Compassion: Conceptualisations, research and use in psychotherapy* (pp. 9–71). Routledge. https://doi.org/10.4324/9780203003459

Gilbert, P., & Choden. (2014). *Mindful compassion: How the science of compassion can help you understand your emotions, live in the present, and connect deeply with others*. New Harbinger.

Gillespie, K., Duffy, M., Hackman, A., & Clark, D. M. (2002). Community based cognitive therapy in the treatment of post-traumatic stress disorder following the Omagh bomb. *Behaviour Research and Therapy, 40*(4), 345–357. https://doi.org/10.1016/S0005-7967(02)00004-9

Gingerich, S., & Mueser, K. T. (2011). *Illness management and recovery: Personalized skills and strategies for those with mental illness* (3rd ed.). Hazelden.

Goldmann, E., & Galea, S. (2014). Mental health consequences of disasters. *Annual Review of Public Health, 35*(1), 169–183. https://doi.org/10.1146/annurev-publhealth-032013-182435

Goldstein, R. B., Smith, S. M., Chou, S. P., Saha, T. D., Jung, J., Zhang, H., Pickering, R. P., Ruan, W. J., Huang, B., & Grant, B. F. (2016). The epidemiology of *DSM-5* posttraumatic stress disorder in the United States: Results from the National Epidemiologic Survey on Alcohol and Related Conditions–III. *Social Psychiatry and Psychiatric Epidemiology, 51*(8), 1137–1148. https://doi.org/10.1007/s00127-016-1208-5

González-Pinto, A., Gonzalez, C., Enjuto, S., Fernandez de Corres, B., Lopez, P., Palomo, J., Gutiérrez, M., Mosquera, F., & Perez de Heredia, J. L. (2004). Psychoeducation and cognitive-behavioral therapy in bipolar disorder: An update. *Acta Psychiatrica Scandinavica, 109*(2), 83–90. https://doi.org/10.1046/j.0001-690X.2003.00240.x

Hamblen, J. L., Norman, S. B., Sonis, J. H., Phelps, A. J., Bisson, J. I., Nunes, V. D., Megnin-Viggars, O., Forbes, D., Riggs, D. S., & Schnurr, P. P. (2019). A guide to guidelines for the treatment of posttraumatic stress disorder in adults: An update. *Psychotherapy, 56*(3), 359–373. https://doi.org/10.1037/pst0000231

Hamblen, J. L., Norris, F. H., Gibson, L., & Lee, L. (2009). Training community therapists to deliver cognitive behavioral therapy in the aftermath of disaster. *International Journal of Emergency Mental Health, 12*, 33–40.

Hamblen, J. L., Norris, F. H., Pietruszkiewicz, S., Gibson, L., Naturale, A., & Louis, C. (2009). Cognitive behavioral therapy for postdisaster distress: A community based treatment program for survivors of Hurricane Katrina. *Administration and Policy in Mental Health, 36*(3), 206–214. https://doi.org/10.1007/s10488-009-0213-3

Hamblen, J. L., Norris, F. H., Symon, K. A., & Bow, T. E. (2017). Cognitive behavioral therapy for postdisaster distress: A promising transdiagnostic approach to treating disaster survivors. *Psychological Trauma: Theory, Research, Practice, and Policy, 9*(Suppl. 1), 130–136. https://doi.org/10.1037/tra0000221

Hamblen, J. L., Roncone, R., Giusti, L., & Casacchia, M. (2018a). *La sofferenza psicologica da disastri naturali e trauma importanti: Trattamento cognitivo-comportamentale, manuale per gli operatori* [Psychological suffering from natural disasters and major traumas: Therapist manual]. Pensiero Scientifico Editore.

Hamblen, J. L., Roncone, R., Giusti, L., & Casacchia, M. (2018b). *La sofferenza psicologica da disastri naturali e trauma importanti: Trattamento cognitivo-comportamentale, quaderno di lavoror per l'utente* [Psychological suffering from natural disasters and major traumas: Client workbook]. Pension Scientifico Editore.

Hensel, J. M., Ruiz, C., Finney, C., & Dewa, C. S. (2015). Meta-analysis of risk factors for secondary traumatic stress in therapeutic work with trauma victims. *Journal of Traumatic Stress, 28*(2), 83–91. https://doi.org/10.1002/jts.21998

Hilton, L., Maher, A. R., Colaiaco, B., Apaydin, E., Sorbero, M. E., Booth, M., Shanman, R. M., & Hempel, S. (2017). Meditation for posttraumatic stress: Systematic review and meta-analysis. *Psychological Trauma: Theory, Research, Practice, and Policy, 9*(4), 453–460. https://doi.org/10.1037/tra0000180

HIV/AIDS. (2020, December 12). In *Wikipedia*. https://en.wikipedia.org/wiki/HIV/AIDS

Holliday, R., Holder, N., & Suris, A. (2018). Reductions in self-blame cognitions predict PTSD improvements with cognitive processing therapy for military sexual trauma-related PTSD. *Psychiatry Research, 263*, 181–184. https://doi.org/10.1016/j.psychres.2018.03.007

Horowitz, M. J. (1975). Intrusive and repetitive thoughts after stress. *Archives of General Psychiatry, 32*(11), 1457–1463. https://doi.org/10.1001/archpsyc.1975.01760290125015

Horowitz, M. J. (1986). *Stress response syndromes* (2nd ed.). Jason Aronson.

Hurricane Katrina. (2020, October 30). In *Wikipedia*. https://en.wikipedia.org/wiki/Hurricane_Katrina#cite_note-9

Hurricane Sandy. (2020, October 30). In *Wikipedia*. https://en.wikipedia.org/wiki/Hurricane_Sandy#United_States_2

Jackson, C. T., Covell, N. H., Shear, M. K., Zhu, C., Donahue, S. A., Essock, S. M., & Felton, C. J. (2006). The road back: Predictors of regaining preattack functioning among Project Liberty clients. *Psychiatric Services, 57*(9), 1283–1290. https://doi.org/10.1176/ps.2006.57.9.1283

Jafari, H., Heidari, M., Heidari, S., & Sayfouri, N. (2020). Risk factors for suicide behaviours after natural disasters: A systematic review. *The Malaysian Journal of Medical Sciences, 27*(3), 20–33. https://doi.org/10.21315/mjms2020.27.3.3

Jankowski, M. K., Rosenberg, H. J., Rosenberg, S. D., & Mueser, K. T. (2011). *Coping with stress: A CBT program for teens with trauma*. Hazelden.

Janoff-Bulman, R. (1989). Assumptive worlds and the stress of traumatic events: Applications of the schema construct. *Social Cognition, 7*(2), 113–136. https://doi.org/10.1521/soco.1989.7.2.113

Janoff-Bulman, R. (1992). *Shattered assumptions: Towards a new psychology of trauma*. Free Press.

Jeon, H. J., Suh, T., Lee, H. J., Hahm, B. J., Lee, J. Y., Cho, S. J., Lee, Y. R., Chang, S. M., & Cho, M. J. (2007). Partial versus full PTSD in the Korean community: Prevalence, duration, correlates, comorbidity, and dysfunctions. *Depression and Anxiety, 24*(8), 577–585. https://doi.org/10.1002/da.20270

Jerud, A. B., Zoellner, L. A., Pruitt, L. D., & Feeny, N. C. (2014). Changes in emotion regulation in adults with and without a history of childhood abuse following posttraumatic stress disorder treatment. *Journal of Consulting and Clinical Psychology, 82*(4), 721–730. https://doi.org/10.1037/a0036520

Johannesson, K. B., Arinell, H., & Arnberg, F. K. (2015). Six years after the wave: Trajectories of posttraumatic stress following a natural disaster. *Journal of Anxiety Disorders, 36*, 15–24. https://doi.org/10.1016/j.janxdis.2015.07.007

Kabat-Zinn, J. (2013). *Full catastrophe living: Using the wisdom of your body and mind to face stress, pain, and illness* (rev. ed.). Bantam Books.

Kaniasty, K., & Norris, F. H. (2012). Distinctions that matter: Received social support, perceived social support, and social embeddedness after disasters. In Y. Neria, S. Galea, & F. H. Norris (Eds.), *Mental health and disasters* (pp. 175–200). Cambridge University Press.

Kanter, J. W., Manos, R. C., Bowe, W. M., Baruch, D. E., Busch, A. M., & Rusch, L. C. (2010). What is behavioral activation? A review of the empirical literature. *Clinical Psychology Review, 30*(6), 608–620. https://doi.org/10.1016/j.cpr.2010.04.001

Kessler, R. C., Barker, P. R., Colpe, L. J., Epstein, J. F., Gfroerer, J. C., Hiripi, E., Howes, M. J., Normand, S.-L. T., Manderscheid, R. W., Walters, E. E., & Zaslavsky, A. M. (2003). Screening for serious mental illness in the general population. *Archives of General Psychiatry, 60*(2), 184–189. https://doi.org/10.1001/archpsyc.60.2.184

Kessler, R. C., Chiu, W. T., Demler, O., & Walters, E. E. (2005). Prevalence, severity, and comorbidity of 12-month *DSM-IV* disorders in the National Comorbidity Survey Replication. *Archives of General Psychiatry, 62*(6), 617–627. https://doi.org/10.1001/archpsyc.62.6.617

Kessler, R. C., Galea, S., Gruber, M. J., Sampson, N. A., Ursano, R. J., & Wessely, S. C. (2008). Trends in mental illness and suicidality after Hurricane Katrina. *Molecular Psychiatry, 13*(4), 374–384. https://doi.org/10.1038/sj.mp.4002119

Kessler, R. C., Sonnega, A., Bromet, E., Hughes, M., & Nelson, C. B. (1995). Posttraumatic stress disorder in the National Comorbidity Survey. *Archives of General Psychiatry, 52*(12), 1048–1060. https://doi.org/10.1001/archpsyc.1995.03950240066012

Kilpatrick, D. G., Resnick, H. S., Milanak, M. E., Miller, M. W., Keyes, K. M., & Friedman, M. J. (2013). National estimates of exposure to traumatic events and PTSD prevalence using *DSM-IV* and *DSM-5* criteria. *Journal of Traumatic Stress, 26*(5), 537–547. https://doi.org/10.1002/jts.21848

Kindt, M., & Engelhard, I. M. (2005). Trauma processing and the development of posttraumatic stress disorder. *Journal of Behavior Therapy and Experimental Psychiatry, 36*(1), 69–76. https://doi.org/10.1016/j.jbtep.2004.11.007

Kleim, B., Grey, N., Wild, J., Nussbeck, F. W., Stott, R., Hackmann, A., Clark, D. M., & Ehlers, A. (2013). Cognitive change predicts symptom reduction with cognitive therapy for posttraumatic stress disorder. *Journal of Consulting and Clinical Psychology, 81*(3), 383–393. https://doi.org/10.1037/a0031290

Konuk, E., Knipe, J., Eke, I., Yuksek, H., Yurtsever, A., & Ostep, S. (2006). The effects of eye movement desensitization and reprocessing (EMDR) therapy on posttraumatic stress disorder in survivors of the 1999 Marmara, Turkey, earthquake. *International Journal of Stress Management, 13*(3), 291–308. https://doi.org/10.1037/1072-5245.13.3.291

Kredlow, M. A., Szuhany, K. L., Lo, S., Xie, X., Gottlieb, J. D., Rosenberg, S. D., & Mueser, K. T. (2017). Cognitive behavioral therapy for posttraumatic stress disorder in individuals with severe mental illness and borderline personality disorder. *Psychiatry Research, 249*, 86–93. https://doi.org/10.1016/j.psychres.2016.12.045

Kristensen, P., Weisæth, L., & Heir, T. (2010). Predictors of complicated grief after a natural disaster: A population study two years after the 2004 South-East Asian tsunami. *Death Studies, 34*(2), 137–150. https://doi.org/10.1080/07481180903492455

Kroenke, K., Spitzer, R. L., & Williams, J. B. (2001). The PHQ-9: Validity of a brief depression severity measure. *Journal of General Internal Medicine, 16*(9), 606–613. https://doi.org/10.1046/j.1525-1497.2001.016009606.x

Krygier, J. R., Heathers, J. A., Shahrestani, S., Abbott, M., Gross, J. J., & Kemp, A. H. (2013). Mindfulness meditation, well-being, and heart rate variability: A preliminary investigation into the impact of intensive Vipassana meditation. *International Journal of Psychophysiology, 89*(3), 305–313. https://doi.org/10.1016/j.ijpsycho.2013.06.017

Kumpula, M. J., Pentel, K. Z., Foa, E. B., LeBlanc, N. J., Bui, E., McSweeney, L. B., Knowles, K., Bosley, H., Simon, N. M., & Rauch, S. A. M. (2017). Temporal sequencing of change in posttraumatic cognitive. *Behavior Therapy, 48*(2), 156–165. https://doi.org/10.1016/j.beth.2016.02.008

Lai, J., Ma, S., Wang, Y., Cai, Z., Hu, J., Wei, N., Wu, J., Du, H., Chen, T., Li, R., Tan, H., Kang, L., Yao, L., Huang, M., Wang, H., Liu, Z., & Hu, S. (2020, March 23). Factors associated with mental health outcomes among health care workers exposed to coronavirus disease 2019. *JAMA Network Open, 3*(3), e203976.

Lancee, W. J., Maunder, R. G., & Goldbloom, D. S. (2008). Prevalence of psychiatric disorders among Toronto healthcare workers one to two years after the SARS outbreak. *Psychiatric Services, 59*(1), 91–95. https://doi.org/10.1176/ps.2008.59.1.91

Lejuez, C. W., Hopko, D. R., Acierno, R., Daughters, S. B., & Pagoto, S. L. (2011). Ten year revision of the Brief Behavioral Activation Treatment for Depression:

Revised treatment manual. *Behavior Modification, 35*, 111–161. https://doi.org/10.1177/0145445510390929

Levitt, J. T., Malta, L. S., Martin, A., Davis, L., & Cloitre, M. (2007). The flexible application of a manualized treatment for PTSD symptoms and functional impairment related to the 9/11 World Trade Center attack. *Behaviour Research and Therapy, 45*(7), 1419–1433. https://doi.org/10.1016/j.brat.2007.01.004

Lewinsohn, P. M. (1974). A behavioral approach to the treatment of depression. In R. M. Friedman & M. M. Katz (Eds.), *The psychology of depression* (pp. 157–185). Wiley.

Li, J., Chow, A. Y. M., Shi, Z., & Chan, C. L. W. (2015). Prevalence and risk factors of complicated grief among Sichuan earthquake survivors. *Journal of Affective Disorders, 175*, 218–223. https://doi.org/10.1016/j.jad.2015.01.003

Lion Air Flight 610. (2020, December 17). In *Wikipedia.* https://en.wikipedia.org/wiki/Lion_Air_Flight_610

Lissek, S., & van Meurs, B. (2015). Learning models of PTSD: Theoretical accounts and psychobiological evidence. *International Journal of Psychophysiology, 98*(3), 594–605. https://doi.org/10.1016/j.ijpsycho.2014.11.006

Lowe, S. R., Chan, C. S., & Rhodes, J. E. (2010). Pre-hurricane perceived social support protects against psychological distress: A longitudinal analysis of low-income mothers. *Journal of Consulting and Clinical Psychology, 78*(4), 551–560. https://doi.org/10.1037/a0018317

Lowe, S. R., & Galea, S. (2017). The mental health consequences of mass shootings. *Trauma, Violence, and Abuse, 18*(1), 62–82. https://doi.org/10.1177/1524838015591572

Manchester Arena bombing. (2020, December 9). In *Wikipedia.* https://en.wikipedia.org/wiki/Manchester_Arena_bombing

Marks, I., Lovell, K., Noshirvani, H., Livanou, M., & Thrasher, S. (1998). Treatment of posttraumatic stress disorder by exposure and/or cognitive restructuring. *Archives of General Psychiatry, 55*(4), 317–325. https://doi.org/10.1001/archpsyc.55.4.317

Matsuoka, Y. J., Nishi, D., Nakaya, N., Sone, T., Hamazaki, K., Hamazaki, T., & Koido, Y. (2011). Attenuating posttraumatic distress with omega-3 polyunsaturated fatty acids among disaster medical assistance team members after the Great East Japan Earthquake: The APOP randomized controlled trial. *BMC Psychiatry, 11*(1), 132. https://doi.org/10.1186/1471-244X-11-132

McEwen, S. (2017). Allostasis and the epigenetics of brain and body health over the life course the brain on stress. *JAMA Psychiatry, 74*(6), 551–552. https://doi.org/10.1001/jamapsychiatry.2017.0270

McFarlane, A. C., & Papay, P. (1992). Multiple diagnoses in posttraumatic stress disorder in the victims of a natural disaster. *Journal of Nervous and Mental Disease, 180*(8), 498–504. https://doi.org/10.1097/00005053-199208000-00004

McGovern, M. P., Lambert-Harris, C., Alterman, A. I., Xie, H., & Meier, A. (2011). A randomized controlled trial comparing integrated cognitive behavioral therapy versus individual addiction counseling or co-occurring substance use and posttraumatic stress disorders. *Journal of Dual Diagnosis, 7*(4), 207–227. https://doi.org/10.1080/15504263.2011.620425

McGovern, M. P., Lambert-Harris, C., Xie, H., Meier, A., McLeman, B., & Saunders, E. (2015). A randomized controlled trial of treatments for co-occurring substance use disorders and post-traumatic stress disorder. *Addiction, 110*(7), 1194–1204. https://doi.org/10.1111/add.12943

McGovern, M. P., Mueser, K. T., Hamblen, J. L., & Jankowski, M. K. (2010). *Cognitive-behavioral therapy for PTSD: A program for addiction professionals.* Hazelden.

McHugh, R. K., Murray, H. W., & Barlow, D. H. (2009). Balancing fidelity and adaptation in the dissemination of empirically-supported treatments: The promise of transdiagnostic interventions. *Behaviour Research and Therapy, 47*(11), 946–953. https://doi.org/10.1016/j.brat.2009.07.005

McLaughlin, K. A., Berglund, P. A., Gruber, M. J., Kessler, R. C., Sampson, N. A., & Zaslavsky, A. M. (2011). Recovery from PTSD following Hurricane Katrina. *Depression and Anxiety, 28*(6), 439–446. https://doi.org/10.1002/da.20790

McLean, C. P., Yeh, R., Rosenfield, D., & Foa, E. B. (2015). Changes in negative cognitions mediate PTSD symptom reductions during client-centered therapy and prolonged exposure for adolescents. *Behaviour Research and Therapy, 68,* 64–69. https://doi.org/10.1016/j.brat.2015.03.008

Meewisse, M., Olff, M., Kleber, R. J., Kitchiner, N. J., & Gersons, B. P. R. (2011). The course of mental health disorders after a disaster: Predictors and comorbidity. *Journal of Traumatic Stress, 24*(4), 405–413. https://doi.org/10.1002/jts.20663

Miller, E. D. (2020). Loneliness in the era of COVID-19. *Frontiers in Psychology, 11,* 2219. https://doi.org/10.3389/fpsyg.2020.02219

Mittal, D., Drummond, K., Blevins, D., Curran, J., Corrigan, P. W., & Sullivan, G. (2013). Stigma associated with PTSD: Perceptions of treatment seeking combat veterans. *Psychiatric Rehabilitation Journal, 36*(2), 86–92. https://doi.org/10.1037/h0094976

Morse, T. (2018). *The mourning news: Reporting violent death in a global age.* Peter Lang. https://doi.org/10.3726/b11523

Mueser, K. T., Gottlieb, J. D., Xie, H., Lu, W., Yanos, P. T., Rosenberg, S. D., Silverstein, S. M., Marcello Duva, S., Minsky, S., Wolfe, R. S., & McHugo, G. J. (2015). Evaluation of cognitive restructuring for PTSD in people with severe mental illness. *The British Journal of Psychiatry, 206*(6), 501–508. https://doi.org/10.1192/bjp.bp.114.147926

Mueser, K. T., McGurk, S. R., Xie, H., Bolton, E. E., Jankowski, M. K., Lu, W., Rosenberg, S. D., & Wolfe, R. (2018). Neuropsychological predictors of response to cognitive behavioral therapy for posttraumatic stress disorder in persons with severe mental illness. *Psychiatry Research, 259,* 110–116. https://doi.org/10.1016/j.psychres.2017.10.016

Mueser, K. T., Rosenberg, S. D., & Rosenberg, H. J. (2009). *Treatment of post-traumatic stress disorder in special populations: A cognitive restructuring program.* American Psychological Association. https://doi.org/10.1037/11889-000

Mueser, K. T., Rosenberg, S. D., Xie, H., Jankowski, M. K., Bolton, E. E., Lu, W., Hamblen, J. L., Rosenberg, H. J., McHugo, G. J., & Wolfe, R. (2008). A randomized controlled trial of cognitive-behavioral treatment of posttraumatic stress disorder in severe mental illness. *Journal of Consulting and Clinical Psychology, 76*(2), 259–271. https://doi.org/10.1037/0022-006X.76.2.259

National responses to the COVID-19 pandemic. (2020, November 7). In *Wikipedia.* https://en.wikipedia.org/wiki/National_responses_to_the_COVID-19_pandemic

Neria, Y., DiGrande, L., & Adams, B. G. (2011). Posttraumatic stress disorder following the September 11, 2001, terrorist attacks: A review of the literature among highly exposed populations. *American Psychologist, 66*(6), 429–446. https://doi.org/10.1037/a0024791

Neria, Y., Gross, R., Litz, B., Maguen, S., Insel, B., Seirmarco, G., Rosenfeld, H., Suh, E. J., Kishon, R., Cook, J., & Marshall, R. D. (2007). Prevalence and psychological correlates of complicated grief among bereaved adults 25–35 years after September 11th attacks. *Journal of Traumatic Stress, 20*(3), 251–262. https://doi.org/10.1002/jts.20223

Neria, Y., Nandi, A., & Galea, S. (2008). Post-traumatic stress disorder following disasters: A systematic review. *Psychological Medicine, 38*(4), 467–480. https://doi.org/10.1017/S0033291707001353

Nillni, Y. I., Nosen, E. L., Williams, P. A., Tracy, M., Coffey, S. F., & Galea, S. (2013). Unique and related predictors of major depressive disorder, posttraumatic stress disorder, and their comorbidity after Hurricane Katrina. *Journal of Nervous and Mental Disease, 201*(10), 841–847. https://doi.org/10.1097/NMD.0b013e3182a430a0

Nordløkken, A., Pape, H., & Heir, T. (2016). Alcohol consumption in the aftermath of a natural disaster: A longitudinal study. *Public Health, 132,* 33–39. https://doi.org/10.1016/j.puhe.2015.11.007

Nordløkken, A., Pape, H., Wentzel-Larsen, T., & Heir, T. (2013). Changes in alcohol consumption after a natural disaster: A study of Norwegian survivors after the 2004 Southeast Asia tsunami. *BMC Public Health, 58*(1), 58. https://doi.org/10.1186/1471-2458-13-58

Norris, F. H., & Davidson, J. (2007). *Short Post-Traumatic Stress Disorder Rating Interview, Expanded Version (SPRINT-E)* [Unpublished instrument]. Dartmouth Medical School.

Norris, F. H., Donahue, S., Felton, C., Watson, P., Hamblen, J. L., & Marshall, R. (2006). A psychometric analysis of Project Liberty's Adult Enhanced Services Referral Tool. *Psychiatric Services, 57*(9), 1328–1334. https://doi.org/10.1176/ps.2006.57.9.1328

Norris, F. H., & Elrod, C. L. (2006). Psychosocial consequences of disaster: A review of past research. In F. H. Norris, S. Galea, M. J. Friedman, & P. J.

Watson (Eds.), *Research methods for studying mental health after disasters and terrorism* (pp. 20–44). Guilford Press.

Norris, F. H., Friedman, M., & Watson, P. (2002). 60,000 disaster victims speak: Part II. Summary and implications of the disaster mental health research. *Psychiatry: Interpersonal and Biological Processes, 65*(3), 240–260. https://doi.org/10.1521/psyc.65.3.240.20169

Norris, F. H., & Hamblen, J. H. (2007). *Project Recovery evaluation: CBT for post-disaster distress*. National Center for PTSD.

Norris, F. H., & Kaniasty, K. Z. (1996). Received and perceived social support in times of stress: A test of the social support deterioration deterrence model. *Journal of Personality and Social Psychology, 71*(3), 498–511. https://doi.org/10.1037/0022-3514.71.3.498

Norris, F. H., Tracy, M., & Galea, S. (2009). Looking for resilience: Understanding the longitudinal trajectories of responses to stress. *Social Science & Medicine, 68*(12), 2190–2198. https://doi.org/10.1016/j.socscimed.2009.03.043

Norris, F. H., Watson, P. J., Hamblen, J. L., & Pfefferbaum, B. J. (2005). Provider perspectives on disaster mental health services in Oklahoma City. In Y. Danieli, D. Brom, & J. B. Sills (Eds.), *The trauma of terrorism: Sharing knowledge and shared care, an international handbook* (pp. 649–662). Haworth Press.

North, C. N., Nixon, S. J., Shariat, S., Mallonee, S., McMillen, J. C., Spitznagel, E. L., & Smith, E. (1999). Psychiatric disorders among survivors of the Oklahoma City bombing. *Journal of the American Medical Association, 282*(8), 755–762. https://doi.org/10.1001/jama.282.8.755

November 2015 Paris attacks. (2020, December 11). In *Wikipedia*. https://en.wikipedia.org/wiki/November_2015_Paris_attacks

O'Donnell, M. L., Lau, W., Fredrickson, J., Gibson, K., Bryant, R. A., Bisson, J., Burke, S., Busuttil, W., Coghlan, A., Creamer, M., Gray, D., Greenberg, N., McDermott, B., McFarlane, A. C., Monson, C. M., Phelps, A., Rusek, J. I., Schnurr, P. P., Ugsang, J., . . . Forbes, D. (2020). An open label pilot study of a brief psychosocial intervention for disaster and trauma survivors. *Frontiers in Psychiatry, 11*, 483. https://doi.org/10.3389/fpsyt.2020.00483

Pandemic H1N1/09 virus. (2020, December 2). In *Wikipedia*. https://en.wikipedia.org/wiki/Pandemic_H1N1/09_virus

Park-Lee, E., Lipari, R. N., & Hedden, S. L., RTI International, Kroutil, L. A., & Porter, J. D. (2017, September). *Receipt of services for substance use and mental health issues among adults: Results from the 2016 National Survey on Drug Use and Health.* https://www.samhsa.gov/data/sites/default/files/NSDUH-DR-FFR2-2016/NSDUH-DR-FFR2-2016.htm

Pasch, R. J., Brown, D. P., & Blake, E. S. (2011, September 15). *Tropical cyclone report: Hurricane Charley.* https://www.nhc.noaa.gov/data/tcr/AL032004_Charley.pdf

Perrow, C. (1999). *Normal accidents: Living with high-risk technologies*. Princeton University Press.

Perrow, C. (2007). *The next catastrophe: Reducing our vulnerabilities to natural, industrial, and terrorist disasters*. Princeton University Press.

Phoenix Australia. (2020). *About SOLAR*. https://www.phoenixaustralia.org/expertise/research/solar/

Pietrabissa, G., & Simpson, S. G. (2020). Psychological consequences of social isolation during COVID-19 outbreak. *Frontiers in Psychology*. https://doi.org/10.3389/fpsyg.2020.02201

Pietrzak, R. H., Goldstein, R. B., Southwick, S. M., & Grant, B. F. (2011). Prevalence and Axis I comorbidity of full and partial posttraumatic stress disorder in the United States: Results from Wave 2 of the National Epidemiologic Survey on Alcohol and Related Conditions. *Journal of Anxiety Disorders, 25*(3), 456–465. https://doi.org/10.1016/j.janxdis.2010.11.010

Pietrzak, R. H., Tracy, M., Galea, S., Kilpatrick, D. G., Ruggiero, K. J., Hamblen, J. L., Southwick, S. M., & Norris, F. H. (2012). Resilience in the face of disaster: Prevalence and longitudinal course of mental disorders following Hurricane Ike. *PLOS ONE, 7*(6), e38964. https://doi.org/10.1371/journal.pone.0038964

Pittsburgh synagogue shooting. (2020, December 14). In *Wikipedia*. https://en.wikipedia.org/wiki/Pittsburgh_synagogue_shooting

Plyer, A. (2016). *Facts for features: Katrina impact*. The Data Center. https://www.datacenterresearch.org/data-resources/katrina/facts-for-impact/

Pollard, M. S., Tucker, J. S., & Green, H. D., Jr. (2020). Changes in adult alcohol use and consequences during the COVID-19 pandemic in the US. *JAMA Network Open, 3*(9), e2022942. https://doi.org/10.1001/jamanetworkopen.2020.22942

Porges, S. W. (2011). *The polyvagal theory: Neurophysiological foundations of emotions, attachment, communication, and self-regulation*. Guilford Press.

Preti, E., Di Mattei, V., Perego, G., Ferrari, F., Mazzetti, M., Taranto, P., Di Pierro, R., Madeddu, F., & Calati, R. (2020). The psychological impact of epidemic and pandemic outbreaks on healthcare workers: Rapid review of the evidence. *Current Psychiatry Reports, 22*(8), 43. https://doi.org/10.1007/s11920-020-01166-z

Prigerson, H. G., Horowitz, M. J., Jacobs, S. C., Parkes, C. M., Aslan, M., Goodkin, K., Raphael, B., Marwit, S. J., Wortman, C., Neimeyer, R. A., Bonanno, G., Block, S. D., Kissane, D., Boelen, P., Maercker, A., Litz, B. T., Johnson, J. G., First, M. B., & Maciejewski, P. K. (2009). Prolonged grief disorder: Psychometric validation of criteria proposed for *DSM-V* and *ICD-11*. *PLOS Medicine, 6*(8), e1000121. https://doi.org/10.1371/journal.pmed.1000121

Prins, A., Bovin, M. J., & Tiet, Q. Q. (2016). The Primary Care PTSD Screen for *DSM-5* (PC–PTSD–5): Development and evaluation within a veteran primary care sample. *Journal of General Internal Medicine, 31*(10), 1206–1211. https://doi.org/10.1007/s11606-016-3703-5

Prins, A., Cimpean, D., & Schnurr, P. P. (2009). Treatment in primary care settings. In K. T. Mueser, S. D. Rosenberg & H. J. Rosenberg (Eds.), *Treatment of posttraumatic disorder in special populations* (pp. 301–314). American Psychological Association.

Rahman, A., Hamdani, S. U., Awan, N. R., Bryant, R. A., Dawson, K. S., Khan, M. F., Azeemi, M. M., Akhtar, P., Nazir, H., Chiumento, A., Sijbrandij, M., Wang, D., Farooq, S., & van Ommeren, M. (2016). Effect of a multicomponent behavioural intervention in adults impaired by psychological distress in a conflict-affected area of Pakistan: A randomized clinical trial. *Journal of the American Medical Association, 316*(24), 2609–2617. https://doi.org/10.1001/jama.2016.17165

Rahman, A., Khan, M. N., Hamdani, S. U., Chiumento, A., Akhtar, P., Nazir, H., Nisar, A., Masood, A., Din, I. U., Khan, N. A., Bryant, R. A., Dawson, K. S., Sijbrandij, M., Wang, D., & van Ommeren, M. (2019). Effectiveness of a brief group psychological intervention for women in a post-conflict setting in Pakistan: A single-blind, cluster, randomised controlled trial. *The Lancet, 393*(10182), 1733–1744. https://doi.org/10.1016/S0140-6736(18)32343-2

Ratcliffe, M., Ruddell, M., & Smith, B. (2014). What is a "sense of foreshortened future"? A phenomenological study of trauma, trust, and time. *Frontiers in Psychology, 5*, 1026. https://doi.org/10.3389/fpsyg.2014.01026

Ready, C. B., Hayes, A. M., Yasinski, C. W., Webb, C., Gallop, R., Deblinger, E., & Laurenceau, J.-P. (2015). Overgeneralized beliefs, accommodation, and treatment outcome in youth receiving trauma-focused cognitive behavioral therapy for childhood trauma. *Behavior Therapy, 46*(5), 671–688. https://doi.org/10.1016/j.beth.2015.03.004

Resick, P. A., Galovski, T. E., Uhlmansiek, M. O., Scher, C. D., Clum, G. A., & Young-Xu, Y. (2008). A randomized clinical trial to dismantle components of cognitive processing therapy for posttraumatic stress disorder in female victims of interpersonal violence. *Journal of Consulting and Clinical Psychology, 76*(2), 243–258. https://doi.org/10.1037/0022-006X.76.2.243

Resick, P. A., Monson, C. M., & Chard, K. M. (2017). *Cognitive processing therapy for PTSD: A comprehensive manual.* Guilford Press.

Resick, P. A., Nishith, P., Weaver, T. L., Astin, M. C., & Feuer, C. A. (2002). A comparison of cognitive processing therapy with prolonged exposure and a waiting condition for the treatment of posttraumatic stress disorder in female rape victims. *Journal of Consulting and Clinical Psychology, 70*(4), 867–879. https://doi.org/10.1037/0022-006X.70.4.867

Ritchie, H., Hasell, J., Appel, C., & Roser, M. (2019). *How many people are killed by terrorists worldwide?* https://ourworldindata.org/terrorism#how-many-people-are-killed-by-terrorists-worldwide

Rosen, C. S., & Cohen, M. (2010). Subgroups of New York City children at high risk of PTSD after the September 11 attacks: A signal detection analysis. *Psychiatric Services, 61*(1), 64–69. https://doi.org/10.1176/ps.2010.61.1.64

Rosenberg, H. J., Jankowski, M. K., Fortuna, L. R., Rosenberg, S. D., & Mueser, K. T. (2011). A pilot study of a cognitive restructuring program for treating posttraumatic disorders in adolescents. *Psychological Trauma: Theory, Research, Practice, and Policy, 3*(1), 94–99. https://doi.org/10.1037/a0019889

Schauer, M., Neuner, F., & Elbert, T. (2005). *Narrative exposure therapy: A short-term intervention for traumatic stress disorders after war, terror, or torture.* Hogrefe & Huber.

Schlenger, W. E., Caddell, J. M., Ebert, L., Jordan, B. K., Rourke, K. M., Wilson, D. B., Thalji, L., Dennis, J. M., Fairbank, J. A., & Kulka, R. A. (2002). Psychological reactions to terrorist attacks: Findings from the National Study of Americans' Reactions to September 11. *Journal of the American Medical Association, 288*(5), 581–588. https://doi.org/10.1001/jama.288.5.581

Schumm, J. A., Dickstein, B. D., Walter, K. H., Owens, G. P., & Chard, K. M. (2015). Changes in posttraumatic cognitions predict changes in posttraumatic stress disorder symptoms during cognitive processing therapy. *Journal of Consulting and Clinical Psychology, 83*(6), 1161–1166. https://doi.org/10.1037/ccp0000040

Schuster, M. A., Stein, B. D., Jaycox, L. H., Collins, R. L., Marshall, G. N., Elliott, M. N., Zhou, A. J., Kanouse, D. E., Morrison, J. L., & Berry, S. H. (2001). A national survey of stress reactions after the September 11, 2001, terrorist attacks. *The New England Journal of Medicine, 345*(20), 1507–1512. https://doi.org/10.1056/NEJM200111153452024

Seow, L. S. E., Ong, C., Mahesh, M. V., Sagayadevan, V., Shafie, S., Chong, S. A., & Subramaniam, M. (2016). A systematic review on comorbid post-traumatic stress disorder in schizophrenia. *Schizophrenia Research, 176*(2–3), 441–451. https://doi.org/10.1016/j.schres.2016.05.004

Seppälä, E. M., Nitschke, J. B., Tudorascu, D. L., Hayes, A., Goldstein, M. R., Nguyen, D. T. H., Perlman, D., & Davidson, R. J. (2014). Breathing-based meditation decreases posttraumatic stress disorder symptoms in U.S. military veterans: A randomized controlled longitudinal study. *Journal of Traumatic Stress, 27*(4), 397–405. https://doi.org/10.1002/jts.21936

September 11 attacks. (2020, November 12). In *Wikipedia.* https://en.wikipedia.org/wiki/September_11_attacks

7 July 2005 London bombings. (2020, December 19). In *Wikipedia.* https://en.wikipedia.org/wiki/7_July_2005_London_bombings

Severe acute respiratory syndrome. (2020, December 18). In *Wikipedia.* https://en.wikipedia.org/wiki/Severe_acute_respiratory_syndrome

Shah, R., Shah, A., & Links, P. (2012). Post-traumatic stress disorder and depression comorbidity: Severity across different populations. *Neuropsychiatry, 2*(6), 521–529.

Shear, M. K., Frank, E., Houck, P. R., & Reynolds, C. F. (2005). Treatment of complicated grief: A randomized controlled trial. *Journal of the American Medical Association, 293*(21), 2601–2608. https://doi.org/10.1001/jama.293.21.2601

Shear, M. K., Ghesquiere, P., & Glickman, K. (2013). Bereavement and complicated grief. *Current Psychiatry Reports, 15*(11), 406. https://doi.org/10.1007/s11920-013-0406-z

Shear, M. K., Jackson, C. T., Essock, S. M., Donahue, S. A., & Felton, C. J. (2006). Screening for complicated grief among Project Liberty service recipients

18 months after September 11, 2001. *Psychiatric Services, 57*(9), 1291–1297. https://doi.org/10.1176/ps.2006.57.9.1291

Shear, M. K., Yuanjia Wang, W., Skritskaya, N., Duan, D., Mauro, C., & Ghesquiere, A. (2014). Treatment of complicated grief in elderly persons: A randomized clinical trial. *JAMA Psychiatry, 71*(11), 1287–1295. https://doi.org/10.1001/jamapsychiatry.2014.1242

Silove, D. M., Baker, J. R., Mohsin, M., Teesson, M., Creamer, M. C., O'Donnell, M. L., Forbes, D., Carragher, N., Slade, T., Mills, K., Bryant, R., McFarlane, A., Steel, Z., Felmingham, K., & Rees, S. (2017). The contribution of gender-based violence and network trauma to gender differences in post-traumatic stress disorder. *PLOS ONE, 12*(2), e0171879. https://doi.org/10.1371/journal.pone.0171879

Silver, S. M., Rogers, S., Knipe, J., & Colelli, G. (2005). EMDR therapy following the 9/11 terrorist attacks: A community-based intervention project in New York City. *International Journal of Stress Management, 12*(1), 29–42. https://doi.org/10.1037/1072-5245.12.1.29

Spanish flu. (2020, November 10). In *Wikipedia*. https://en.wikipedia.org/wiki/Spanish_flu

Steel, C., Hardy, A., Smith, B., Wykes, T., Rose, S., Enright, S., Hardcastle, M., Landau, S., Baksh, M. F., Gottlieb, J. D., Rose, D., & Mueser, K. T. (2017). Cognitive behaviour therapy for posttraumatic stress in schizophrenia: A randomised controlled trial. *Psychological Medicine, 47*(1), 43–51. https://doi.org/10.1017/S0033291716002117

Stevanovic, P., & Rupert, P. A. (2004). Career-sustaining behaviors, satisfactions, and stresses of professional psychologists. *Psychotherapy: Theory, Research, & Practice, 41*(3), 301–309. https://doi.org/10.1037/0033-3204.41.3.301

Suarez, R., Mills, R. C., & Stewart, D. G. (1987). *Sanity, insanity, and common sense: The groundbreaking new approach to happiness*. Fawcett Columbine.

Sullivan, M. B., Erb, M., Schmalzi, L., Moonaz, S., Taylor, J. N., & Porges, S. W. (2018). Yoga therapy and polyvagal theory: The convergence of traditional wisdom and contemporary neuroscience for self-regulation and resilience. *Frontiers in Human Neuroscience, 12*, 67. https://doi.org/10.3389/fnhum.2018.00067

Tan, G., Dao, T. K., Farmer, L., Sutherland, R. J., & Gevirtz, R. (2011). Heart rate variability (HRV) and posttraumatic stress disorder (PTSD): A pilot study. *Applied Psychophysiology and Biofeedback, 36*(1), 27–35. https://doi.org/10.1007/s10484-010-9141-y

Tang, B., Deng, Q., Glik, D., Dong, J., & Zhang, L. (2017). A meta-analysis of risk factors for post-traumatic stress disorder (PTSD) in adults and children after earthquakes. *International Journal of Environmental Research and Public Health, 14*(12), 1537. https://doi.org/10.3390/ijerph14121537

Tarrier, N., & Sommerfield, C. (2004). Treatment of chronic PTSD by cognitive therapy with exposure: 5-year follow-up. *Behavior Therapy, 35*(2), 231–246. https://doi.org/10.1016/S0005-7894(04)80037-6

Thordardottir, E. B., Valdimarsdottir, U. A., Hansdottir, I., Resnick, H. S., Shipherd, J. C., & Gudmundsdottir, B. (2015). Posttraumatic stress and other health consequences of catastrophic avalanches: A 16-year follow-up of survivors. *Journal of Anxiety Disorders, 32*, 103–111. https://doi.org/10.1016/j.janxdis.2015.03.005

Timeline of the COVID-19 pandemic. (2021, February 28). In *Wikipedia*. https://en.wikipedia.org/wiki/Timeline_of_the_COVID-19_pandemic

Tolin, D. F., & Foa, E. B. (2006). Sex differences in trauma and posttraumatic stress disorder: A quantitative review of 25 years of research. *Psychological Bulletin, 132*(6), 959–992. https://doi.org/10.1037/0033-2909.132.6.959

2004 Indian Ocean earthquake and tsunami. (2020, December 20). In *Wikipedia*. https://en.wikipedia.org/wiki/2004_Indian_Ocean_earthquake_and_tsunami

2009 L'Aquila earthquake. (2020, October 21). In *Wikipedia*. https://en.wikipedia.org/wiki/2009_L%27Aquila_earthquake

2011 Norway attacks. (2020, November 10). In *Wikipedia*. https://en.wikipedia.org/wiki/2011_Norway_attacks

2017 Las Vegas shooting. (2020, December 5). In *Wikipedia*. https://en.wikipedia.org/wiki/2017_Las_Vegas_shooting

U.S. Department of Homeland Security. (n.d.). *Declared disasters*. https://www.fema.gov/disasters/grid/year

van der Kolk, B. A., Stone, L., West, J., Rhodes, A., Emerson, D., Suvak, M., & Spinazzola, J. (2014). Yoga as an adjunctive treatment for posttraumatic stress disorder: A randomized controlled trial. *The Journal of Clinical Psychiatry, 75*(6), e559–e565. https://doi.org/10.4088/JCP.13m08561

van Dis, E. A. M., van Veen, S. C., Hagenaars, M. A., Batelaan, N. M., Bockting, C. L. H., van den Heuvel, R. M., Cuijpers, P. & Engelhard, I. M. (2020). Long-term outcomes of cognitive behavioral therapy for anxiety-related disorders: A systematic review and meta-analysis. *JAMA Psychiatry, 77*(3), 265–273. https://doi.org/10.1001/jamapsychiatry.2019.3986

Van Rheenen, T. E., Meyer, D., Neill, E., Phillipou, A., Tan, E. J., Toh, W. L., & Rossell, S. L. (2020). Mental health status of individuals with a mood-disorder during the COVID-19 pandemic in Australia: Initial results from the COLLATE project. *Journal of Affective Disorders, 275*, 69–77. https://doi.org/10.1016/j.jad.2020.06.037

Vlahov, D., Galea, S., Ahern, J., Resnick, H. S., Boscarino, J. A., Gold, J., Bucuvalas, M., & Kilpatrick, D. G. (2004). Consumption of cigarettes, alcohol, and marijuana among New York City residents six months after the September 11 terrorist attacks. *The American Journal of Drug and Alcohol Abuse, 30*(2), 385–407. https://doi.org/10.1081/ADA-120037384

Vlahov, D., Galea, S., Ahern, J., Rudenstine, M. S., Resnick, H. S., Kilpatrick, D. G., & Crum, R. M. (2006). Alcohol drinking problems among New York City residents after the September 11 terrorist attacks. *Substance Use & Misuse, 41*(9), 1295–1311. https://doi.org/10.1080/10826080600754900

Wagner, A. W., Jakupcak, M., Kowalski, H. M., Bittinger, J. N., & Golshan, S. (2019). Behavioral activation as a treatment for posttraumatic stress disorder among returning veterans: A randomized trial. *Psychiatric Services, 70*(10), 867–873. https://doi.org/10.1176/appi.ps.201800572

Wagner, A. W., Zatzick, D. F., Ghesquiere, A., & Jurkovich, G. J. (2007). Behavioral activation as an early intervention for posttraumatic stress disorder and depression among physically injured trauma survivors. *Cognitive and Behavioral Practice, 14*(4), 341–349. https://doi.org/10.1016/j.cbpra.2006.05.002

Wang, Q., Xu, R., & Volkow, N. D. (2021). Increased risk of COVID-19 infection and mortality in people with mental disorders: Analysis from electronic health records in the United States. *World Psychiatry, 20*(1), 124–130. https://doi.org/10.1002/wps.20806

Weathers, F. W., Blake, D. D., Schnurr, P. P., Kaloupek, D. G., Marx, B. P., & Keane, T. M. (2014). *Clinician-Administered PTSD Scale for* DSM-5. National Center for PTSD.

Weathers, F. W., Bovin, M. J., Lee, D. J., Sloan, D. M., Schnurr, P. P., Kaloupek, D. G., Keane, T. M., & Marx, B. P. (2018). The Clinician-Administered PTSD Scale for *DSM-5* (CAPS–5): Development and initial psychometric evaluation in military veterans. *Psychological Assessment, 30*(3), 383–395. https://doi.org/10.1037/pas0000486

Weathers, F. W., Keane, T. M., & Davidson, J. R. T. (2001). Clinician-Administered PTSD Scale: A review of the first ten years of research. *Depression and Anxiety, 13*(3), 132–156. https://doi.org/10.1002/da.1029

Weathers, F. W., Litz, B., Keane, T. M., Marx, B. P., & Schnurr, P. (2013). *PTSD Checklist for* DSM-5 *(PCL–5)*. National Center for PTSD.

Westphal, M., Olfson, M., Gameroff, M. J., Wickramaratne, P., Pilowsky, D. J., Neugebauer, R., Lantigua, R., Shea, S., & Neria, Y. (2011). Functional impairment in adults with past posttraumatic stress disorder: Findings from primary care. *Depression and Anxiety, 28*(8), 686–695. https://doi.org/10.1002/da.20842

Wood, C. M., Salguero, J. M., Cano-Vindel, A., & Galea, S. (2013). Prevalence of panic attacks and panic disorder after mass trauma: A 12-month longitudinal study. *Journal of Traumatic Stress, 26*(3), 338–344. https://doi.org/10.1002/jts.21810

Woolfolk, R. L., Sime, W. E., & Barlow, D. H. (2008). *Principles and practice of stress management* (3rd ed.). Guilford Press.

Zalta, A. K., Gillihan, S. J., Fisher, A. J., Mintz, J., McLean, C. P., Yehuda, R., & Foa, E. B. (2014). Change in negative cognitions associated with PTSD predicts symptom reduction in prolonged exposure. *Journal of Consulting and Clinical Psychology, 82*(1), 171–175. https://doi.org/10.1037/a0034735

Zang, Y., Hunt, N., & Cox, T. (2013). A randomised controlled pilot study: The effectiveness of narrative exposure therapy with adult survivors of the Sichuan earthquake. *BMC Psychiatry, 13*(1), 41. https://doi.org/10.1186/1471-244X-13-41

Zang, Y., Hunt, N., & Cox, T. (2014). Adapting narrative exposure therapy for Chinese earthquake survivors: A pilot randomization controlled feasibility study. *BMC Psychiatry, 14*(1), 262. https://doi.org/10.1186/s12888-014-0262-3

Zatzick, D., Rivara, F., Jurkovich, G., Russo, J., Trusz, S. G., Wang, J., Wagner, A., Stephens, K., Dunn, C., Uehara, E., Petrie, M., Engel, C., Davydow, D., & Katon, W. (2011). Enhancing the population impact of collaborative care interventions: Mixed method development and implementation of stepped care targeting posttraumatic stress disorder and related comorbidities after acute trauma. *General Hospital Psychiatry, 33*(2), 123–134. https://doi.org/10.1016/j.genhosppsych.2011.01.001

Zika virus. (2020, December 19). In *Wikipedia*. https://en.wikipedia.org/wiki/Zika_virus

Zlotnick, C., Bruce, S., Weisberg, R. B., Shea, M. T., Machan, J., & Keller, M. (2003). Social and health functioning in female primary care patients with post-traumatic stress disorder with and without comorbid substance abuse. *Comprehensive Psychiatry, 44*(3), 177–183. https://doi.org/10.1016/S0010-440X(03)00005-1

Index

About the Authors

Jessica L. Hamblen, PhD, is a clinical psychologist and associate professor in the Department of Psychiatry at the Geisel School of Medicine at Dartmouth. She is also the deputy for education at the U.S. Department of Veterans Affairs' National Center for PTSD. Her research interests are in developing, evaluating, and disseminating evidence-based treatments for posttraumatic stress disorder. Dr. Hamblen has a national reputation as an expert in the long-term mental health response following disaster and has conducted trainings after major national disasters, including the September 11, 2001, terror attacks and Hurricane Katrina in 2005.

Kim T. Mueser, PhD, is a clinical psychologist and professor at the Center for Psychiatric Rehabilitation at Boston University. Dr. Mueser's clinical and research interests focus on the treatment of posttraumatic stress disorder in vulnerable populations and in psychiatric rehabilitation for persons with severe mental illness. He has given numerous workshops on this work, nationally and internationally, and has coauthored more than 10 books and more than 300 journal articles and book chapters. He has received a number of awards, including the Armin Loeb Research Award and the Emily Mumford Medal for Distinguished Contributions to Social Science in Medicine.